940.5315 Trep
Trepman
Among men and beasts

DATE DUE			
JUN. 17. 1984			
AUG - 7 1985			
DEC 2 4 1985			
SEP 1 1987			
APR 1 4 1990			
OCT 2 9 1990			
JAN 2 7 1994			
MAY 2 0 1997			
MAY 2 4 2000			

DISCARDED

JUL 2 7 1979

AMONG MEN AND BEASTS

The author, Paul Trepman, in his prisoner outfit as Pawel Kolodziej-czyk three weeks after his liberation in Bergen-Belsen.

Among Men and Beasts

PAUL TREPMAN

TRANSLATED FROM THE YIDDISH BY
SHOSHANA PERLA AND GERTRUDE HIRSCHLER

South Brunswick and New York: A. S. Barnes and Company
London: Thomas Yoseloff Ltd
and
Bergen Belsen Memorial Press of the
World Federation of Bergen-Belsen Associations, Inc.
New York—Tel Aviv

© 1978 by Paul Trepman

Library of Congress Catalog Card Number: 77-89648

A. S. Barnes and Co., Inc.
Cranbury, New Jersey 08512

Thomas Yoseloff Ltd
Magdalen House
136–148 Tooley Street
London SE1 2TT, England

World Federation of Bergen-Belsen Associations, Inc.
P.O. Box 333, Lenox Hill Station
New York, New York 10021

Second Printing 1979

ISBN 0-498-02168-8
Printed in the United States of America

In loving memory of Josef Rosensaft,
fellow survivor, friend, mentor, and leader

CONTENTS

ONE

PART ONE

1

A Summer of Foreboding

ALL THROUGH THE summer of 1939 Warsaw was in the grip of a strange malaise. No one had the heart to think about going to the country. People were afraid to leave the tight, safe little circle of home and family.

Every day my mother talked of some other neighbor who was hoarding food. The grocery stores were doing a brisk trade.

Mother had advised me to stay home that summer, but I went with some friends to spend my vacation in Mikuliczyn near Jaremcze, in the eastern Beskidy mountains.

I had known Mikuliczyn for many years. It was an enchanting little mountain village on the main highway between Jaremcze and Vorochta, scarcely touched by modern civilization. Here among the half-illiterate peasants, in the midst of the virgin forests and on the banks of the River Prut, exhausted city dwellers could find relaxation and peace of mind. Maccabi, the Jewish athletic club, had its central camp for instructors there, and many of the Jewish high schools in towns such as Stanislawow, Horodenka and Kolomyja sent their students to Mikuliczyn for the holidays. In short, it had always been a nice place for a summer vacation.

But in the summer of 1939 Mikuliczyn was dreary and deserted. The few tourists who came felt uncomfortable in this small Polish-Ukrainian village. Shopkeepers stood yawning all day long in their empty stores waiting for customers. Singing in the streets had been

1

forbidden by the police. A few couples danced to the music of a small band in Shor's dance hall. Hotel owners and managers went out to the railroad depot to meet incoming trains, in the hope that some guests might have arrived, but those few stalwart souls who turned up were invariably greeted with surprised looks and ironical smiles as if the villagers were asking them: "Why on earth did you come here now?"

Only the River Prut was as gusty and stormy as ever.

People discussed politics and, having analyzed the situation, hurriedly packed their bags and went back home to the city.

In a meadow outside the village the Poles who belonged to the National Guard practiced shooting while the Ukrainians went around grinning at each other, confident that their dreams of freedom would soon come true.

We decided to go home to Warsaw.

When the train pulled into the station and we got out at Ammunition Square, I could hardly recognize the streets; even the houses looked different. The people also had changed beyond belief; the fear of impending catastrophe had etched grim lines into their faces.

My schoolmates were busy with mysterious preparations—for what, they did not tell me at the beginning. The office where I had been working was closed. When I went to my boss to ask him what was going on, he told me that since no merchandise had been coming in from abroad, he saw no point in sitting there, just looking at the bare walls. People by the thousands stood in front of the Postal Savings Bank, waiting to withdraw their money. The grocery stores were packed with customers; outside, there were long lines of others waiting to get in. Men and women rushed about to and for, but no one knew where, or for what. At night, the windows were blacked out and the street lights dimmed.

The usual good-night greeting in town was, "See you in the morning—I hope."

My mother had a large workshop where she made fancy lingerie. Now she had received an order from the Polish army to sew haysacks for the cavalry. The work went on day and night, without a stop. I helped out, too; I wanted to keep busy in order to cast off the frustration and the sense of helplessness that had taken hold of me because of my enforced unemployment. All the Jewish youth groups—not to speak of their Polish counterparts—had been ordered to send their members out to help dig air raid trenches. One of our neighbors got a telegram from his wife, who was still vacationing in Krynica, informing him in veiled language that she was unable to get home because all the trains had been requisitioned for army transports.

On the Wednesday and Thursday before the war finally came, general mobilization orders, signed by President Mościcki, appeared on the walls of Warsaw's buildings.

Meanwhile, in Parliament, Foreign Minister Józef Beck was attacking Hitler, and Marshal Rydz-Śmigly declared belligerently that Poland would not surrender so much as a coat button to the Germans.

The radio was playing old Polish songs. Loudspeakers in the streets blared forth patriotic speeches and popular marching songs of the Polish Legion.

When Mother saw the mobilization orders, she wept. Fortunately for her, I was not in the age group that had been ordered to report for induction, but some of my schoolmates were already in the army.

Those were days of bleak despair in Warsaw, particularly among the Jews, who knew that the outbreak of war would mean their end.

"We might as well jump into the Vistula," our neighbor, Hannale Berkowitz, sobbed.

2

The War Begins

FRIDAY, SEPTEMBER 1, 1939, was a brilliantly sunny day. The cloudless sky was a deep, dazzling blue. The ground was burning hot. A steamy humidity had spread out over the streets of Warsaw. People were panting and sweating as though they were about to be strangled by some unspeakable monster. Though the day had dawned so brightly, their hearts were heavy.

That Friday morning I had slept later than usual. When I finally awoke at 8:30, I reached at once for the radio and turned on Station Warsaw Two for the latest news. "I don't care what happens, just don't let there be any war," I prayed. Why did the Poles have to be so stubborn about giving up the Corridor? [1] Wasn't this all that Hitler wanted? Were they in a position to resist the German armies? Were they willing to bring disaster upon our country? Why not let Hitler have his Corridor and be done with it? Thousands of other Jewish boys, along with their fathers and mothers, were asking the same questions. An entire people was entreating Providence to avert catastrophe.

Over the radio a voice was announcing in a low monotone: "Ko-

---

[1] A strip of Polish territory which separated East Prussia from the rest of Germany. Hitler used the "Polish Corridor" problem as a propaganda pretext for his invasion of Poland.

Ma 33 is arriving. Za-Mi 74 has passed. Do-La 11 has come in."
Strange-sounding announcements with an ominous ring; bizarre
code-words in place of the customary morning exercises.

I got dressed quickly and ran out into the street. I passed people
gathering in little knots discussing and analyzing every phrase that
issued from the Parliament House on Wiejska Street. There was
a run on the grocery stores. On Ptasia Street some policemen had
sealed the doors of four stores whose owners had violated the price
controls. Now they were putting up posters announcing that anyone
found guilty of black market dealings would be sent to the concentration camp of Bereza-Kartuska. The Postal Savings Bank was
no longer paying out money to depositors. When a rumor spread
that Shereshewsky's Bank was still open, everybody seemed to be
scurrying off in that direction. Colorful posters appeared on the
walls, with patriotic slogans addressed to "Brother Poles, Ukrainians and Jews." All the elementary school buildings in Warsaw
had been converted into recruiting stations and army supply depots.
The Greater Warsaw area had been divided into sectors for civilian
defense. Polish boy scouts could be seen digging trenches together
with youngsters from Jewish youth organizations.

On Żelazna Street the secret police had arrested a priest who had
kept a small camera hidden somewhere in his coat; the priest had
turned out to be a German spy. Another spy, this one disguised
as a chimney-sweep, had been caught standing on a rooftop signal-
ing with his arms at something in the sky. He was shot on the
spot.

I went home. I wanted to be with my mother. She was pacing
restlessly from the apartment to the workshop and back again and
didn't say a word. I think she intended to calm me by her silence,
as if to say, "Look, my child, I'm not even talking about the war.
All this commotion doesn't bother me, so you shouldn't let it worry
you, either."

But try as I might, I could not stay home for long. I went to the
house of my friend Reisfuss on Leszno Street. Some of our schoolmates were already there. We sat down at a table with a map of
Poland and the latest extra edition of the *Kurier Czerwony* to study
the military situation. My friend's bedroom looked like the map

6

room of army headquarters. Most of the other homes in Poland looked like that, too, in those early days of the war.

At twelve noon that day Warsaw had its first air raid. The people did not even try to find an air raid shelter; they just stood in the streets gazing up at the German planes. Some kept insisting that these were not German planes but bombers of the Polish air force going through maneuvers in the sky above Warsaw. Not even the wailing of the sirens could convince them that this was the real thing. But half an hour later the radio brought reports of heavy damage in the suburbs of Mokotow and Praga. When the next air raids came, not a soul was to be seen in the streets. I spent whole days at my friend's house talking about the war, though all my thoughts were with my mother at home. From the very beginning it was clear that, compared to the Germans, the armed forces of Poland were mere toy soldiers. Bad news came each day from the western front, reports of heavy losses, of continuous German advances, and of devastation sowed by the Nazi air force upon the towns and villages of our country. We took heart at the news of General Bortnowski's heroic resistance in Danzig but our hopes were short-lived. Poland was rushing headlong to its ruin.

One of our friends, the daughter of a well to do fruit dealer who lived on Ptasia Street, told us in great secrecy that her father and brothers had asked a seamstress to sew some knapsacks for them. When the Germans got close to Warsaw, the men would flee along with the retreating Polish army, the girl explained. This news came as a shock. We exchanged quick looks. The next day all the Jewish men were having knapsacks made up post-haste. As if in obedience to some mysterious command, the men—particularly the Jewish men—in the city prepared to leave their homes and to travel into the unknown.

The first five days of the war, days of terror, of feverish planning and utter despair, dragged on like years.

I desperately cast about for some consolation. On Sunday, September 10, something happened to lift my spirits and revive my hopes. The news had come to Warsaw that Britain had declared war on Germany. Now we are saved, I thought. Crowds from all parts of the city were moving toward the British Embassy on Nowy

Świat Street. Patriotic songs rang out, especially the old Polish battle hymn "We Shall Never Surrender Our Soil." Cheers and hurrahs filled the air and echoed through the streets. Poles and Jews, extreme Polish nationalists and youthful hasidim, marched together, arm in arm, like brothers. That Sunday, streets on which no Jew had ever dared show his face before welcomed the black-clad hasidim with their broad-brimmed hats and bouncing earlocks. The British ambassador appeared on the embassy balcony and said a few words of greeting. Afterwards the crowds filled the restaurants and cafés; they sat at sidewalk tables and in summer gardens, their hearts lighter than they had been in days, drinking cups of strong, black coffee. German war planes appeared in the sky, but nobody paid any attention to them. At that moment the Nazi air force was vanquished by the joy of the people of Warsaw. The knowledge that we were no longer alone in our battle gave us new courage and confidence.

But this holiday mood lasted only a few hours. Toward evening there was another air raid. That night, as we patrolled the streets with the Civil Defense League, we saw thousands of refugees from Mlawa, Ripin and other towns and villages where the Germans had literally mowed down the Polish troops. We could not believe our eyes. We had not expected it to happen so fast, so soon.

By Tuesday night the mood in Warsaw had become tense and nervous. The radio announcers no longer made any attempts to calm the people. Colonel Umiastkowski, who had been giving morale-boosting talks over the Raszyn radio station, was still on the air, but now he was speaking in somber tones. He no longer called for perseverance and endurance; instead, he ordered every young man capable of holding a gun or a shovel to leave Warsaw and march eastward with the retreating Polish army, and join its ranks.

At about midnight I was awakened at home by my friend David Reisfuss. He told me to pack some things at once because we would be leaving in an hour's time. By "we" he meant our "Brotherhood of Four" who had sworn to remain together in life and death. My immediate reaction was that I could not go with them. How could I leave my mother who stood at the door waiting for me whenever

I got home ten minutes later than I had promised? Reisfuss did not attempt to argue the point with me but ran back to his own home to pack his belongings, leaving me standing in the middle of my room in my pajamas, still not realizing what was going on, and unable to act.

But Mother had already begun to take clothes from my wardrobe—some underwear, shoes, a suit—and to pack them into my knapsack.

"Go, Pinye dear," she said. "Go and may luck be with you. Don't worry about me. How much longer do I have to live, anyway? You have to save yourself. I have brought you this far but from now on you'll have to decide your own fate. You still have your whole life ahead of you." But then her self-control left her, and she burst into tears. "Woe is me," she sobbed, "to have to live through this in my old age!"

She kept on crying and talking, kissing me and holding me tightly in her arms. I did not know what to do. I had never really been away from my mother before. Even when I had been away at school in Vilno she had come every few weeks to spend a couple of days with me. Formerly, I had needed her, but now the roles had been reversed. How could I leave her when she needed me so badly? But the call of duty to join the battle against the Germans had to be answered. The war was in full swing and all young men were badly needed to fight the invaders. For what seemed hours, we struggled with ourselves and with each other, but in the end she prevailed and I left. I walked out the door quickly, leaving my widowed mother alone and in terrible danger. To this day I can see her tear-streaked face and hear the broken sobs with which she sent her only son out into the black abyss of war.

At the Reisfuss home, my three friends were waiting for me, ready to start out: Shlomo Damazer, David Yakubovich and David Reisfuss. Mrs. Reisfuss was crying; her two daughters were moving about nervously, packing food for us to take along. David's father, who had always seemed so stern and unemotional, was wiping his eyes. "Start out with your right foot first for good luck, and may God protect you," he murmured in a husky voice.

9

Here we were, our "Brotherhood of Four," hardly past childhood, setting out for an unknown fate.

Shlomo Damazer was the son of a Warsaw sausage manufacturer. He was short, and his hair had a way of tumbling into his plain, pale face. He was nervous and absent-minded and we, his friends, had our hands full keeping him calm and petting him like a child; he practically demanded it of us. His strange behavior had probably been due to the fact that although his family was well off and had a fine, comfortable home, Shlomo had always felt that he did not really belong anywhere. He had never had any luck. There had been constant fights with his brothers. He had not been popular with girls. As a matter of fact, none of us could picture Shlomo actually hugging a girl. He felt a bitter resentment toward his parents. He had never graduated from the Finkel High School because he had been over-sensitive; for him, every little classroom upset had been a major catastrophe. The only person for whom he seemed to have genuine affection was our friend Jerzy "Jappa" Grynstein, who had gone to Palestine in 1938. It was apparently on account of Grynstein that Shlomo had originally joined our group. Basically, Shlomo had fine human qualities; he was always ready to help others. Now, as we were about to leave Warsaw, he placed himself entirely into our hands. It was as if he were saying: "Wherever you'll go, I'll go, too. You can do with me whatever you like."

David Yakubovich, or "Yakubek," as we called him, was the best-looking of the four of us; he was as handsome as any movie star. Yakubek had a rare sense of humor which never deserted him, not even in the hospital when he had his left kidney removed. He had been the moving spirit in all our secret gatherings and had been known for his ravenous appetite. At one time, his family had been rich, but they had lost all their money and had had to sell their remaining possessions to send Yakubek to the Krinsky High School, where he had been the best student in his class, and later to the Warsaw Polytechnic Institute, where he also had an outstanding record. With his jokes, his witty remarks and his unshakable optimism, David Yakubovich was an inexhaustible source of faith and courage for the rest of us.

10

But our undisputed leader was David Reisfuss, whom we called "Srayek." He was short, even shorter than Shlomo Damazer, but that was an insignificant detail. Srayek was smart; his mind was clear and sober and he never started out on any venture without carefully planning every detail. Whenever he had a new idea, he would take off his glasses, wipe them, bite his lips, and then, very softly, proceed to tell us his views, which invariably met with our approval. His father had been working hard as a cutter at the PEPEGE rubber boot factory, but nothing had been too good for his Davidek. After graduating from the Trzeci Związek Państwowy High School, Srayek had gone away to Italy to study medicine because it was extremely difficult for a Jew to get into the University of Warsaw. He had spent his summer vacation in Michalin and had been about to return to his studies in Pisa when the war broke out. He had been unable to go back to Italy, and now he was going away with us—only God knew where.

* * *

It was late at night by the time we left the Reisfuss home at Leszno Street. It was pitch dark outside. The windows had been blacked out in accordance with the orders of the military authorities. We could hardly see each other, but we could sense the haste, the panic, and the confusion which had taken hold of the people of Warsaw that night after Colonel Umiastkowski's radio announcement calling on all able-bodied males to follow the army eastward.

We set out in the direction of Bielanska Street. In passing, we said a mute good-bye to No. 2 Leszno Street, once the headquarters of the Jewish Artist's Union, and to Gertner's famous Central Bar, in front of which we had stood in our younger days watching the actors of the Yiddish theater going in and out. On Tlomatzka Street, to our right, was No. 13, the clubhouse of the Jewish Writers' Union. To our left, we took silent leave of the Ahiasaf Hebrew Publishing Company and of the house where the Zionist leader Itzhak Grinbaum had lived before he left Poland back in 1932 and settled in Palestine. To our right again, we had a last look at the Great Synagogue, the Judaica Library, and the Raphael Photographers' Studio at whose windows we had stopped so many times

11

to admire the portraits of movie stars and other celebrities. Now, for the last time, we passed these buildings, dark and silent, but bright with memories of our childhood.

On Bielanska Street the blind fear was more obvious than anywhere else in town. Here the people were no longer walking but running, though no one seemed to know where to go. We followed the crowd across Bielańska Street where in the peaceful past we had flirted with the girls from the Saksova, Landau and Yehudiah high schools. As we ran past No. 9, the Nowości Theater, I could make out posters and pictures advertising the new production of Goldfaden's *Shulamith*. I had seen the operetta just two days before the war and had thought it quite marvelous. Where were all these actors now, I wondered. We passed familiar store signs and billboards: "Abramski, the Best Shoes in Town"; "Alter Katzizna Photographers," "Baum and Forbert, Pioneers of Yiddish Films in Poland," "Ludwig Spiess and Son, Pharmacists"—memories of hopes and dreams which we were leaving behind, forever.

But we had no time for such thoughts as we rushed on, caught up in the crowds of refugees. The skies above us were filled with the terrible roar of German bombers. Searchlights crisscrossed the sky. All at once we found ourselves on the Poniatowski Bridge that spanned the River Vistula. We had to watch our step so as not to fall into the river below, because the bridge had already been badly damaged. The Poles had mounted guns at close intervals, manned by artillery soldiers—some sad and somber-looking, others whistling army tunes. As we sped across the bridge, the area commander, a colonel, called out to us cheerfully: "See you soon!" Then he turned briskly back to his men.

By the time we reached the suburb of Praga, dawn was breaking over the city. The highway was jammed with thousands who, like ourselves, were fleeing from the Germans. We were amazed to see high-ranking Polish officers driving civilian cars carrying their wives and maids, suitcases and even dogs. We naively wondered why these officers should want to take their families and their belongings with them to the battlefront. We did not realize then that they were not going off to fight the Germans but that they were running like mice from the war zone. As they sped along, forcing everyone

12

else off the highway, they were followed by the shouts and curses of wretched refugees who were trying desperately to drag themselves to safety on foot. The seething mass of humanity filled every inch of the highway. We were forced into the trails and ditches on the side of the road. There were thousands—tens of thousands— pushing bicycles piled high with bedding and bundles, and horse-drawn wagons filled with two or three families and their belongings. These were the lucky ones. What of the others who had neither bicycle nor horse and had to rely on their own two legs? They, too, were laden with bundles crammed with their last possessions; they, too, had little children, ailing wives and aged mothers. How far would they be able to go without collapsing? But we had no time for such thoughts. We had no choice except to move on.

Suddenly, German planes appeared overhead. Swooping down upon the highway, they began to machine-gun the refugees. In the turmoil that followed, men and women fell over one another, trampling each other, screaming, while the pilots of the German air force dropped incendiary bombs on the woods nearby, where hundreds of refugees had taken cover. It was a massacre followed by a flaming inferno. I saw one man with both legs torn off, and another with his entrails exposed. One woman had gone stark raving mad; another woman was screaming, her hair and clothes on fire. And then, in an instant, all was still. The planes had disappeared. Those who had been spared pushed forward, deaf to the pleas of the badly wounded not to leave them behind. At such times people think only of themselves, and of their own families. Those who could not keep up with the others were left by the roadside. All along the highway were carcasses of horses, bicycles with broken wheels and tires ripped to shreds. There were also cars of the best American, Italian, Czech and German makes, which had been abandoned by their owners because they had run out of gasoline.

Suddenly a troop of mounted Polish cavalry appeared around a bend in the highway, galloping in the opposite direction from the stream of refugees—toward Warsaw, not away from it. The refugees began to cheer; some even stopped to pick wild flowers on the edge of the highway to toss at the horsemen. The officer in the lead gave them a salute and shouted, "We'll drive the Prussians out!" A few in the crowd laughed bitterly, but most of us believed him, because we wanted so much to believe what he was saying.

The hit-and-run scene was to be repeated over and over again. German planes attacked the helpless civilians at brief intervals, sowing panic, suffering and death. We were hardly able to make any headway because we spent most of the time seeking cover from the German bombers.

We decided to leave the main highway and move along the side roads, believing that we would be safer off the beaten track, away from the mainstream of refugees who were under constant bombardment from the Nazi planes. Thus, we entered, and passed, the town of Otwock. Although we were not the only ones using this route, things were much quieter there than on the main highway. We dug up some carrots, onions and parsnips in the fields along the way to appease our hunger.

But before long, new trouble caught up with us. Shlomo Damazer collapsed; he could not go on any more. He said he no longer cared what would happen to him; he wanted to return to the city. He had developed a sore between his legs from sitting in the damp moss in the woods, where we had rested from time to time, and each step was sheer agony for him. Of course we would not hear of his going back to Warsaw alone. We grabbed him by the arms and pulled him along with us. After a while we stopped and laid him on the ground on his stomach. Yakubek took off his pants and dusted his sore with talcum powder. This helped a little, but it lost us two hours, and we had no time to lose. The news we picked up along the way kept getting worse. Shlomo was worried that we might fall into the hands of the Germans on his account. Just then a horse-drawn wagon drew abreast of us with a man, a woman and two children—a Gentile family. We stopped them and begged them to give our sick friend a lift. The man said that he belonged to the anti-Semitic "Endek" party, but that in times like these we all would have to stand united against our common foe. So, he allowed Shlomo to climb onto the wagon, while we three others followed on foot, helping push the wagon from behind. After we had dragged ourselves along in this fashion for half a day,

14

we were stopped by an army patrol and ordered to get back on the main highway because the side-roads had been closed to all non-army traffic.

The main highway was about three kilometers away, and it was almost impossible to get there because it was blocked with refugees; besides, the wagon had trouble making it over the sandy ground. Both Shlomo and the woman had to get off the wagon because the horse was at the end of its strength. The leather harness had cut deep into its skin, but, hurt and bleeding though it was, the poor beast was making a valiant effort to go on, as if it knew the danger threatening us from the approaching Germans.

Shlomo lay down on the ground and refused to go on. We stayed with him. After a while a column of Polish tanks came lumbering by, each piled high with young men. The column stopped and the tank drivers told us to climb aboard. With some effort, Shlomo Damazer and David Reisfuss climbed the lead tank; David Yaku-bovich mounted the second, and I, the third. The four of us agreed to meet in Garvolin. Little did I know then that I would never see any of my three friends again.

After some time, the tank on which I was riding came to a stop. The officer in charge announced that we would have to get off about two kilometers before Garvolin and that the boys aboard the tanks—some 70 in all—would have to walk the rest of the way into the town. On our arrival there, the officer added, we would be inducted into the army.

A truck passed by, showering us with packs of cigarettes. I grabbed as many as I could, stuffing them into my knapsack and into my pockets. A moment later we moved on. The clanging and the roar of the tanks was deafening. The heat of the motor seared our bottoms while the hot September sun burned our faces. But we did not care, because the tanks were taking us away from our enemies.

Eventually our ride came to an end and we were ordered off the tank. The first two tanks were nowhere in sight. The officer told us that they had gone ahead. I was now alone among stran-gers, in a world full of nameless terrors.

*   *   *

The stores in Garvolin were open for business as usual. The Jewish storekeepers were surprised to see refugees from Warsaw. Had the world really turned upside down, they asked. Money was pouring into their tills; articles that had been gathering dust on their shelves for years were snapped up eagerly by the transients.

The town was fairly overrun with refugees. All the restaurants and taverns were packed. People sat on the sidewalks, wherever they found a little space to rest, or to eat. The stores had run out of bread and crowds laid siege to the bakeries waiting for a fresh batch. As soon as the loaves were removed from the ovens, they were seized by hungry travelers.

Suddenly German planes appeared in the sky. They circled very low, almost touching the rooftops so that we could clearly see their pilots. Immediately, machine guns and even revolvers opened fire on them from the ground. One of the planes was hit and crashed in flames at the outer edge of the town. The crowds in the streets went wild. They seized the lucky marksman, a Jewish infantry soldier, and lifted him high into the air. He was thoroughly hugged and kissed and acclaimed over and over again as the "Jewish hero."

I had spent all my time looking for my three friends, but after this experience with enemy reconnaissance I decided to get out of Garvolin as soon as possible.

About midnight I came to the little town of Luków. I could hear the muffled sound of explosions from the distance. Later, I met some dazed refugees from Garvolin who told me that not a single house had been left standing in their town.

Despite the lateness of the hour, Luków was wide awake. On the way out of Garvolin I had attached myself to a group of young Jewish men; it made me feel safer, and a little less lost, on the road. A Jewish family gave us a room in their house, and welcomed us with a full meal of freshly-baked hallah, fish and meat. The delicious food gave us a new lease on life. Afterwards, we went to our room and took off our shoes to give our feet a rest.

Back in Otwock my toes had already begun to hurt but I had not stopped to take off my shoes to look for the cause of the trouble. When you are running for your life, you tend to ignore

16

such things. But now, when I wanted to take off my socks, I found that they were glued to my toes and soaked with blood, so that I literally had to tear them off. As I did so, my toenails came off along with them. I bit my lips so as not to cry out with the pain. My new friends washed my wounds, applied iodine and goat grease and then carefully bandaged my feet.

The next morning the others left, but I remained behind because walking was impossible for me. I heard rumors that the Germans had already taken Warsaw. That evening, I dragged myself painfully out of the house and into the street to hear the latest news. I moved one step at a time—each step was sheer agony—until I got to the highway. There I stopped and watched the masses of refugees move past. As I stood there grimacing in pain, I noticed a familiar figure standing not far away from me. It was Mr. Keller, the father of my friend Krishya. At that very moment, he noticed me, too, and we rushed to each other with outstretched arms.

Keller had owned and operated a forwarding business in Warsaw, with four moving trucks, several flatcars and twelve teams of horses. His daughter Krishya had been our good friend, our favorite, in fact, although she was quite a bit younger than we were. She was a pretty girl, with a pleasant singing voice and a delicate, lady-like manner. Her house at 32 Grzybowska was the place where our bunch had always met on Saturday nights, to dance and to enjoy the refreshments which her mother, Mrs. Keller, had prepared for us. On more than one occasion Krishya's parents had joined in our fun, dancing, sipping drinks and telling jokes. Now and then they even went with us to one of the night spots such as the popular Adria or the FF Club.

Now, in the midst of all the panic and confusion, here was Krishya's father. He told me how he had decided to get out of Warsaw, leaving behind his wife and Krishya, the apple of his eye, because they had not wanted to leave their home. He, Keller, had driven out of Warsaw in one of his trucks but very soon a Polish army patrol had stopped him and taken away his truck, leaving him stranded on the highway with all his belongings. "But, as you know," he told me with a smile, "I always manage somehow. I walked to the nearest village and in return for a couple of quarts

17

of liquor I got myself a horse and wagon. So here I am in Luków, along with David, a boy who works for me. He wouldn't let me go alone. Tomorrow morning we'll move on. You're welcome to join us, if you want to. We have plenty of canned food with us."

I burst into tears. I had been utterly alone, without my friends, barely able to walk, and here Mr. Keller had suddenly come to my rescue. I fell on his neck and kissed him, crying bitterly. Then I went back to my lodgings and took my knapsack over to his room. David was happy to hear that I was going to join them, because I would make things easier for the two of them; ever so often, they had had to get off their wagon and push it.

We agreed to start out at dawn the next morning. However, we found ourselves leaving a good deal earlier because a little later that night the Germans started to bomb the town. In a flash we harnessed the horse, tossed our bags into the wagon and took off at a gallop. The horse, rested and well fed, fairly flew. Behind us, all hell had broken loose; we could hear the explosions for quite some time. The Nazis were wiping Luków off the map.

All night long we hurried on, never stopping once. We passed long Polish army transports and had to make our way between cannons, army wagons and cavalry units. A melancholy tune reached our ears. It was a Polish cavalry officer, singing softly in the dark about the little village where he had grown up and about his sweetheart, who was waiting there for his return. To this day I can see that cavalryman silhouetted against the starlit sky and hear his plaintive song.

At one point, Keller put the reins into my hands and told me to go on without him for a while. He then got off the wagon and disappeared somewhere off the highway. I thought he had gone to relieve himself. But when he reappeared, he was leading a horse. He quickly harnessed it to our wagon, leaped into the saddle and in a wink he had both horses running at full gallop. He had taken the horse from an army unit that had gone past, herding a hundred such horses to some unknown destination. It was, he explained, no more than fair payment for the truck which the army patrol had taken from him. Keller was one of those fortunate people who can get along in any situation. He was a decent, honest man, but when you are in a war you have to think of saving your own skin before anything else.

All through the next day we hurried ahead. We passed village after village where only blackened chimneys still stood erect, mute witnesses to the thorough job the Nazi air force had done. We stopped outside a village church near Kock to eat something. Just then the German planes appeared and within seconds the entire place, including the church, was in ruins. The rain of bombs, the roaring and whistling that preceded every hit, nearly drove us out of our minds. After each explosion Keller would raise his head from the grass and shout, "Trepman, are you alive? David, are you alive?" and when we answered that we were all right he heaved a sigh of relief. "Thank God," he said. Keller, the unbeliever, was murmuring the *Shema Yisrael* prayer along with us. The Christians nearby crossed themselves and cried out to Jesus. All around us we could hear the wild screams of the wounded and the neighs of the terrified horses. Trees crashed to the ground, crushing those who had sought shelter beneath them. After the planes had gone, we picked ourselves up from the grass and saw that the three of us—Keller, David and I—were alone in the midst of hundreds of corpses. Without a word we jumped onto the wagon and hurriedly fled from the nightmarish scene.

We took the highway leading to Międzyrzec. But after we had traveled only a few kilometers, we were stopped by soldiers who advised us not to go on to Międzyrzec because the place was being bombed by the Germans. Since the road to Radzyn—our original goal—had been closed by the army to all traffic moving from our direction, we turned back and took a side road leading to Zelechow. We stopped to rest in an abandoned schoolhouse. From the disarray in the classrooms and in the principal's office we could tell that the building had been occupied by soldiers who apparently had fled in a hurry. Keller, never once losing his presence of mind, calmly went off to look for oats to feed our two weary horses. He came back lugging a barrel of kerosene. I did not understand why he should want to burden our horses with this additional load. But Keller explained that in wartime kerosene was worth its weight in gold. He was so right! From that point on we were able to get all

19

the food we needed for both the horses and ourselves. For one quart of kerosene peasants along the way gave us two loaves of bread, a pitcher of milk, ten eggs and a chunk of lard. Keller's good sense kept us alive.

We got to Zelechow toward evening. The town looked more like a cemetery than a place of human habitation. The doors of all the houses were shut tight, the shutters were locked, and everything was in pitch darkness. Not a soul was to be seen. We came to a bakery where men were baking bread for the Polish army. We managed to wheedle two warm loaves of bread out of them and continued on our way. The officer who was apparently supervising the work advised us to go on to Radzyn. He told us that an army was being organized there which would definitely stop the Germans. We followed his advice because this was exactly why we had left our homes: we had wanted to join the army and fight the Nazis.

On the way we stopped off at the estate of a nobleman for a rest. Several hundred soldiers and civilians were already there, and the lady of the house was serving them bread and milk. "God bless you and keep you from all harm, and may you have the strength to drive out the German swine," she said to each soldier as she passed by. Among the refugees Keller recognized a man he knew from Warsaw, Janek Tom, brother of the conductor and composer of popular music, Conrad Tom. They hugged and kissed each other and inquired about mutual friends. Janek joined us on our way but he caused us plenty of trouble. Tall and thin, he was totally unaccustomed to hardships. His fears and his egotism made the going rough for the rest of us. He had lots of money with him, but whenever a couple of pennies were needed, he pretended not to hear and never contributed anything. More than once Keller regretted having taken him along with us.

A few years later I was to meet Janek again—in the Warsaw ghetto, where he was an officer in the Jewish ghetto police. When I was brought to the Jewish police station at 13 Twarda Street I was taken to Janek, who pretended not to know me and added my name to a list of individuals to be sent on to a concentration camp. I reminded him of our journey together in Keller's wagon, but

Janek only smiled and muttered, "Oh, it's you," as he motioned to the police officer on duty to take me away. He did not even bother to look at me again. Unfortunately, such unsavory individuals turned up here and there in those years, but they were very few.

Radzyn was swarming with soldiers who had become separated from their units. Everything was in complete chaos. Cavalrymen rode about without saddles and weapons, barefoot, dirty and hungry. Infantrymen were looting stores and homes. Officers were shouting orders without any authority to back them up. Headquarters seemed to be functioning after a fashion, but there was a total absence of organization and discipline. No high-ranking officers were around, and the non-coms seemed to be afraid of the privates. Here, in the little town of Radzyn, we could see the full measure of Poland's defeat.

We stopped one of the sergeants and asked him to induct us into the army. He told us to cross the River Bug and go to Wlodawa because there were no uniforms available in Radzyn; the enemy was too close.

But before we could get out of Radzyn we were caught once again in a German air raid. Flying very low, almost brushing the rooftops, the Nazi planes followed up their hail of bombs with a spatter of machine-gun fire directed at the crowds milling about the town. The resulting turmoil was beyond description. In an instant human beings had turned into trapped wild beasts. They pushed, shoved and screamed, trampling each other and running wherever their legs carried them. The four of us leaped over the fence of a churchyard. With hammering hearts we listened to the shrieks of the falling bombs, wondering each time whether our number had come up. We fully expected to die at any moment. I buried my head in the grass in a vain attempt to block out the scene around me. We lay like this for about an hour, glued to the ground, scarcely breathing. When the bombing finally stopped, we got to our feet and ran to our wagon. To our surprise, everything was still there as we had left it; nothing had been stolen or destroyed. Our horses were standing quietly where we had left them, nibbling at the grass. We quickly jumped onto our wagon

21

and drove away. The road out of Radzyn was covered with the torn, charred bodies of men, women and children. Those who had survived, including the soldiers, were fleeing in panicked disarray. It was clear that no new Polish army was going to be organized in Radzyn now.

The thousands of fleeing soldiers and civilians on the highway were acting like fugitives from an insane asylum. Some of them had turned tail and were rushing back in the direction of Warsaw. Others hurried on, eastward, across the River Bug. And still others, like ourselves, were scurrying back and forth without rhyme or reason within a narrow radius of about eight square kilometers. We could not make up our minds where we should go or whom we should believe. One of the officers we met told us that Warsaw was in flames so that there was no point in going back because we would not find anyone alive there. We therefore hurried on toward Wlo-dawa. But on the way we met a group of civilians who told us that the town commander had ordered all able-bodied men to proceed to Warsaw immediately to help defend the city. By this time we were thoroughly confused, but since orders were orders, especially in wartime, we turned back. After we had traveled about ten kilo-meters in the direction of Warsaw, we were stopped by two Polish government officials. "Where are you going, citizens?" the taller of the two asked us. "Straight into the arms of the Germans to get butchered? You'd better turn around and go to Kowel. From there you can travel on to Rumania. Our government and our general staff are all there. The Rumanian government allowed them to come in and organize a new Polish army on Rumanian territory. So—in the name of our people and in the name of our President—I say to you: Go to Rumania!" All the people crowding around us in the middle of the highway began to cheer and tossed their caps into the air, and everybody turned and headed back for Kowel and Rumania. The four of us—Keller, Janek, David and I—did likewise but, in order to avoid the crush of the main highway, we decided to travel along side-roads.

This was the start of a new stage in our journey. The Germans were stepping up their bombings. The fields we passed were covered with dead cows and horses and with the bodies of children who had probably taken care of the cattle. The Germans were bombing schools, churches and hospitals. Scarcely an hour passed that we did not have to stop, hitch our horses to a tree, and take cover in the tall grass, in a cornfield or—when we were lucky—in a little forest. The drone of the Nazi bombers had become so familiar to our ears that we had learned to distinguish between the Messerschmitts and the Czech-made Skodas. Most of the bombers were Skodas. Not once did we see Polish planes in the sky; we saw them only on the ground, where they had been shot down in dogfights with the Nazis.

We sped past gutted, abandoned villages. In one village the peasant women stood forlornly on the doorsteps of their houses. When they saw us, they burst into a chorus of weeping and wailing, for us and also for their sons and husbands who had been taken into the army. It was becoming increasingly dangerous to travel by day, so we decided to travel only by night.

Some twenty kilometers before Wlodawa we met a friend of Keller's, Henryk Gold. Henryk had been the conductor of Poland's best jazz band and had composed many popular tango tunes. Now he was wearing an army uniform but he had become separated from his unit. Keller invited him to join us but Gold declined. He said he was a soldier and therefore had to stay with the army. Incidentally, he reminded us that it was the eve of Rosh HaShanah, the Jewish New Year. However, he agreed to let us take him to the nearest village where, he said, he would have to report to army headquarters. On the way, Keller and Gold exchanged reminiscences and talked about their hopes for the future. Then Gold got off, bade us farewell, and disappeared into the darkness.

We decided to by-pass Wlodawa because the town was in flames. When we reached the bridge on the outskirts of the town and were about to cross the River Bug, we were stopped by Polish gendarmes who informed us that the bridge had been mined and would blow up at any moment. When we argued that we had seen other refugees cross the bridge only moments before, the gendarmes got angry and threatened to shoot us. In the end, however, they permitted us to cross, asking only that we drive slowly. But as we started to cross the bridge, an axle of our wagon broke and we had to stop. The gendarmes shouted at us to get off the bridge immediately because if we didn't get off, we'd kill both them and ourselves. German planes were constantly flying low over the bridge, ready to machine-gun anything they saw moving there. We got off the wagon and tried to push it across, but we could not budge it. We had no other choice but to unload our baggage and start carrying it across the bridge piecemeal. We made several trips back and forth, to the steady accompaniment of the officers' curses, until finally we had brought all our belongings, including the wagon and the horses, safely to the opposite bank of the river. Just then, the German bombers appeared in the sky again, but they did not spot us. Keller leaped onto one of our horses and disappeared. He was gone for several hours. Meanwhile, the three of us—David, Janek and I—pulled off our clothes and jumped into the river while the Poles were not looking. We were afraid of the German bombers but we could no longer stand the dirt and grime on our bodies. Ignoring the danger, we took a refreshing bath in the cold water of the River Bug.

Finally, Keller came back—with a new wagon. He had found a village blacksmith who had sold him the wagon and shod our horse for 6,000 zlotys. At first, the blacksmith, a White Russian, had not wanted to take the Polish money. "What good is this trash now?" he had said to Keller. "Poland is finished, thank God, and so is the Polish money."

So now we had two enemies to contend with—the Germans on the one hand, and the White Russians, who hated the Poles, on the other. We had heard of incidents in which the White Russians had summarily gunned down Polish soldiers and civilian refugees.

There was yet a third foe—the gypsies who would wait by the side of the roads and offer to guide refugees along a shorter route through the forest for just a few zlotys and a loaf of bread. Once deep inside the forest, they would kill the refugees and make off with their money and their belongings. But Keller was equal to this challenge also. He took off the Polish army medal he had been wearing in his coat lapel and began talking to the peasants in a mixture of Russian, Polish and Ukrainian. In this way we were able to travel on unmolested. However, from then on we were careful not to stop in villages but only in the open fields.

* * *

The refugees whom we met on the highway seemed to be in good spirits. Word had spread that on September 17 the Red Army would occupy the eastern sector of Poland as far to the west as the River Bug. Deliverance seemed at hand. Already the roads and highways were guarded by a people's militia recruited from among the local peasantry. We were told that many Poles had turned around at Wlodawa and started back for Warsaw. It seemed that our wanderings, our fears, and the bombings, would soon be at an end.

We continued further on our way. Before long, our wagon rolled into Kamien-Koszyrski, a little town some 40 kilometers from Kowel, with a large Jewish population. Kamien-Koszyrski, too, was full of soldiers and refugees. Most of the soldiers, along with many Polish civilians, had packed their belongings and fled when they heard that the Russians were coming. But the Jews had stayed put. Keller drove our wagon into the courtyard of one of the Jewish families and got oats for our horses, while David and I watched our belongings. At this point Janek Tom told us good-bye; he said he was going back to Warsaw.

After a while I began to look for a room. Keller had already found one for himself. As I walked through the town, I met some people I had known in Warsaw. One of them was Szymek Laufer, the cousin of a friend of mine. The two of us decided to travel together. I had to part from Keller, who said that since the situation seemed to be stabilizing, he would return to Warsaw, pick up his wife and daughter, and bring them back with him into the Russian sector. We bade each other a fond farewell, and I promised never to forget how he had saved my life.

A year later I was to meet Keller and his family in Rohatyn, where they were working at jobs with the Soviets. They were in good spirits, happy that they had all managed to remain alive. In 1942 I was to see them again, this time in the Warsaw ghetto. When the Germans had captured Rohatyn from the Russians,

Keller had taken his family back to Warsaw, into the ghetto, believing that if you had to live under the Nazis anyway, it was better to be in your own home town. Eventually, the three Kellers went underground and found lodging in the Aryan sector of the city. Later I heard that Keller had found work as a street cleaner and that his daughter Krishya had gotten an office job. They had good "Aryan" papers and, even more important, faces that could easily pass for 'Aryan.' In this manner, the Kellers were able to settling in Toronto, where Mr. Keller died a few years later. Krishya and Mrs. Keller live in Toronto and we see each other from time to time.

* * *

Szymek and I finally found some kind people who gave us a room in their house. They were the owners of the local mill; their name ,as I recall, was Chait. They attended to our cuts and sores, washed our clothes and shared their food with us as if we had been their own children. Their only son treated us like brothers. Every evening the better-class youth of the town gathered at the Chait's for games and good talk. They did their utmost to cheer us up and to allay my fears for my mother, who was still in Warsaw, in the hands of the Nazi conquerors. In view of her age, there could be no thought of smuggling her out of the Nazi-held area and bringing her to Kamien-Koszyrski.

The day after our arrival in the town, the Russians came. Nahorny, the new town commissar, ordered all those having weapons or ammunition of any kind to turn them over to the Russion occupation authorities within 24 hours. Nahorny was a pleasant man, cultured and courteous. Late every afternoon he would step out onto the balcony of his headquarters and give the townspeople information on current problems. The streets of the town were filled with refugees. We would gather in the market place and stand there in groups, comparing notes about our war experiences and how we had managed to survive them. In the courtyard of the synagogue the local women cooked meals for the refugees. Men who had been prominent merchants, noted doctors, lawyers, actors, writers and Jewish community leaders back in Warsaw and in other cities sat down quietly and shamefacedly at the long tables and ate the food with a heavy appetite. Each Friday night the hasidic *rebbe* of Modzyc led the Sabbath services in the synagogue, which was filled with worshippers. Who could have foreseen that here, in the midst of our wanderings, we would have an opportunity to hear this famous sage to whose hasidic "court" in Otwock we had traveled every year for Yom Kippur?

Each passing day brought new rumors. Some said that the Russians would occupy Polish territory as far west as the Warsaw suburb of Praga. Others, less optimistic, felt that they had better keep on moving eastward because the Germans could not be trusted to content themselves with the River Bug as their boundary line but would almost certainly attempt to push further to the east. Still other refugees insisted that a great Polish army, organized in Rumania and armed by the British, was moving toward Poland. And all the time the men were longing for the wives and children they had left in the German-occupied sector. The young people wanted to turn back and go home. But there was nothing we could do except wait. Most of the Jews decided to "stay with the Russians," as they put it, but first they wanted to return to their German-held home towns and get their families out. Some even planned to move further east, deep into Russia proper, because they felt that Poland was not safe enough.

I stayed in Kamien-Koszyrski for nine days. When I learned that the milk train was running again I thought it best that Szymek and I should move on to Kowel. I bade my hosts a warm farewell. Tears running down her cheeks, Mrs. Chait walked with me to the garden gate. Up to the last minute, she had tried to talk me out of leaving. "Bring your mother here and stay with us," she pleaded. "You'll have everything you need at our house." Difficult though it was to resist such an invitation, I was bent on moving on to Zoblotow, a town only 20 kilometers from Kolomyja, on the Rumanian border. When Mrs. Chait saw that I was determined to go, she gave me a large package of food she had prepared for Szymek and me and kissed me good-bye as if I had been her own son. Her husband and son, too, embraced and kissed me. I was never to see them again, for in 1941 the Germans occupied Kamien-Koszyrski and killed all the Jews in the town.

3

Hammer and Sickle

THE MILK TRAIN took Szymek and me to Kowel. The weather had turned cloudy and cold. The few leaves that were still left on the trees clung limply to the frozen branches while the grass was dying in rusty brown patches on the ground. The Asiatic chill worked its way deep into our bones.

Our train consisted entirely of open freight cars. The summer clothes in which we had left home early in September were not warm enough to protect our bodies from the biting cold; we huddled together like Siamese twins to keep warm. We could see Russian marines standing near the tracks, beside trucks mired deep in mud. They waved to us, smiling broadly and occasionally throwing us some of their cheap *machorka* tobacco wrapped in scraps of paper. At a time when other soldiers were killing people like ourselves, it was good to know that there were also soldiers like these kind-hearted Russians. But the fierce cold had dulled our emotions. We sat pressed as close as possible to one another, a frozen, scarcely breathing mass of refugees whom fate had brought together and was now herding into the unknown like so many head of cattle.

In Kowel, we found the stores jammed with people. We could not get so much as a piece of bread. The streets were clogged with refugees. We did not stop anywhere but hurried to the central railroad station from where a train was scheduled to leave for Lwow at 5 o'clock that afternoon. It was only 10 o'clock in the morning,

29

but we thought that in the station we might find a warm place to rest while we waited for our train.

When we got to the station, however, we found that it was packed with refugees like a can of sardines. All the benches and tables were occupied by people sleeping or trying to sleep. Every bit of space on the floor, too, was taken. Children cried, women moaned, and here and there an old man or woman fainted. The air was rank with the stench of blocked toilets. Lacking bathroom facilities, people were relieving themselves wherever they happened to be in the station. Szymek and I kept looking for a spot to rest, but there was none.

Five o'clock came at last, but the train was nowhere in sight. After a while, it was announced that the Lwow train had been delayed and would not arrive until midnight. However, we did not dare to leave the station and risk missing the train. Local militiamen with red armbands, rifles slung over their shoulders, were keeping order in the waiting room. We remained standing near the gate to the train platform, motionless, hour after hour, until at long last, midnight came. But still there was no train. One o'clock, then two, and three, and still nothing happened. Finally, at 4 a.m., the stillness suddenly exploded; the train was pulling into the station. Everyone grabbed bags and knapsacks; the men helped the women to their feet and picked up the small children, ready to board the train. When the platform gate was opened, bedlam broke loose as people fought and pushed their way to the train. Screaming and shouting, shoving, elbowing and trampling those who got in the way, the mob stampeded forward, each person wanting to be first to board the train, afraid of being left behind.

I could not breathe, and I had lost sight of Szymek. People were clambering into the train through the windows of the cars because the doors were blocked. Suddenly I heard someone call my name. It was Szymek, shouting to me from the window of one of the cars to hand him my knapsack and to get aboard. In all the terrible crush he had managed not only to board the train but to find two seats, one for himself and another for me. Had it not been for him, I would never have got out of Kowel. I tossed my knapsack to him; he caught it and began to haul me up through the window, stopping only long enough to beat off some men who were pulling me by the legs in the opposite direction to keep me out of the train. Some sharp blows were exchanged, but at long last I found myself inside the car, pain and exhaustion forgotten in the relief of having reached my goal.

Our car was packed with people sitting and standing jammed together between the legs of those fortunate few who had found seats, in the aisles and even in the washrooms—human beings from Warsaw, Cracow, Lódz, Częstochowa and smaller towns of western Poland, all fleeing for their lives. There were even a few Polish soldiers, sailors and policemen who had put on civilian clothes and joined the exodus. The ten seats in our section were already crowded with fourteen passengers, with others still pushing their way in, some climbing over our heads to find a perch on the baggage rack. From time to time those with seats got up to let the standees sit down for a while.

Among the passengers in our section there was a family from Bielsko. It was obvious from their clothes, their luggage and their other belongings that they were definitely not poor people. They opened their bags and took out fancy sausages, cold cuts, preserves and other delicacies which they generously shared with all the others in the compartment. We became friends and started to talk about the war, about when all this was going to end, and our chances of ever seeing our families again.

Every few kilometers we tried to get a little fresh air into our lungs. Someone in the compartment would open one of the windows and put out his head. The sun was shining, and the wind tousled our hair and stung our faces. The train passed little thatched cottages standing lost in mysterious silence. Everyone was quiet but you could feel the tension in the air. People were clinging to the steps and even to the roofs of the cars. Every now and then the train stopped in the middle of nowhere; no one knew why, but we found these stops most welcome because they gave us a chance to relieve ourselves after hours of agonizing self-control.

We passed through towns and villages, some familiar from the map, others with names we had never heard before. The train seemed to be playing a game of hide-and-seek with us, going round and round in a way we could not understand—from Kowel to Lutzk, on to Pinsk and finally to Luniniec, where it stopped for two whole days. From there, we were told, the train would proceed directly to Brody by way of Sarna, Rowno, Zdolbunow and Dubno. Would our journey ever end? Everywhere, dead silence. The railroad stations through which we passed were deserted. The signals were not working, and the trains were running without direction or control. There was no drinking water. Only war and death, inter-twined like lovers, lay along our seemingly endless path.

We traveled for four days without ever being asked for tickets. Later, we found out that the Soviet military authorities had ordered all the trains in eastern Poland to carry refugees free of charge. This piece of news was very encouraging; it seemed that somebody still considered us as humans after all.

As we neared the city of Brody our hearts grew lighter. The highways were still crowded with Polish soldiers, peasants and refugees, but over and above these we could see units of the Red Army. Dozens of Red echelons moving along with tanks, artillery and airplane parts waved at us as we passed. The Russian soldiers tossed tobacco and cans of soup into our cars. At one station, someone bought a Ukrainian newspaper, and we noted that this issue was already one published by the Soviet authorities. Eagerly scanning the paper for the latest news, we were happy to see a report from Tass, the official Soviet news agency, that the Russians were going to occupy all Polish territory to the east of the Vistula River. We took this to mean that we would be able to go back as far west as Praga, close to Warsaw, our home town. I began to hope again that I might be able to smuggle my mother across the Vistula into the Soviet zone. Although the weather outside had not improved, the day seemed brighter and sunnier to me than it had been at any time during our journey.

But the next day was dreary again, because the newspapers denied the previous day's reports and announced that the Soviets would move no further west than the River Bug.[2]

---

[2] As a matter of fact, the River Bug was to remain the boundary line between the Russian and German zones of divided Poland until war broke out between Germany and the Soviet Union, in June 1941.

We were sad and dispirited as our train pulled into Lwów—or Lemberg, as the city had been known prior to World War I.

We stayed in Lwów until the evening. The central gathering places for the refugees in Lwów were Saleski Plaza and the Café de la Paix. There, Szymek and I met many old friends and acquaintances. Quite a few of them were planning to travel north to Vilno. in Lithuania, from where, it was said, one could take clandestine routes to Palestine. They persuaded me to join them, but in the summer before the war, at the Zionist camp in Mikuliczyn, I had met a girl from Zoblotow, and I felt I had to go there rather than to Lithuania.

We left the café and spent the rest of the day strolling around the city. At almost every turn we ran into friends from Warsaw. There were the Sadowski brothers, fruit wholesalers who had been close to our family; several Jewish cabaret artists including a brother of the Polish novelist Adam Nasielski; Professor Moses Schor,[3] chief rabbi of Warsaw's Great Synagogue; Eliyahu Mazur, president of Warsaw's Jewish community council, and the noted Jewish scholar, my former teacher Dr. Ostersetzer. Now they and we were in the same boat; the streets of Lwów, warmed by the autumn sun, had become our temporary residence. In one street, you could buy a loaf of bread; in another, a little butter; and in yet another, a piece of meat. Not every store carried everything you wanted. You had to search for a place that had what you needed, and at a price you could afford. Each refugee carried all his household goods— a pocket knife, a spoon and a toothbrush —on his person. A refugee with bulging pockets was immediately tagged as a person of means.

Our journey from Lwów to Zoblotów was shorter and more comfortable than the trip from Kowel to Lwów. The trains seemed to be running on schedule. We traveled with peasants and others from nearby towns and villages who were on their way home after a day of brisk business in Lwów. Some of them had already learned how to profit from wartime shortages. They had brought to the city food and farm produce such as flour, butter, lard, eggs,

---

[3]Rabbi Schor was to die in a Soviet prison camp.

chickens and potatoes, and exchanged these for soap, shoes, clothing, liquor, razor blades, kitchenware, and other articles that had become scarce in the countryside. At first the Soviet occupation authorities seemed to turn a blind eye to this illegal trading, but as the weeks more on. Soviet soldiers began to stop trains and to order all the passengers to get out for a thorough search of their baggage and clothing. This procedure would take hours. In the meantime, the train would move on, leaving the unfortunate passengers stranded out in the open and with no other choice but to walk for miles in the dark of the night to the nearest railroad station. There, they frequently had to wait until the next day to make a train connection. Under such circumstances, this sort of trading became more difficult each day. Yet the natural urge to fend off starvation broke through the barriers raised by the Soviets. People risked their health, their lives and even the lives of their families to find the money they needed to buy bread, meat or a little corn flour. They bribed Red soldiers and high Soviet officials to take smuggled goods to Lwów and other cities in Red Army or government trucks which presumably were immune to searches. In the end it seemed that even the mighty Soviets were powerless in the face of the human will to survive.

All those individuals who commuted between Lwów and smaller surrounding towns and villages to ply their dubious trade were lumped together under the description of "speculators." Yet most of them were not professional black marketeers but only ordinary law-abiding citizens whom the new Soviet order had robbed of the means of making an honest living. For instances, there was Mr. A. D., a Jew, who had been employed in a law office before the war. He had earned a fair salary which had enabled him to provide quite decently for his wife and two children—a girl of 20 and a boy of 14—but which had certainly not been enough to make him rich or even to allow him to accumulate substantial savings. When the Soviets took over, he found himself out of work at the age of fifty. In those days the Russian authorities gave jobs only to young people. As a result, hunger became a regular visitor at the Dr. home. Mr. D. was aware of what others in a similar position were doing but he shuddered at the very thought of breaking the law. However, when he realized that his family was starving, he finally broke down and decided to try his luck. One evening he tied several pounds of tobacco in little bags around his waist under his clothes and, with much fear and trembling, set out for Lwów. Everything went smoothly and his trip proved most profitable, for he was able to get not only bread, but also meat, fish and fruit for his family. This is how A. D. and hundreds of others like him in the Ukraine became "speculators."

Eventually, the Soviets set up factories which offered steady employment to people like A. D., but during the early weeks and months of the war, thousands of people were arrested and sentenced to long prison terms for having engaged in black market operations.

* * *

Zoblotów, the next stop on our journey, is a small town midway between Kolomyja and Sniatin. At the outbreak of the war, the population of that area consisted largely of Ukrainians, with a sprinkling of Polish officials and a substantial number of Jews in the towns and villages. During the cold winter months, the Ukrainians wore long sheepskin coats, tall sheepskin hats and leather boots. In the summer, they put on white pants of coarse hand-woven linen with hand-embroidered overblouses, over which they wore short sheepskin vests even when it was very hot. This was their Sunday best. For work, they wore plain coarse shirts and tight pants. To visitors from the west they looked like figures out of the Middle Ages. The Ukrainians in that part of Galicia followed the customs of the Ruthenian mountain folk who smoked long pipes, rode about on ponies, made Brindza cheese and were ready to sell even their mothers for a consideration.

The town itself was a tidy little place. As one approached the depot on the train from Kolomyja, one could see at left the railroad tracks which linked the town with Lwów and the great world beyond, and at right the swiftly-flowing River Prut. In the distance across the river were the mountains that extended far into Sub-carpathian Ruthenia and Rumania. The Chomow mountain, which stands guard over the town, was considered sacred by the Ukrainians; later, it also became sacred to the Jews as the final resting place of 600 Jewish men, women and children who were gunned down by the Nazi murderers in 1941.

Before the war, the Jews of Zoblotów had made an honest living, weaving and selling rugs, selling groceries and dry goods, tilling the soil, and buying cattle from the local peasants which they shipped to big cities like Cracow and Vienna. They sent their children to high school in Sniatin and Kolomyja, and even to the University of Lwów. On Thursday nights and Friday mornings the women would bake their own bread and rolls, potato cakes and fruit pastries. In the wintertime, they were busy fattening ducks, geese and turkeys. Some of them still yearned for their girlhood days in Czernowitz,[4] boasted of their German and could recite from memory all the poems of Friedrich Schiller. In addition, a fine, new generation of Jews, was growing up in Zoblótow—pretty, raven-haired girls, sturdy lads, and gifted students who had all but forgotten their Yiddish and would speak only Polish. The young people proudly sported the uniforms representing the various Zionist, socialist and religious youth organizations. There were youthful romances and broken hearts, small-town poets and painters, and future rabbis, doctors, intellectuals and business tycoons. In short, Zablotów before World War II had been a fine and happy Jewish community.

When the Soviet forces entered Zoblotów. they were welcomed with open arms. Every evening the people of the town crowded into the market place where the Red Army had set up a mobile outdoor movie theatre showing films on Communist achievements in the Soviet Union. Afternoons, the market place was the scene of mass meetings at which the townspeople were told of the reforms about to be introduced into "the happy life of liberated Zoblotów." Everybody came to these rallies, for though attendance was not compulsory, most people felt it was wise to be seen there. Everyone in Zoblotów was eager to show neighbors, friends and enemies alike, that he was happy under the new Soviet order.

---

4 Before 1918 Czernowitz, capital of Bukovina (a region partly in the western Ukraine) had belonged to the Austro-Hungarian Empire.

Comrade Kurochka, who had been appointed acting town commissar by the army, ordered storekeepers to empty their shelves and sell all their merchandise as quickly as possible. Immediately, long lines formed in front of the stores. Soviet government employees and soldiers and officers of the Red Army did not have to wait in line. The townspeople watched with envy and anger in their eyes as the Russians came out of the stores laden with enough merchandise for at least ten families. The people of Zoblotów were permitted to buy only enough for their own individual needs; they could not even shop for their husbands, wives or children. The storekeepers began to hide some articles, selling them "under the counter" to their friends at night. Many found themselves spending entire days in the street, standing in one line after the other. People pushed, quarrelled, traded insults and made lifelong enemies, all in an attempt to move one place ahead in the line.

The town's tobacco factory was taken over by a unit of the Red Army. Whole families were deprived of their citizenship rights and hid out in dark corners like frightened mice. In time, even avowed local Communists who had been big shots during the early days of the occupation were summarily arrested or dismissed from their positions and replaced by Soviet citizens. Strangely enough, the town council, which was not permitted to take any action without the express approval of the Soviet authorities, included many Ukrainians who had been Fascists before the war. Those Jews who had joined the Communist ranks shook their heads in dismay but did not say a word.

Several weeks after the arrival of the Russians, postal service was resumed under the direction of a Russian postmaster. Food cooperatives were opened where matches were available in unlimited quantities, but bread only in the early morning hours, and sugar only once in a great while. The privately-owned stores soon closed down because they had sold out all their stock and were unable to pay the exorbitant taxes demanded by the Soviet authorities. A "polyclinic" was set up where local doctors treated patients free of charge. The director of the clinic was the town's dentist, Dr. Spiegelglass, who had obtained the appointment because of his known Communist sympathies. The public health services of the entire Zoblotów district were placed under the direction of one Dr. Gross, who had attended medical school in Italy but had never graduated. He, too, owed his position to the fact that he was a Communist. As a result, Dr. Nussenblatt, who was Jewish, and Dr. Porotko, an Ukrainian, both of them fine specialists, frequently had to follow orders which ran counter to their professional knowledge and experience. The polyclinic was housed in the building that had belonged to the Jewish Club but had been requisitioned by the Soviet authorities. Since the Russians were permitted to requisition any building they wanted, many Jewish families suddenly found themselves without a roof over their heads.

Only a very few people in Zoblotów were really happy under the new order; most of these were anti-Semites who had been given leading positions in the Communist party hierarchy and now hoped to settle their accounts with the Jewish businessmen and other people of property who had been destroyed in the reshuffling of the class structure. "Poland is no more," the newly-promoted "comrades" declared. "Your good times are over! Now it's our turn to have roast goose and fruit pies!" But they, too, were to be bitterly disappointed. The prominent Jews of the town had lost their homes and possessions, but this brought no advantages to the newly-consecrated proletarian elite; their life-style did not become any better than it had been under Polish rule.

For several months Zoblotów was almost devoid of life; the empty, closed shops looked for all the world like tombstones in the deserted streets and alleys. Gradually, the Soviets tried to make things a little livelier with daily parades, for which every house in town had to be decked with red flags, portraits of Stalin, and propaganda posters depicting the fall of Poland and the high morale of the Soviet citizens. Every night a band played dance music in the former clubhouse of the Polish "Sokól" youth organization; there, Ukrainian girls danced with Polish and Jewish boys, and Ukrainian boys with Polish and Jewish girls. The town intelligentsia was flattered to be invited to these dances.

Interestingly enough, business also began to pick up in the churches and synagogues; before long, both were packed wall to wall with worshippers. It seemed that the godlessness of the new regime only served to make the people more religious.

The Soviets permitted three schools in Zoblotów, one for each "nationality group": Ukrainian, Polish and Jewish. The children in each of these groups were taught in their own mother tongue; in the Jewish school, the language of instruction was Yiddish. The curriculum in all three schools was identical in content and philosophy: it was devoted to the ideas and doctrines of Communism, and Russian was a compulsory "foreign language." In this respect, the Ukrainian children had an easier time of it than the students of the Jewish and the Polish school: they only had one foreign language to learn, while the Polish and Jewish children had two— Russian and Ukrainian. since Zoblotów had officially become a part of the Ukrainian Soviet Socialist Republic.

The Ukrainian school was located in the same building which it had occupied before the war. The teaching staff, too, remained the same as before, except that several new teachers had been added. Oddly, the new principal appointed by the Russians was Kostiuk, Banderowiec and a well-known Fascist. In fact, most of the teachers at the Ukrainian school were avowed reactionaries; yet they were retained to teach Communism under the Soviets, and remained until the western Ukraine was occupied by the Germans.

The new seven-grade "Jewish Intermediate School" occupied the entire first floor and the main floor of the right wing in the building which before the war had housed the Polish school. As for the Poles, they were permitted only a four-year elementary school because there were barely enough Polish children in town even for the first four grades.

The man whom the Soviet authorities appointed as principal of the Jewish school was Moshe Dunst, a veteran Communist who had been the moving spirit behind many strikes staged under the Polish regime and had been arrested several times by the Poles. Dunst came from a hasidic family and was well-versed in Talmudic studies and in the Hebrew language, having studied at a Talmudical academy before exchanging his religion for Communism. Unlike many of his party comrades, however, Dunst was a thoroughly honest man who never exploited his new position for personal gain. He was sincere in his convictions and took his work very seriously. Evidently, his character did not fit into the new Soviet reality. His appointment as principal of the Jewish school had, in fact, been a demotion, for he had begun his career under the Soviets as a member of the Zoblotów city council. In 1941 he was to be relieved of his principalship and demoted to the position of ordinary teacher. Dunst's steady descent down the party ladder frightened the Communist bigwigs in town. "If this could happen to Moshe Dunst," they whispered to each other, "what will become of the rest of us?"

Aside from Moshe Dunst, the faculty of the Jewish school in Zoblotów was an interesting mixture of ages, backgrounds and party connections. Żyro had already been an active Communist before the war, and had served a five-year prison sentence for his Communist activities at the government-supervised Jewish Teachers' Seminary in Warsaw. Amele Berler, too, had already been a party member before the war; a carpet dealer by trade, he had never studied beyond the seven-year intermediate school. Young Mrs. Bloch, the daughter of a wealthy landowner whose property had been confiscated by the Russians, had earned a certificate of matriculation. She was not even able to read Yiddish, the language of instruction at the school, nevertheless she got the position because her brother-in-law held a prominent post in the local party leadership. Then there was Burg, a student at the University of Lwów, a young man of remarkable intelligence, who had come from a poor family and sympathized with the Communist ideology. He was a warm human being, much liked by his fellow teachers. The other members of the faculty were Muster (Amele Berler's father-in-law) and Mrs. Shafir, both of whom had taught in Polish schools for many years; Miss Starzecka, a devout Polish Catholic, an expert in the Ukrainian language and the pride of our school;[5] and finally, myself.

Although the Jewish school was in urgent need of teachers I

---

[5] Eventually, Miss Starzecka was exiled to Siberia because she insisted on going to church in defiance of explicit orders from the NKVD, the Communist secret police.

was not accepted immediately because my credentials—a matriculation certificate from a Polish *gymnasium* and a diploma from the Tachkemoni Rabbinical Seminary of Warsaw—had aroused suspicion. Moreover, some of the Jews in Zoblotów remembered me as the young man who had conducted a Zionist summer camp in Mikuliczyn for four summers in a row before the war; this certainly was no recommendation for one who was supposed to help educate a new generation of anti-religious, anti-nationalist Communists. But in the end, due to the efforts of Dunst and Żyro, I was accepted and duly inscribed on the faculty roster of the Jewish school of Zoblotów.

Teaching at this school was not easy and proved to be a considerable strain on my nerves. Our first school year under Russian rule was a period of groping in the dark and of heated disputes with the Zoblotów Regional Executive Committee. Every teacher was expected to find, or devise, his own Yiddish terminology for use in teaching such general academic subjects as mathematics, geography and zoology. We consulted some of the old textbooks that had been issued by the Zionist Youth Organization, but we could do that only in utmost secrecy because these books had been declared strictly taboo under the Soviet regime.

The teachers applied themselves to their tasks with selfless devotion, encouraged by the fact that, all the difficulties and restrictions notwithstanding, the government had placed the Jews on a par with the other nationality groups by supporting the Jewish school. Even Mr. Muster, who had spent 32 years teaching at Polish-language schools, kept stressing this point, adding that now, at long last, he felt secure, no longer an outsider among teachers of other nationality groups.

The school work during that first year consisted largely of extracurricular activities such as drawing pictures of Stalin, making up designs featuring the Hammer and Sickle; drilling for parades, discussions of such inspirational topics as Soviet leaders, the Red Army, and the aims of socialism and learning dozens of Soviet songs, such as *The International, The Three Tank Drivers, The March of the Partisans, A Hymn to Stalin, and others.*

The unquestioned master in this aspect of our work was Amele

41

Berler, who threw himself heart and soul into the task of "re-educating" both teachers and students along Communist lines. He worked hard at making himself popular at the school, for he knew that if his students liked him it would enhance his overall standing in town. None of us, not even Mr. Dunst, the principal, dared to call him to task for an error in his presentation or for a false note in one of the party songs he was teaching to his class, for Berler sat firmly in the saddle. His way of talking, his movements and his dealings with people reflected his arrogance, and he had every reason to feel superior: in the first place, he had behind him many years of Communist activity; secondly, he was younger and better-looking than our boss, Dunst; and thirdly, his sister-in-law was secretary of the Red militia of Zoblotów. As a result, the walls of the classrooms were covered with party portraits and slogans, and the students vied with one another in demonstrating their knowledge of "the great and glorious Soviet Union."

Although I had to watch my step in the presence of some of them, I felt quite at home among my colleagues. Except for isolated instances, I felt that they were doing their best to help me, a stranger in town. I became particularly friendly with Burg, Zyro and Dunst, who introduced me to their families and frequently invited me to their homes.

Before long, they had a chance to prove their friendship for me, and they passed the test with flying colors. A young man named Yingster, the son of a *shohet* [6] and himself a former rabbinical student, had reported me to the NKVD, explaining that I was a Zionist and therefore not fit to educate young people in the Communist ideology. It seems that Yingster was eager to get a position at our school and, learning that all the positions had been filled, decided to create an opening by getting one of the teachers dismissed. Since he was afraid to do anything against such big shots as Berler, Dunst or Burg he decided that I, a refugee from Warsaw, would be the easiest mark. As a result, I was called to the NKVD headquarters several times for questioning. The interrogations invariably took place sometime during the night. I would be rudely

---

[6] Slaughterer of kosher meat.

awakened and taken to headquarters, where I would be kept for several hours. The officer who questioned me, a short, stocky Georgian with beady little eyes, treated me with the utmost courtesy. He would offer me the best brand of Soviet cigarettes, a cup of good, strong coffee and some tasty cookies. We spent a good deal of time talking about such innocuous subjects as women, and the merits of health resorts in Russia. Then, toward the end of our talk, the little Georgian would throw in some innocent-sounding questions about my past: Did I have relatives abroad? What did I think of the Soviet school system? In the course of one such talk, the officer asked me whether I had ever had any dealings with a Polish political party known as "Ozon." I answered that since "Ozon" had been a reactionary, anti-Semitic party that had viciously fought the Jews at every turn, I could not very well have belonged to it. His reply was simple. "You were a Zionist and a nationalist. 'Ozon' was a nationalist party," he said. "And everybody knows that all the nationalists are working hand in hand against the Revolution." I explained to him that I was a Zionist simply because, as a Jew, I wanted to have a land to call my own, just as any Russian, Ukrainian or Georgian wanted to be a citizen of his own land. But I noticed that my reply did not satisfy him.

My last meeting with this smiling little Georgian was brief and strictly official. He handed me a paper to sign, but gave me no time to read what I was signing. He told me to remember who I was, that the Soviet authorities had entrusted me with the education of the young Communist generation, and that I must not disappoint the Soviet people. Finally, he ordered me to report to the local militia once each week. Then he dismissed me. Only later did I learn that the NKVD had asked Dunst about me. I also learned that Dunst and Zyro had gone in person to NKVD headquarters and declared that I was a "very good and devoted teacher" whereas Yingster was a disruptive influence at our school. I was told that Amele Berler had refused to intervene on my behalf, even though Dunst had asked him to do so. He probably did not want to stain his Communist conscience by interceding on behalf of a Zionist.

My first year at the Jewish school passed very quickly. It was not only a year of very hard work but also one in which I had

43

to be constantly on the lookout for informers, concealing my true feelings and worrying about my family, particularly my mother, who was still in Warsaw. I disliked a good many things that were part of the Soviet reality; some of the Soviet decrees really shocked me and dealt a severe blow to my faith in the basic goodness of man.

Looking back now, it seems to me that during this period of my life I lived like an animal, happy to have some food, a place to sleep, and glad that I was allowed to survive. I dreamed of my mother nearly every night; I saw her face before me, her eyes red with weeping. My friends and I kept up our spirits by telling each other that things could not possibly go on like this for long and that someday we would see a better world arise on the ruins of the old. The Jews of Zoblotów were not so optimistic. "Better to depart for a better world," they used to say, "than to go on living like this."

All the citizens living in areas "liberated" by the Soviet Union were required to have passports. Refugees from the German-held area were ordered to fill in special questionnaires which included a question as to whether they wished to become citizens of the Soviet Union. Those who replied in the negative were eventually deported to Siberia. On the advice of my non-Communist friends in Zoblotów I declared my intention to apply for a Soviet passport. I received a passport, but it included what became known as "the infamous Clause No. 11." This clause, or paragraph, appeared only in the passports of individuals who were regarded as suspicious characters or security risks: members of the bourgeoisie, land-owners, manufacturers, businessmen, counter-revolutionaries, criminals and refugees from the German sector.

On the morning after I had received my passport, I was ordered by the militia to leave Zoblotów immediately, on the grounds that individuals with "Clause No. 11" in their passports were permitted to live only in towns situated more than 100 kilometers away from the border, and Zoblotów was just a few kilometers from the border between the Polish Ukraine and Rumania. Later, I learned that some 20 other refugees like myself had been permitted to stay in Zoblotów because they had been able to bribe the right officials or because they had the proper connections with the local Soviet authorities. But I had no such luck and was told that I would be liable to severe punishment if I were ever seen in Zoblotów again, even as a visitor.

Depressed and tired, I had to pack my meager belongings once again and look for another place to stay. My work at the Jewish school in Zoblotów had not been good for me. The Communist anti-religious ideas which we teachers had to inculcate into the minds of our students had definitely not fostered my mental and emotional well-being. We were forced to keep our school open on Saturdays; Sunday was the only free day allowed. In other words, the Ukrainians and Poles were able to observe their traditional day of rest, while we Jews were not permitted to keep our Sabbath. Inspectors and supervisors made a point of visiting our school on Saturdays to make sure we were not neglecting our anti-religious activities. We were forced to teach the youngsters that the Jewish Law was decadent, that Sabbath observance made no sense, and that the rabbis and the rabbinical schools were a menace to society.

My one comfort in all this deceit was the reaction of my students. They would exchange winks or grimace with disgust; some even cried. No child could be excused from school on Saturdays; even the rabbi was afraid to have his daughter stay at home on Saturadys because other parents who had attempted to keep their children out of school on the Jewish Sabbath had been severely punished. So the little girl would sit before me in my class even on the Sabbath with a sad and resentful look in her face as she heard me ridicule all the traditions which her parents held sacred. I had never been what one might call extremely Orthodox but as I bombarded my young charges with atheistic propaganda which they did not know how to challenge, I felt that I was a traitor to the memory of my late father, to my family, and to everything I had been taught in my childhood. Sometimes I would try to find relief by soundlessly mouthing the words of a Zionist song or the names of Jewish religious and Zionist leaders as I stood in front of my class. On more than one occasion I felt an overpowering urge to resign from my position, but this impulse was smothered each time

45

by the realization of what would happen to me if I were to do that. Under the Soviet regime, refusal to accept a position or voluntary resignation from employment was punishable by long prison terms or deportation for life.

I will never forget what we had to do at the Jewish school on Yom Kippur. Dunst, the principal, had received instructions from the authorities that the school was to operate as usual even on this, the holiest day the Jewish calendar, which is marked by solemn worship and a 24-hour fast. Dunst ordered all of us teachers to bring our lunches to school and to eat them in front of our pupils so that the youngsters might be inspired to emulate our example. I still remember how I stood in front of my class eating my lunch and thinking of Frischmann's famous Hebrew story, "Three Who Ate." What a difference, I thought bitterly. In Frischmann's story the rabbi and the elders of the community partook of food on Yom Kippur in front of their flock so that the congregation would follow their example and thereby be spared from the plague that had stricken the town. Here, at our Jewish school, the teachers were breaking the Yom Kippur fast not in order to save their pupils' lives but to poison their minds. The children stared at me with angry eyes; yet, I did not feel that they bore me any resentment. Suddenly a boy named Altman, who sat in the front row of the room, jumped up and said to me: "Comrade Pinkas Lazarovich, we know you're eating today not because you want to, but because you've been ordered to do it. We also know that all the horrible things you've been telling us about the Bible and the Sabbath are not true and that you yourself don't really believe them. You've been telling us these things only because you're afraid. If you teachers really believe what you've been teaching us, why does Mrs. Dunst light candles every Friday night, and why did Amele Berler go to a rabbi to get married?" As Altman sat down, the other boys and girls nodded in mute approval of his little speech. Altman's outburst gave me new courage because it showed that these youngsters sensed what was going on in my heart every time I parroted the brutal doctrines of atheism as part of their daily lessons. I felt a new rapport between myself and my students, especially Altman. Some of the other teachers confided

46

to me that they had had similar experiences with their pupils. Berler suggested that I adopt more effective methods of purging the "opiate of the masses" from the minds of the children in my class.

In response to an appeal from my school, the local militia agreed to waive "Clause 11" temporarily in my case and to permit me to stay in Zoblotów until the end of the school year. After I had finished the term, I set out for the nearby town of Bursztyn, where I knew some people. I was immediately offered a position at the Ukrainian school; there was no Jewish school in Bursztyn. The Jews of the town blamed this state of affairs on the superintendent of the regional school system and on the first secretary of the Communist regional committee, both of whom were avowed anti-Semites. But my personal problems were not yet at an end. In order to be able to accept the position I had been offered, I had to present a note from the militia certifying that I was not an undesirable character or a security risk. But the militia refused to give me such a certificate because Bursztyn, too, was quite close to the Rumanian border. As a result, I had to leave Bursztyn and move on to Rohatyn, the nearest town beyond the northern 100-kilometer limit.

Rohatyn was buzzing with refugees. Here the Soviet authorities had gathered together all the refugees in the Lwów and Stanislawów districts who had received Soviet passports. Those without Soviet papers had already been deported to Siberia.

In Rohatyn the refugees lived in cellars, attics and stables. The town was not large enough to accommodate the Jews who had converged upon it from all over Poland. I met many of my friends from Warsaw, among them Mr. Keller, who had saved my life back in Luków the year before. I also saw Mr. Broch, who had taught me German and English at the Tachkemoni Rabbinical Seminary [7] back in Warsaw, and who had been much loved and admired by all his students. I found him in a terrible state. He was wearing a tattered Polish army tunic, torn shoes tied to his feet with filthy rags, and a ragged shirt. No one paid any attention to

---

[7] In addition to the full rabbinical course, the curriculum at this seminary included secular high school subjects.

him because nobody knew him in Rohatyn. He had lost his wife and child in one of the first air raids on Warsaw. I took him to a restaurant for a meal. At the table, this once vigorous, cheerful man with the build of an athlete sat facing me in the servile posture of a beggar waiting for a handout and cried bitterly. I would never have believed that a strong man like Broch could break down so completely. I tried to calm him and, as I parted from him, slipped 200 rubles into his shirt pocket without his noticing it. I met him many more times in Rohatyn. His situation did not improve. Broch, that excellent teacher and linguist, was unable to find employment under the Soviets because his passport, like mine, contained "Clause No. 11."

Eventually, the authorities sent me as a teacher to Kleszczywna, a village in the middle of the forest between Rohatyn and Prze-myślany. This village with its 200 huts was surrounded by dense, jungle-like forests which seemed to have communicated some of their primeval savagery to the villagers. These disciples of Petlura, Konowalec and Bendera [8] lived like barbarians. Had I not lived among them myself and observed them closely for half a year, I would never have believed that the Middle Ages could still have been so much alive in the midst of twentieth-century Europe. The talk of the villagers was ingratiating, but their intentions and deeds were unspeakable. They loved everything Ukrainian and detested anything associated with other nationality groups. They robbed each other, and slept with each other's wives and little daughters. They killed their closest friends for trifles, and any stranger who ventured into their midst was in mortal danger.

It was among these Ukrainian villagers that I was supposed to disseminate Communist culture, which they hated with all their souls. I was afraid to go out among them after sundown. I got a room at the home of Isak Karpfen, the only Jew in Kleszczywna. The village school consisted of four grades. The principal, Mikhail Hotra, should still have been attending elementary school himself. The second teacher was an elderly Polish woman who lived with

---

[8] These three men were notorious Ukrainian Fascist leaders in the 1920's and 1930's.

her two illegitimate children in the school house, which was next to the church. She had been the principal of the school before the coming of the Soviets and deeply resented having been displaced by Hotra. The third member of the faculty was a young Polish girl. She was very pretty; her blond hair, blue eyes and full-bosomed figure drew men to her like flies. Hotra was madly in love with her and the two were frequently discovered in positions unbefitting serious members of the teaching profession.

The six months I spent in Kleszczywna dragged on interminably. I was repelled by the atmosphere of the place, by the people and by my work. One morning I arrived at school to be met by a gruesome scene. The school house was crowded with frightened, weeping men and women. The elderly schoolteacher, her two illegitimate children, and her maid lay together on the bed in their room; their heads, hands and feet had been hacked off and tossed alongside their bodies. I was told that they had been slain by an "unknown" killer as an act of vengeance; it was suspected that the old woman had been reporting her fellow villagers to the NKVD. Mrs. Karpfen, my landlady, told me that the "unknown" killer or killers were definitely somewhere among the tearful mourners who had gathered in the school house. Needless to say, this bloodcurdling experience did not increase my love for Kleszczywna.

There were other problems, too. At least 60 per cent of the children in my class were infested with lice which were in perpetual motion not only on their bodies but all over the chairs and desks. Often I had to brush the thick black bugs from my own desk as well. Not a week passed without some mother or father rushing into the classroom and falling upon a child with a cane or a whip, shouting: "So it's learning you need, do you? And who will take the cattle out into the pasture? Get out of here quick, take the whip and go to the cows, pronto!" And they would throw me a look as if I had been to blame for all their troubles.

The villagers of Kleszczywna were giving the Soviets a hard time. Whenever a supervisor or other representative of the Communist party arrived from Rohatyn, the word went around that "Avraham" was on his way, implying that all the Communists were Jews and should therefore be hated as infidels.

49

When I was notified at long last by the Bursztyn militia that I had been granted permission to live in the Bursztyn region, I heaved a deep sigh of relief and made all haste to go to Rohatyn for an official permit to live and work in Burstyn. I was overjoyed to be able to leave Kleszczywna, that nest of savages.

It turned out that there was no work available for me in Bursztyn proper. I was sent to Ludwikówka, some three kilometers away. The population of this village consisted almost entirely of Poles, the so-called Mazurs, whose main occupation was weaving. There was a four-grade Polish school with two female teachers who before the war had been, and secretly still were, faithful members of the rabidly anti-Semitic "Endek" party. Rokoszynski, the president of the village council, a blacksmith by trade and a fanatical Communist by conviction, was the horror of the village because the Mazurs hated the Communists with all their souls.

At first, the villagers of Ludwikówka did not trust me, either, although they were impressed with my pure Polish pronunciation and my non-Jewish appearance. But later, when they finally became convinced that if someone was a Jew it did not necessarily mean that he was a Communist, their feelings toward me changed for the better. They invited me to their weddings and feasts, complained to me in confidence about the new regime, and talked to me freely about Rokoszynski, the blacksmith, who loved the Soviets more than he did his own Polish countrymen. The villagers were poor people who eked out a bare subsistence weaving linen for the peasants of the surrounding villages in return for staple foods. They had no soil to till. I strongly sympathized with the weavers of Ludwikówka, particularly with their grief over the fate of Poland, their motherland, which now lay vanquished and bleeding.

I found a place to live in Bursztyn, and walked to my work in Ludwikówka and back each day. It was now the early spring of 1941. A year and a half had passed since the Soviets had taken over the western Ukraine. By that time, many Communists, including some who had served long prison sentences under the Polish regime because of their party activities, had had second thoughts and given up their Communism; many of them had already been deported to Siberia as a result.

Soviet law had the populace of the "liberated areas" in its iron grip. Tardiness at work was a punishable crime. A "first offender" would be tried as a "saboteur" and invariably sentenced to pay the government 25 per cent of his monthly wages for a period of six months; a second offense was punishable by one year in prison, and a third, by five years. Hoarding was strictly forbidden, but quite a few sacks of flour, sugar, sausages and other delicacies which the ordinary folk had not seen in the stores for a long time had been discovered at the home of the Regional Director of Supplies, a party member.

People often spent nights away from home because they were afraid of being arrested and deported to Siberia. Smuggling a bit of flour into Lwów and trading it for a length of dress or suit fabric was punishable by five years imprisonment. The unfortunates caught in the act would be marched through the town to the railroad station under armed guard like dangerous criminals. Obtaining meat, eggs or butter on one's own initiative was also defined as "black market trading" although it was not possible to get these and other staples from the government stores. Meanwhile, the party bigwigs went home every day laden with bags full of food and clothing. None of them was ever arrested.

Small wonder, then, that the people of the western Ukraine had long since lost whatever enthusiasm they had felt for the Soviets during the early days of Russian occupation. People walked in the street on tiptoes and talked in near-whispers, as if afraid of the sound of their own voices. The Jews still had some good clothes from the "Polish" days, but they were afraid to be seen wearing them because it was obvious that anyone having good clothes had to be a member of the bourgeoisie—or a high Soviet official. On Saturdays, the Jews would sneak into the local synagogue furtively, like thieves fearful of being discovered. The front door of the big house where the hasidic *rebbe* of Bursztyn lived was always locked on the Sabbath; his disciples would enter by the back door to visit him. The hasidim made certain that their rabbi and his family did not go hungry. And a hasid who traveled out of town, no matter

51

where, invariably brought back with him a sack of flour, a piece of butter, or a little money for the *rebbe*. Hasidim frequently risked their very lives for the welfare of their spiritual leader.

Zionist groups, too, were determined to survive. One day in the summer a friend informed me that the young Zionists of the town would hold a secret gathering to mark the anniversary of Theodor Herzl's death. When the news came that another great Zionist leader, Vladimir Jabotinsky, had died in America in the summer of 1940, his disciples, the Revisionists, arranged a clandestine memorial meeting. Only the most trustworthy individuals were invited to these functions, and it was interesting to see how members of opposing Zionist parties would forget their ideological differences and appear together at these occasions, united by common ideals and by a common sense of isolation. Such was Jewish life in the town of Bursztyn during the early part of 1941.

I recall one particular incident that showed the tension under which we were living during that period. I had made some new friends in Bursztyn, whom I often visited at their home. One day, as we were sitting in their living room talking about things that had nothing to do with politics, their son, a little boy of eight, suddenly burst into the room trembling with fear. "Don't talk so loud," he said in a terrified whisper, "the NKVD will hear you!" Even small children were living in terror of the Communist secret police.

Another time, an elderly Hebrew teacher was arrested by the Bursztyn militia for "counter-revolutionary activities." All his life he had been teaching the Bible and the Hebrew prayers to the Jewish boys in town. The authorities had repeatedly warned him that such "reactionary" pursuits would get him into trouble, but he did not understand how teaching little boys to pray could be against the law. As a result, he was sent to rot in jail. The local priest was sentenced to 15 years at hard labor for a similar offense. I happened to be in the courtroom when that priest was sentenced. The prosecutor hurled endless accusations and insults at him but the young man remained calm throughout the trial and accepted the verdict with quiet dignity. The Hebrew teacher did not even get a courtroom trial.

But as the year 1941 wore on, the disquieting rumors that reached us from the western banks of the River Bug almost caused us to forget our troubles with the Soviets. Our worst fears were realized on June 22, 1941, when the Soviet Union was attacked by Nazi Germany.

4

The First Pogrom

WITHIN ONE NIGHT, the Russians were gone from our town. All the preceding day the people in the various Soviet offices had been busy burning their papers and tying up their most important documents into small bundles to take away with them. Officers and party officials had been ordered not to go anywhere without their guns, not so much for fighting off the German invaders as for defense against attacks from armed bands of Ukrainians. In various cities, particularly in Lwów, the Ukrainians had already seen off the departing Russians with barrages of bullets and hand grenades. In 1939 they had welcomed the Red Army with flowers and cakes, but during the months preceding the Nazi attack they made secret contact with the Germans and now, with the Red Army in full retreat, they had turned into a powerful, dangerous Fifth Column.

The Russians left Zoblotów in the dead of night. They took with them only those individuals who had held key positions in the Soviet regime. The few cars they had at their disposal could not accommodate all the people who wanted to escape from the advancing Germans. The Jews of Zoblotów felt like orphans, abandoned in the middle of nowhere. They dreaded what would happen now, because the Ukrainians had been telling them all along, "Just you wait until the Bolsheviks leave!"

The morning after the Reds had left, the streets of Zoblotów

55

were decked out in the blue and yellow colors of the Ukrainian national flag. The three-pointed symbol of the Ukraine suddenly sprouted in the lapels of young and old. Local police functions were taken over by Ukrainians recruited from the ranks of the lowest underworld characters and the most rabid Jew-haters. Huge posters, printed in Lwów, appeared on the walls of buildings, with an appeal from the highest authorities of the Greek Catholic Church, urging the "sons of the great and mighty Ukrainian people to assume power at long last over their own Motherland and to carry on in the spirit of God and of their glorious Ukrainian tradition." All over the Ukraine, people wept from sheer joy, for at long last they were rid of the Poles and also of the Red Russians, whom they hated even more. Ukrainian hoodlums broke the windows of Jewish homes, and we began to hear frightening reports from the neighboring towns and villages. One Jewish family had been burned to death inside their own house; a Jew had been dispossessed of his flour mill by neighbors whom he had regarded as his good friends; Jewish women had been brutally raped. The home of a Jewish merchant had been looted by Ukrainian police; another Jew had been robbed of all his cows and stores of grain, and Korn's tavern had been ransacked by the police, who then drank up all of Korn's liquor.

For eleven days, the Ukrainians had their way with the Jews. All over Galicia,[9] Jewish lives were not worth a penny.

Then, suddenly, on a sunny Wednesday morning, a troop of Hungarian soldiers appeared on the highway leading from Kolomyja to Zoblotów. Blowing their bugles, they rode into the town on horses and in Galician trucks. Their arrival in Zoblotów raised new, unexpected hopes in the hearts of the Jews. They remembered the good old days of Austro-Hungarian rule under which Jews had enjoyed equal rights along with their Gentile fellow citizens. Little did they know that the Hungarian occupation was only a temporary arrangement between Hungary and Germany; they had forgotten that Admiral Horthy, the regent of Hungary, had allied himself with the Germany of Adolf Hitler.

The commander of the Hungarian unit that occupied Zoblotów

---

9 Galicia is the northwestern part of the Ukraine.

seemed to the Jews a saint in human disguise. A man of noble birth, he abhorred injustice, no matter who did it or to whom it was done. When the officer went out for a stroll through the streets of the town, he courteously acknowledged every greeting, and it seemed to the Jews that he responded to their salutes with a particularly friendly smile. Some of the Jews tried to go to him and tell him what the local Ukrainians had done to them. But this was not so easy, for despite his friendly manner and sympathetic attitude, the Hungarian officer was realistic and exercised great circumspection in his dealings with the Ukrainians. Eventually, however, two of Zoblotów's leading Jewish residents managed to obtain an interview with him, shortly after he had issued an order to the effect that anyone found "guilty of disrupting public law and order in these days of unrest" was subject to execution by hanging. The Jews and Poles heaved a collective sigh of relief, while the Ukrainians shook their heads in dismay as if to say, "What else can you expect of the Hungarians, who are torturing our brothers in the Carpathian mountains?"

The Hungarian commander saw to it that his orders were carried out to the letter. When a Ukrainian mob in a neighboring village burned down a Jewish home, killing all its occupants, he sent a punitive expedition which put up a gallows and summarily hanged the culprits. A Ukrainian policeman who had "expropriated" a suit from the wardrobe of a Jewish home was dismissed from the police force and put into prison.

The Jews prayed that Galicia would be permanently annexed by Hungary and that their friend, the Hungarian commander, would remain in Zoblotów until the war was over. They were not afraid of the Hungarian soldiers. On the contrary, they invited them to stay with them and, in fact, most of the soldiers, including the commander, were billetted at the homes of Jews. A few Hungarian officers even fell in love with Jewish girls. It became an open secret that some of the Hungarian officers and soldiers were ridiculing the Germans and predicting that Hitler's armies would go down in ignominious defeat.

The Poles, too, were happy with this unexpected turn of events. After the Russians had left the area, many of the Poles had packed their bags and tried to move to towns and villages where their countrymen constituted the majority of the population. But when the Hungarians arrived, they happily unpacked their belongings again and went back to their little farms. After all, hadn't the Hungarians and Poles been friends for hundreds of years, beginning with the 15th century, when the rulers of the Polish Batory dynasty had also been rulers of Hungary?

Only the Ukrainians felt that they had cause for fear. They had always hated the Magyars and were terror-stricken by reports of Ukrainian homes burned to the ground by the Hungarians in retaliation for Ukrainian potshots at Hungarian soldiers. Even more, however, they resented the measures taken by the Hungarian occupation authorities to stop the attacks of the Ukrainian nationalists against the one group which until then had been least able to defend itself—the Jews.

Unfortunately, this period of peace and quiet for the Jews was short-lived. One day, some six weeks after the Hungarians had come to Zoblotów, official notices blossomed forth on walls all over town declaring that all of Galicia was now under the jurisdiction of the German *Generalgouvernement*.[10] The Hungarian troops were to be replaced by Ukrainian police under the command of a German *Gauleiter*[11] and the Nazi *Sicherheitsdienst*.[12] At this news the Ukrainians went mad with joy, while the Poles trembled in fear and the Jews realized that their darkest hour was at hand.

The departing Hungarians bade the Jews a friendly farewell, and the Hungarian commander advised the Jews to find hiding places for their valuables. This was a timely piece of good advice, for as soon as the last Hungarian soldier had left Zoblotów, the Ukrainian hoodlums got to work beating up the Jews and looting their homes.

At that time no one knew for sure what the Germans were really doing to the Jews. Poles who came to Zoblotów from Warsaw or

---

[10] Official designation for the Nazi-held sector of Poland.
[11] Lit. "Regional Director." Chief official of a political district under Nazi control.
[12] "Security Service." The Nazi party intelligence service.

Cracow to sell their wares told us that German soldiers were beating up Jews, that German storm troopers with skull-and-crossbones emblems on their caps had been taking Jews away, presumably to forced-labor camps, and that these Jews had not been heard from since. But we refused to believe that such outrages could continue for very long. It was, we reasoned, probably no more than a way of allowing the German soldiers to let off steam before they were sent to the front lines. The Russians had behaved in much the same way under similar circumstances, and the Polish and Austrian soldiers also had not acted exactly like saints when they went off to battle. It was all, we told each other, no more than a front-line soldier's idea of "fun."

The first Germans to arrive in Zoblotów were not fighting men but a unit of the *Technische Nothilfe*,[13] assigned to repair or rebuild the bridges and highways that had been blown up by the retreating enemy. The commanding officer of this unit, a man past 60, had been a prison guard before the war. Most of the 80 engineers under his command were also men above the age of compulsory military service. The unit took over a building which had previously housed the Soviet "Regional Executive Committee." First, the Germans called for some Jewish girls to attend to their housekeeping chores. Next, they issued an order commanding all Jewish males, without exception, to report "voluntarily" for work on the bridge which the Soviets had blown up as they retreated. The German commander "authorized" the local Ukrainian police to supervise the Jewish workers. In the meantime, Ukrainians continued raiding Jewish homes, beating up their occupants and stealing whatever property they could find. No one stopped them; after all, they were rendering a signal service to the German *Reich*.

Finally, the Jews of Zoblotów felt that they could no longer endure the beatings and chicanery of their former friends and neighbors. They therefore sent a delegation to call on the German commander, asking him to allow the Jews to assume full responsibility for supplying the daily quota of 300 Jewish workers, and for their performance and punctuality, so that they might be rid of the

---

[13] Emergency Engineering Force.

Ukrainian ruffians who were acting as their overseers. At first, the officer hesitated, but a handsome gift of cash soon softened his patriotic heart. As a result, a Jewish *Arbeitsamt*[14] was created which undertook to recruit Jewish labor for the *Technische Nothilfe* and later on also for Ukrainian public works. The bureau was headed by the leaders of the Jewish community who exercised their influence to persuade the Jews not to attempt to evade recruitment. Each morning 300 Jewish men marched down to the River Prut where, to the accompaniment of blows and insults, they worked at raising the bridge that had been blown up and sunk by the Russians. Every Jewish male in town was forced to contribute two days of labor per week to hasten the victory of the German *Reich.*

When the bridge had been rebuilt, the *Nothilfe* unit left Zoblotów and moved on, leaving the Jews to wonder what would happen next. One of the men in the unit had boasted to one of the Jewish workers that the time would come when the Jews would recall the *Nothilfe* days with longing. The Jewish *Arbeitsamt* continued to function; it had to fill a request from the Ukrainian mayor and police chief for additional Jewish workers to repair and refurbish various buildings, notably the tobacco factory which, they claimed, had been practically destroyed by "the friends of the Jews," namely, the Soviets. The Jews were also forced to pay a special city tax, which was collected by the *Arbeitsamt.*

Meanwhile, terrifying reports reached us from neighboring communities. It was said that in Sniatin the Germans had seized 100 Jews, loaded them onto trucks like cattle and driven them into the forest. No one knew for sure what had happened to these unfortunates, but one Ukrainian, who had passed by the place a few days later, said he had noticed that the soil at the edge of the forest had been freshly dug up and that, in places, he had seen the soil moving. In Kossow and Kuty, too, the Germans had seized Jews and dragged them off to forced labor. All the Jewish families in another village had been gunned down on the slopes of a nearby mountain. In Kolomyja all the Jewish intelligentsia—doctors, teachers, lawyers, accountants and engineers—had been rounded

---

14 Employment bureau or labor exchange.

up in the middle of the night and taken to the city jail. The next morning they were led out to the prison yard and shot.

At first, the Jews refused to believe these stories; some even laughed and called them "old wives' tales." But it was known for a fact that all the Jews in the Kolomyja area were forced to wear yellow patches cut in the shape of a Star of David; later, this was changed to a white armband marked with a blue Star of David. Jews were forbidden to use the railroads or even to travel on foot from one town or village to another. These reports were brought to us by Ukrainians who claimed to be our good friends. At nightfall, such an individual might turn up at the home of a Jewish neighbor and advise him to find himself a good hiding place because the Germans were going to conduct similar operations in our town also. The panic-stricken Jew would then pass the word to another Jew and so forth until Jewish families throughout the town were trembling with terror. Some cooler heads, however, suspected that these direct warnings were simply a Ukrainian ruse to get the Jews to give them valuables "for safekeeping."

Many Jews, in fact, agreed to entrust their good clothes, china, bed linens and jewelry to the care of their neighbors, asking only that the Ukrainians find hiding places also for them and their families. But in most instances the Ukrainians drew the line at this point: They were willing to safeguard Jewish property, but not Jewish lives. A few Ukrainians took Jews into their homes, but did not hesitate to deliver them up to the Gestapo agents on demand.

The mayor of Zoblotów was a Ukrainian lawyer, Dr. Maletzki, who before the war had earned his livelihood exclusively from Jewish clients. He had been a close friend of Dr. Teicher, a Jewish colleague, who now served as the *Judenälteste*[15] of the town. Every afternoon a car marked "Police" drew up in front of the mayor's house; a couple of high police officials got out of the car and disappeared into the residence, where they sat closeted with the mayor for several hours. What they discussed, no one, not even Maletzki's closest associates, knew. At about that time a rumor spread through Zoblotów that the Ukrainians were digging deep trenches in a

---

15 "Elder of the Jews." A Jewish individual placed in charge of a ghetto.

place beyond the town limits, near the Chomow mountain. Now, for the first time, the Jews of Zoblotów lost their nerve; they were sure that the "trenches" were intended as mass graves for them. Were this not so, they felt, they, the Jews, would have been sent out to dig the trenches, because such heavy work was normally assigned only to Jewish slave laborers, never to Ukrainians. Jews began to flee to Kuty and Sniatin in the belief that since those communities had already had their pogroms, they would not be subjected to a "repeat performance." Before long, these unfortunates were to learn how wrong they had been.

At the other extreme were those who insisted that the trenches were being dug for anti-aircraft guns, for had not the Soviets threatened to bomb the entire Stanislawów area to the ground because the Ukrainians had dared shoot at the retreating Soviet troops? No one knew where these optimists had obtained their information, but everyone wanted to believe them.

The Jews began to set up hiding places for themselves and their families in attics and cellars, and in barns under piles of hay or straw. By this time the Germans had set up a *Judenrat* [16] in Zoblotów. Three times each week German gendarmes appeared at *Judenrat* headquarters to leave "orders" for specific items such as boots, suit materials, rings, jewelry, gold and silver. Two or three days later they would return to call for the articles, which the members of the *Judenrat* had collected from the wealthier Jewish residents of the town. Eventually, the more affluent Jews had nothing left to give, but the Nazis kept increasing their orders. The officials of the *Judenrat* now were compelled to go from door to door, searching every Jewish home, begging, ordering and finally forcing the householders to give up their remaining valuables to save the community from disaster. Like most of our people in those days, the *Judenrat* officials, too, still thought that they could stave off catastrophe with money and expensive gifts. A few of the Jews employed by the *Judenrat* for this purpose were unsavory characters who managed to slip not a few of the items into their own pockets. The

---

[16] "Jewish Council." Jewish body set up by the Nazis to administer a ghetto.

Jews of the town cursed not only the Germans but also the *Juden-ratnikes* who, they claimed, were in cahoots with the Nazis.

Yet, even in their greatest panic, none of the Jews ever suspected that reality would prove even more gruesome than their direst premonitions.

It happened on a Sunday, a sunny, golden day—December 21, 1941. I was standing with my landlord—the owner of the house in which I lived—on our porch, watching the smug, solemn Ukrainians making their way to church. Our house was not far from the post office, and about two kilometers from the railroad station. The wheat had already been gathered in; the fields were bare, but they still seemed to shine with the afterglow of the golden corn. The homes of the Jews were tightly locked, looking for all the world like so many scarecrows set up to frighten the birds away from the sheaves of wheat that still could be seen here and there. Their owners were in constant terror of uninvited visitors. The bells of the church tolled steadily, calling the worshippers to prayer. Ukrainian girls, wearing blouses embroidered in all the colors of the rainbow, passed by, giggling shrilly, shamelessly flirting with the young men while the older folk discussed the events of the day as they walked along. In the procession, we spotted a few German gendarmes. We quickly took off our hats and bowed, as Jews were supposed to do whenever they saw a German official, and the Germans responded with "saccharine" smiles. Much to our relief, this chance encounter passed without blows. The gendarmes kept on walking in the direction of the railroad station, and we remained standing on our porch, without a thought of trouble, watching the Ukrainians pass by on their way to church.

About twenty minutes later we saw a Jew running toward us from the direction of the railroad station. He was a sorry sight: he had been beaten black and blue and was unable to catch his breath. He barely managed to blurt out that the Germans were going from house to house, dragging out all the Jews. Old Mrs. Fischel, who had been sick in bid, had been shot dead on the spot. We and the others heard the news but remained standing like clay figures, not knowing what to do.

By then others, too, came running from the market place with the same report. Then, at last, we understood that the German gendarmes who had smiled at us in passing were, in fact, out to kill us.

My landlord and I rushed to the house of our neighbor, Mrs. Shafir, a poor seamstress whose house had a cellar well concealed beneath a sunken room. My landlord's wife, her two children, Mrs. Shafir and her two children, and I, hurried down into that cellar. Then my landlord and Mr. Shafir, who had stayed upstairs, quickly lowered the trapdoor back into place and covered it with a pile of firewood. We could clearly hear the logs being dropped into place above our heads. Afterwards, the two men crept into the barn of a Ukrainian neighbor where they buried themselves beneath a mound of hay.

Meanwhile my landlady, Mrs. Shafir and I had our hands full calming the four children. A moment later, through a crack in the wall close to the ground where thick logs lay piled up, we heard a burst of gunfire, then the sound of weeping; a little while after that, a woman's tearful pleading voice, and a man's loud, mocking laugh in reply.

Each passing moment seemed like a lifetime. Then, again, wild shouts: *"David, heraus! Schmul heraus! Moische heraus!"* [17]

Through the crack, we could see the Nazis going to my landlord's house, accompanied by grinning Ukrainian youths. While the U-krainian thugs banged on the doors and windows of the house, the Germans stood a little to the side, laughing and drinking liquor from large bottles, letting the Ukrainians do the searching. My landlady was able to make out an old friend, a simple Ukrainian householder with whom her family had owned a field in partner-ship and who had come to her house on a friendly visit only the day before.

"Manya," she asked her daughter. "Look! Is this Vassily or isn't it?"

"It's our dear friend Vassily, all right," the girl replied. We heard the tinkle of breaking glass and saw the Ukrainians rushing into our house, the Germans sauntering in after them. A few min-

---

[17] "Out with you, David! Samuel! Moish!"

utes later they emerged and came toward the house in which we were hiding. We heard them tramping around overhead. We began to whisper the *Shema Yisrael;* it was an odd upsurge of religious feeling, and it kept us sane after a fashion.

And then, suddenly, the hooligans were gone. From far off, we heard what we first took to be hammer blows; before long we realized that it was gunfire. Late at night my landlord came to us in the cellar and told us that it was safe to come out. "It's all over," he announced. Meanwhile, the Ukrainian police were celebrating their success. They had ordered a fine feast at Lissowsky's Restaurant for their honored guests, the Germans. The eating, drinking and carousing went on into the wee hours of the next day.

In the morning the *Judenrat* was ordered to pay not only for the feast but also for the bullets which the killers had spent on the Jews. Moreover, the Jews were told that every Gestapo man in town was entitled to a gift, if the Jews did not want the *Aktion* [18] to continue for another day. Faced with this grim choice, the *Judenrat* had no other alternative but to foot the bill.

All day long I helped gather up the dead from the homes of the Jews, innocent human beings who had been shot in their beds: old people, sick people and little babies.

The trench near the Chomow mountain was filled with the bodies of Jews. Later, Jews who had been spared came and covered the bodies with soil and lime. One Ukrainian woman who lived near the mass grave went out of her mind and had to be committed to the mental hospital of Kolomyja.

In one day, 600 Jews had died in Zoblotów alone.

---

[18] "Operation." Nazi term for pogrom, for the wholesale deportation of Jews to concentration camps, or for a mass murder operation in the gas chambers.

5

Return to Warsaw

AFTER THAT FIRST POGROM I could not bear to stay on in Zoblotów. I could not look into the eyes of the Ukrainians in the town, or face the peasants from the neighboring villages, who had been doing business with the Jews the day before, and murdered them on the next. I decided to leave Zoblotów and return to Warsaw, from where I had fled when the Germans had marched in two years before. The problem was how to make the journey, because Jews were forbidden not only to ride on trains but also to travel on foot from one town to another.

The Jews of Zoblotów were acting like wounded animals. They boarded up the doors and windows of their homes and stores. What little cooking they did was done at night so that the smoke from their chimneys should not attract the attention of the Germans or of the Ukrainian police. The market place lay deserted and dead. Except for those who had to report to a forced labor detail for work on the bridge or at the railroad station, no Jew was seen in the streets. Once in a great while a Jew might dart by, scurrying along an alley, but in a wink he would disappear again into the home of a friend or a neighbor. Inside their homes, the Jews were devising ways of keeping alive and of obtaining a piece of bread, a couple of eggs, or a little meat for their families. Some talked of building bunkers near a stable or out in the field, far from the center of town. Others, still under the illusion that some places in

Nazi-held Poland were "safer" than others, cast about for a chance to send their wives and children to relatives in another town or village.

A few weeks went by, weeks of comparative quiet. True, Germans and Ukrainians periodically looted Jewish homes, Ukrainian policemen beat up a Jew here and there, and *Sicherheitsdienst* officers from Kolomyja still paid regular visits to the *Judenrat* with demands for large sums in cash or gifts of gold. But the Jews felt that such things could be borne, just as long as there was no "repeat performance" of what they recalled in muted whispers as the "Chomow affair." Little by little, the Jews emerged from their hiding places. Here and there a little Jewish grocery store reopened and did business with the local peasants. The peasants had exploited the plight of "their" Jews, acquiring Jewish-owned fields and flour mills in exchange for a sack of corn flour or potatoes and pious promises to continue providing the "sellers" with food. Of course, once they had gained possession of the coveted property the "purchasers" promptly forgot all about their promises. The Ukrainians were without shame. Werhun, an engineer by profession and head of the Ukrainian intelligence in Zoblotów, and his wife, a schoolteacher, went about town beating Jews and looting their homes. The pleas of the Jews for help fell on deaf ears; their Ukrainian neighbors tacitly approved of what the Germans and the Ukrainian police were doing to them.

At that time I met two young Poles from Cracow who were smuggling saccharine into town, selling it quickly and at a high profit. We became friendly and before long I began to work with them. At first I merely acted as their broker, but later I simply bought out their stock wholesale and sold it for my own account. It was a highly profitable venture and though after only six weeks the two young men stopped coming, the money I had earned was to come in handy during the months that followed.

I was more determined than ever to return to Warsaw. I contacted Tomek Ziemba, my friend from Bursztyn. Three days later Tomek and I were sitting together in my room, working out a step-by-step plan for my journey. Ziemba went back to Bursztyn and returned two days later with an "Aryan" birth certificate for me, made out to one Jan Krzus, a Pole who had died some time before. Ziemba had obtained it free of charge from his parish priest who knew very well what purpose it would serve.

We started out the next morning. We decided to journey on foot as far as Kolomyja, because we felt that despite my new "Aryan" birth certificate it would not be safe for us to get on a train in Zoblotów, where I was too well known to "pass" as an Aryan.

Once outside the town, I removed the "Jewish armband" from my sleeve, tore it up and threw it into a sewer. Whenever we saw anyone coming toward us on the highway, Ziemba and I deliberately began to converse loudly and to laugh boisterously.

Toward evening we reached the railroad station of Kolomyja and boarded the next train for Warsaw. Our train was packed with "traveling salesmen"—smugglers, to be exact—who supplied the various communities with food items obtained on the black market. We heard the clucking of live chickens and smelled the strong aromas of liquors and sausages. The German railroad policemen turned a blind eye to the smuggling because they were not exactly losers in these deals.

The crush aboard the train was a piece of luck for me because it kept the Germans from checking the tickets or examining the passengers. But when we got to Chodorów it seemed to us that the train was making an unusually long stop, and the smugglers became uneasy. Then, a shot rang out and, a moment later, the train began to move again. We heard whispered reports that the train police had discovered a Jew in one of the cars. The unfortunate man had carried "Aryan" papers and looked Polish to the core, but a Polish woman, an old hand at smuggling, had been alerted by his Yiddish accent and reported him. The police had taken him off the train at the station in Chodorów and shot him on the spot.

For the rest of the journey no one in our car dared to utter a word. The faces of the passengers had grown rigid with fear. It was in this state of mind that we reached Warsaw the next morning.

My heart was beating as with a hundred little hammers. All sorts of thoughts raced through my brain. I had many Gentile friends and acquaintances in Warsaw: would anyone recognize me? How would I find my mother? I had not seen her in two years. How had she managed to survive, and what was she living on? What about my friends whom I had left behind when I fled from the city in September, 1939?

Ziemba and I went to the home of his cousin in Ochota, where we stayed for two days and made plans for getting into the Warsaw ghetto with our "Aryan" papers. Michal Bojczek, the husband of Ziemba's cousin, was active in the "People's Army," a Polish underground organization. He left the house and returned several hours later with a friend. We became very friendly with the Bojczeks and also with their visitor, who did not tell us his name. Before he left, this man said to me: "I like your looks, and also your way of speaking Polish. Why don't you join our organization?" I agreed to join, but told him that I first wanted to go to the ghetto and find my mother.

In the ghetto, my mother and I had an emotional reunion. We sat up until dawn and told each other what we had gone through during the two years we had been separated, and we wept together for those of our relatives who had died.

The next morning Ziemba insisted that I must leave the ghetto. "There's no future here for you," he kept saying. My mother agreed with him and begged me to leave. "Go and save yourself, so that at least you will survive," she sobbed. "There's no way out for me. You have a chance to stay alive—but not here, in the ghetto. If you stay here you'll only die with the rest of us."

Nevertheless, I stayed in the ghetto for two weeks. I wanted to have at least that much time with my mother. But Tomek Ziemba left before me. I accompanied him as far as the ghetto wall on Muranowska Street. He made his exit without any trouble.

Mother could not accept the risk I was taking in order to be with her. Day after day she pleaded with me to leave the ghetto. Finally, I agreed to go. Once outside the ghetto, I destroyed the "Aryan" papers, resumed my Jewish identity and reported to a small labor camp not far from the city where, according to a close friend who was employed with the Jewish *Arbeitsamt,* the working conditions were good.

At the camp I was assigned to a group of some 60 men and taken by truck to a chicken farm in Falenty, which had once belonged to a wealthy Pole but had been requisitioned by the German S.S. We were led into a large stable which reeked of cow dung although, in fact, it was empty. This stable became our new home. We spent our first two days at the farm nailing together old boards which we covered with straw to serve as our beds. That first night, none of us was able to sleep. We sat in the straw fully dressed and considered our situation. Would we really be put to work here, as we had been told at the Jewish labor exchange at 84 Leszno Street, or would we be shot in a day or two?

On the third day we Jews were put to work in a huge vegetable garden, where we found a number of Polish civilians already on the job. These Poles—all Gentiles—were very kind to us. They warned us which of the S.S. men to watch out for, and showed us how to use our tools properly. They asked us whether we had anything to "sell" in return for a piece of butter, some bread, or a little meat, and we gladly gave them some of our clothing in exchange for food. In the course of our work we became very friendly with the Poles. I conceived a particular liking for one of them, a girl named Christina, who seemed to sympathize with us in our plight. I was attracted by her blue eyes and dark blonde hair, but above all by her hearty laughter and her frank and fearless way of dealing with our S.S. guards. Within a few days Christina and I had become firm friends. She kept asking how she could help me. She continuously told me that the Germans were being soundly beaten on the battlefront, and that we must be strong and not break down because our liberation was at hand. I was aware, of course, that her hopes were not based on fact and that she said these things only in order to cheer me up. Every day she brought me another gift— a piece of boiled meat, some marmalade, and sometimes even a pack of cigarettes. She promised to contact the Bojczeks for me because I had confided in her that I wanted to get out of the S.S. labor camp before it was too late. We Jews suspected that once the summer was over and we would no longer be needed on the farm we would either be shot or deported to the Maidanek concentration camp.

One morning Christina informed me that she had gone to the Bojczeks' house the evening before but had found the place dark and locked. Some neighbors had told her that the Gestapo had taken Michal away and that his wife, Ziemba's cousin, had decided to leave the apartment and move in with relatives in a nearby village. The news that I had lost this valuable contact was a terrible blow. I worked all day as usual, but my thoughts kept wandering up and down the streets of Warsaw, recalling names and addresses of good Polish friends from before the war, until, suddenly, they stopped at the name of Rysiek Maciura. Rysiek was a fellow from a very good Polish family. His father had been a high official in the municipal government of Warsaw. That night I locked myself in the lavatory and wrote Rysiek quite a long letter telling him of my present plight and my plans to escape from Falenty. The next morning I gave the letter to Christina, who quickly slipped it into her dress while our S.S. guard was busy beating up one of the Jews. She personally took my letter to Rysiek, who promised her to do all he could to help me.

Four days later Christina brought me a new "Aryan" identification card made out to "Pawel Kolodziejczyk" along with an employment card certifying that I was a traveling salesman for a picture-frame factory in Kielce and was entitled to move about freely anywhere in the *Generalgouvernement* of Poland. As I later learned, the factory belonged to a *Volksdeutsch*,[19] a man who had done important espionage work for the Germans in Poland before the war.

I began preparations for my escape from Falenty, being extremely careful not to give the slightest hint of my plans, not even to the other Jews in the camp. The only two people who knew my secret were Christina, and a young Jewish fellow from Lodz named Littman, who had become a close friend. Littman also wanted to escape but in his case this was not so easy, because he definitely looked Jewish; he had a long nose, black hair and a dark complexion. Besides, he pronounced his "r"s in the sharp "Jewish" way. Christina made arrangements to have me stay at the home of her uncle, Stefan Michalik, who was the janitor of an apartment building on Wilcza Street in the "Aryan" sector of Warsaw.

---

[19] A German by ethnic identity.

One day, after work, Littman and I grabbed our bundles and, under cover of darkness, left the labor camp. The guard at the gate made no effort to stop us; he probably took us for Polish civilian workers. This was an "open" camp, without barbed wire fences. The Germans probably could not conceive of any Jew daring to escape and figured that if any Jew would be crazy enough to try, he would soon fall into the hands of the police who were scouring every nook and cranny of Warsaw's "Aryan" sector for "illegals."

We traveled on foot as far as the suburb of Okencie. From there, we continued to Warsaw by street car. I noticed the way the passengers were staring at Littman. The ride seemed endless.

Finally, we arrived in the heart of the city. The houses, the stores and the streets had not changed, but I felt like a stranger here in my own home town. I began to regret that I had chosen to "pass" as an Aryan again and to escape from Falenty. Why had I done it, I wondered. Any minute now, I would be caught, taken away to Gestapo headquarters, and then—good-bye, beautiful world! In Falenty, I might have survived at least until the end of the summer because the S.S. needed us to care for their gardens and fields. But now there was no turning back; we had to go on, no matter what.

Deep in these dismal thoughts, I did not even realize that the street car had come to the stop at Wilcza Street. I quickly jumped up from my seat and got off, with Littman behind me. We made our way to the address Christina had given me. Her uncle, Mr. Michalik, gave us a friendly welcome and led us to his basement apartment. His wife showed us our room which contained a folding bed, a table and a bench. We sat down with a sigh of relief, not knowing what to do next.

Late that night Mr. Michalik came into our room, sat down beside us on the bench and began to tell us how the Germans were hunting down Jews who were trying to "pass" as Aryans. Not a day went by, he reported, that the "Schmaltzies" did not discover such fake "Aryans" and turn them over to the Gestapo. We understood what he was trying to tell us and we felt no resentment toward this simple but genuinely kind and honest man who, unlike

73

many another Pole, wanted to help the Jews but was afraid for his own life.

The next morning Littman said that he would go and look up one of his Gentile friends who had been a customer of his father's. He left his bundle in our room and promised to be back toward evening. I stayed in the room because I was expecting Christina to come that day. Littman did not return that evening, nor the next day. I never saw him again.

Christina also did not show up at her uncle's place that night. On the fourth day after my arrival in Warsaw I felt I could not stand it any longer in my room and went out for a walk around the city. I was sure something had happened to Christina, that she had been caught by the Germans at some illegal act, because her two brothers were deeply involved in the Polish underground. I spent half the day walking about the streets of Warsaw. The houses were as I had remembered them, except for a gaping hole here and there, where a German bomb had scored a direct hit. German soldiers, policemen and black-uniformed Gestapo officers were everywhere. The restaurants were packed. The prices they charged were ten times what they had been before the war. I went into a restaurant on Krakowskie Przedmieście and had a good dinner, for which I paid 120 zlotys. All around me at the other tables sat Germans with pretty young Polish girls. But now I was not afraid of getting caught. I was dressed in the latest style: long brown leather coat, breeches, and shiny black officers' boots. I carried myself proudly, my head held high and a smile on my lips, although my heart was heavy with sorrow.

The day I spent roaming the city gave me a lift and a sense of security. That evening, at last, Christina turned up at her uncle's house. I was overjoyed to see her and we kissed each other affectionately while her uncle watched in amazement. Half an hour later a man arrived whom Christina introduced to me as her fiancé. He turned out to be the man whom I had met at the Bojczeks' house and who had suggested that I join his underground organization. We greeted each other like old friends and he gave me an address at which I was to report the next morning. Then he and Christina left. I never saw them again. I do not know what

74

became of Christina and her fiancé, but I will never forget them. If they are dead, let this story be their memorial. If they should still be alive somewhere, let their names be added to the roll of heroes of World War II who risked their own lives in order to save others from death.

The contact to whom Christina's fiancé had sent me was a Polish metal worker who was also active in the underground. I stayed at his house for a whole day. Toward evening, a young lady came in who was introduced to me as the escort who would take me to Lwów. My "contact" gave us two train tickets, several thousand zlotys and an address in Lwów where, he told us, good friends would be waiting to receive us.

At nine o'clock the next morning the girl and I arrived in Lwów. We went on foot to the address we had been given. There, we were let in by an elderly Polish woman who gave us a hot breakfast. She sat with us while we ate and talked about inconsequential things. In the afternoon, her son came in. He was a painfully thin, sickly-looking man of about 30. After greeting us warmly, he explained to me what work I was to do as a member of the "People's Army."

I was henceforth to be in the silver business, buying silver articles from the Jews in the ghettoes and transporting them, with the aid of my underground "contacts," to a peasant in the village of Drzewce near Nalenczow, a health resort in the Lublin district. From there, the silver was to be smuggled into Hungary and sold. The money the silver brought was used to buy ammunition for the underground.

PART TWO

6

The Wise Men of
the Warsaw Ghetto

RISING LIKE SOMBER RAMPARTS in the midst of the seething city, the walls of the Warsaw ghetto struck terror even into the hearts of the Gentiles. It was not that they were so sorry for the Jews, but the thought that at any moment the half-million human beings behind these walls might be wiped out in one stroke by the Nazi conquerors caused the Poles to wonder what would prevent their own people from falling victim to the same fate.

Within the ghetto, life had been reduced to vegetation. Hunger and disease took their unremitting toll each day. As they wept over their dead, the families in the ghetto murmured a strange new prayer: "Thanks be to God for having permitted him to die in his own bed." Those who remained alive looked more like starving animals than like human beings. Solid citizens of the Jewish community who had enjoyed prestige and even a measure of affluence before the war dragged themselves through the ghetto alleys, their bodies shrunken to skin and bones, the cracked skin of their swollen feet oozing pus and blood. "Help me get up, somebody, please, I haven't any strength left! Please, somebody, throw down a crust of bread—just a little moldy bread!" These were the street cries of the Warsaw ghetto. Meanwhile, Mottel Pinkert, "the King of the Dead," grew prosperous, very properous indeed, attending to the corpses.

Every other day or so the ghetto police rounded up young

people in the streets, dog-catcher fashion, and dragged them away "to work someplace." None of them ever returned.

During the winter months, the people in the ghetto stayed in bed all day because it was even colder indoors than it was in the street. There was no wood left to burn; every bit of wooden furniture in the ghetto had long since been chopped up for firewood. To be sure, firewood could be bought, but no one could afford the prices. In the summer, the people also stayed indoors, because no one could bear the searing sun and the stifling heat outside. And all year long, summer and winter, the Jews prayed that they might die in their own beds and not under some unspeakable tortures. But they also felt an urge to survive, to live to see the rise of a new and better world.

Even in the midst of these inhuman conditions there still were in the ghetto men and women with sufficient spirit and stamina to risk their own lives to aid the weak and the dying. They worked in the soup kitchens, smuggled food into the ghetto from the outside, cared for the sick and looked after the homeless. Even more important, they found the intellectual strength to devote time and thought to the training of the younger generation. One of the most magnificent chapters in the tragic annals of the Warsaw ghetto was written by the Jewish scholars and educators who, weak though they were from cold and hunger, strove to teach their students to remain strong and of good courage in the midst of death and despair and to uphold the timeless heritage of the Jewish people.

Before long, these valiant men and women had developed an extensive underground network of elementary schools, where the children of the ghetto were given not only an education but also food. Some of the most prominent figures in the ghetto provided the funds for this purpose so that the children would not have to go hungry—at least not while they were in school. Each school had its own committee of sponsors that hunted up the potatoes, flour, kasha, bread and *ersatz* honey from which the women were able to prepare an amazing variety of dishes—meals that filled empty stomachs and saved many a child from starving to death.

The ghetto schools were not all alike. In some of them, the language of instruction was Polish; in others it was Yiddish or

Hebrew. The course of study in the Polish-language schools was modeled on that of the pre-war Polish public school system. The Hebrew and Yiddish-language institutions were the direct heirs of the Yavneh, Tarbut, CYSHO and Beth Jacob schools that had flourished in Poland between the two World Wars.[20] Although in the ghetto these schools were not permitted to advertise the ideologies they represented, they offered parents an opportunity to educate their children along the lines they would have chosen if there had been no war.

All the ghetto schools were under the direction of the education department of the *Judenrat* headed by a highly respected, noble-minded educator named Orenstein. At the headquarters of the department—one room in the Jewish community center building on 26 Grzybowska Street—one could meet everybody who was anybody in Jewish education in the Warsaw ghetto. There was Rosenblum, a vigorous young man who acted as director of physical education, and Mira Jakubowicz, well known for her achievements in athletics. One might also find Janusz Korczak, the ever-smiling elderly director of the Jewish orphanage, who was known in the ghetto as "the father of the Jewish children;"[21] the two historians, gray-haired Professor Meir Balaban and the erudite Dr. Ignatz Schipper; the noted Bible scholar Dr. Meir Tauber; the eminent scientist and former professor at the University of Warsaw, Dr. Centnerszwer; or dozens of other, younger teachers, including some who had given little thought to their Jewish heritage before the war but whom fate had brought together in the ghetto. Now they all came to 26 Grzybowska Street to pick up the extra half-loaf of bread that teachers got in addition to the

---

20 The pre-1939 Jewish day schools in Poland, which offered secular and Jewish studies under one roof, catered to every shade of Jewish opinion. The Yavneh schools were run by the Mizrachi (Orthodox Zionist) movement; the Tarbut school network had a general Zionist platform; CYSHO schools were Yiddish-language secularist institutions supported by the Yiddishist *Bund* and the Left Po'ale Zion; the Beth Jacob schools were girls' schools of the ultra-Orthodox Agudath Israel.

21 Janusz Korczak (1878–1942) was deported to Treblinka along with the children in his orphanage. (See also Chapter 16.)

regular ghetto rations, and to discuss new courses of study or recent developments in the field of education.

Classes at the *gymnasium* [22] or university level were not permitted in the ghetto, because the Germans did not consider that the *Lumpenvolk*,[23] as they called the Jews, needed any education beyond the four-year elementary school. But even on the brink of extermination the *Lumpenvolk* defied the Nazis. All over the ghetto, high school classes, conducted by educators who had taught at the city's Jewish high schools before the war, met clandestinely at the homes of the students. Those who graduated were given temporary diplomas with the promise that they would be able to exchange them after the war for official, government-approved "certificates of maturity" which would permit them to enter a university or other institution of higher learning.

In the same clandestine fashion the young people in the ghetto were even offered an opportunity to continue their studies on a university level. The professors were Jews who had taught at the University of Warsaw before the war; most of them had been completely assimilated until Hitler drove them back to their Judaism and into the ghetto. The underground university included faculties of medicine, mathematics, philosophy and jurisprudence, and it was said that the dean was none other than Adam Cherniakow, president of the *Judenrat*.[24]

Bread, firewood and books were frequently sold side by side in the streets of the ghetto, and thin, pale young men would stop at the flimsy booths not to buy bread but to pick out a college text or rummage for some rare edition of a classic. The Jews of the Warsaw ghetto might be starving for lack of food, but this did not divert them from their hunger for learning.

The greatest threat to the survival of the ghetto schools lay in

---

[22] Eight-year academic high school catering to pupils between the ages of 10 and 18.
[23] Riffraff, rabble.
[24] An engineer by profession, Cherniakow had worked for the Polish government before the war and had also been a leading figure in Poland's pre-war Jewish community. He committed suicide in July, 1942.

the fact that the ranks of the teachers were steadily thinned by starvation and disease. Fearful that the schools and the clandestine study groups might have to be discontinued for lack of teachers, the leaders of the ghetto sought and found a way of replacing those who had died.

Professor Edmond Stein, a scholar widely known for his research in Jewish and Greek philosophy, who had taught at the Institute of Jewish Studies on Tlomacka Street before the war, founded the *Pedagogium,* a teachers' training school which was intended not only to offer young men and women a higher education but also to ensure that there would be an adequate number of qualified teachers for the children of the ghetto. Dr. Stein set up the *Pedagogium* with the help of members of the *Judenrat.* Since a school of this type was forbidden by the Nazi authorities, it was disguised as a soup kitchen for young working people. Registration began early in March, 1942. The requirement for admission to the *Pedagogium* was a "certificate of maturity," a graduation diploma from the eight-year *gymnasium.*

Classes were held in a school bulding at 17 Chlodna Street, next to the ghetto wall. The *Pedagogium* consisted of two departments— one for Jewish studies and one for mathematics and general science. Its students—120 young men and women—were taught by some of the best educators of the prewar Jewish community. Dr. Stein, who acted as dean, made sure that both the teachers and the students received a hot meal every evening. The food was provided by Mr. Blajman, who was known in the ghetto as the "King of the Bakers" and also as the Warsaw Manischewitz, headed the group of sponsors that supported the *Pedagogium.* Dr. Stein's wife got several women to come to the school every evening to prepare and serve the meal. The students looked upon Mrs. Stein as a substitute mother, and the *Pedagogium* became their second home. Young people whose parents were dying or had already died turned to the *Pedagogium* for the comfort and warmth of a closely-knit Jewish family circle.

Classes were held each day for three hours, from four in the afternoon until the seven o'clock curfew. These hours had been chosen to allow the students to work during the day. Even if they could not earn enough to support themselves, it was considered vitally important that they should have regular employment and "working papers" to prove to the authorities that they were aiding the German war effort. As long as they were doing some work in a small factory, a machine shop, or in one of the institutions of the ghetto community council, they were considered "useful" Jews and therefore, it was thought, would be safe from deportation to labor camps. Later on, Dr. Stein prevailed on the *Judenrat* to classify regular students at the *Pedagogium* as "useful" workers so that they no longer had to accept employment during the day. During that early period, when the Jewish ghetto police rounded up young people to fill the Nazi quota of Jewish slave laborers, they generally did not take those who could show certificates from the *Judenrat* stating that they were enrolled at the *Pedagogium.*

The lectures at the *Pedagogium* provided the students not only with knowledge but also with inspiration and hope. This was particularly true of the course taught by Dr. Stein, who guided his listeners through the intricacies of Jewish thought. He traced the influence of the teachings and traditions of Judaism on Jewish life over the centuries, and dwelled at some length on the glory and honor of Jewish martyrdom through the ages. Obviously, he had planned his lectures to meet not only the intellectual requirements but also the moral and spiritual needs of his students. Dr. Stein always spoke in a soft, muffled voice as if he were discussing secret plans for an underground revolt. But his words were as powerful as the blows of a sledgehammer. When the mass deportations began in July, 1942, and formal classes could no longer be held at the *Pedagogium,* the students continued to rally around Dr. Stein until fate finally parted them forever.

Meir Balaban, historian, former dean of the Warsaw Rabbinical Seminary Tachkemoni and professor at the University of Warsaw, came every other day to lecture at the *Pedagogium.* The little old gentleman still had his good-natured smile but that smile could not hide the deep sorrow in his heart. He was 65 years old and had seen his whole word crumble about him. First, his beloved wife had died. He had taken that loss very hard. After his lectures at the *Pedago-*

gium he would go to the synagogue to recite the *kaddish* prayer in her memory. During that period I would come to the ghetto as often as I safely could, to visit my mother. Usually, I would manage to stay a few days and take the opportunity to attend some of the lectures at the *Pedagogium*. Many of the lecturers, including Dr. Balaban, had been my own teachers at the Tachkemoni School. Many times, I would accompany Dr. Balaban on his walk to the synagogue; he would hold on to my arm and talk all the way, telling me of the tragic turn his life had taken in the ghetto. The Germans had ordered him to write a new history of Jewish life in Poland, "revised" to fit the Nazi propaganda line. They had even given him an official permit to commute between the ghetto and the library of the University of Warsaw to do his research. But under the circumstances his beloved university, where he had taught hundreds of young people before the war and had formed friendships with many Gentile students and professors, had become a prison for him. He told me that the hours he had to spend in the library seemed to him like the last hours of a criminal who had been sentenced to death. He was not permitted to make the trip by street car; not even "useful" Jews were allowed to do that. The pavements were also off limits to Jews. Professor Balaban therefore had to walk in the middle of the street, dodging horses and automobiles. Many Poles walking along Królewska or Krakowskie Przedmieście Streets recognized the bent little scholar with the white "Jewish armband" on his sleeve, painfully making his way to or from the university, and they would avert their faces. Once in a great while, when no German policeman was in sight, a former Gentile student or colleague would stop to greet the professor and then quickly walk away.

Dr. Balaban would arrive at the *Pedagogium* exhausted. He would enter the classroom and sit down at his desk, still in his overcoat, to catch his breath for a few minutes before starting his lecture. The course he taught was entitled "The Rise and Development of the Ghetto in Jewish History." His aim was to refute the connotation of shame and humiliation customarily given to life in the ghetto. Living in the ghetto, he pointed out, had not always been a condition imposed upon the Jews against their will; in some

85

communities Jews had actually petitioned the authorities for permission to live together in one special street or neighborhood. Later, the course of events had broken down the ghetto walls in Italy, Germany and even in Poland. In the same way, Dr. Balaban said, the walls of the Nazi ghettoes, too, would crumble in time, and our foes would fall with them. He enlivened his talks with humorous anecdotes from ghetto life in bygone centuries. He probably never realized how much faith and hope he instilled into his students. Sometimes, as we sat listening to him, we found ourselves imagining that the world was still good and beautiful, that the Jews were living in freedom and peace, and that the word "ghetto" existed only on paper and in Dr. Balaban's lecture notes.

Another luminary who became a lecturer at our *Pedagogium* was Dr. Ignatz Schipper, journalist, orator, historian and Zionist leader. Before the war he had written several definitive works on the history of Polish Jewry, had helped found the Labor Zionist party in Poland, and had been a member of the Polish parliament. Now in his late fifties he, too, was in the Warsaw ghetto. But his spirit and his zeal for scholarly research had remained free and unfettered. His first lecture course at the *Pedagogium* dealt with the history of the Khazars. Dr. Schipper demonstrated that traces of the cultural heritage of the Khazars, who had settled in the south of Russia during the 8th century and had embraced Judaism, still existed in a number of Slavic countries. It was his theory that at one time the Khazars had advanced deep into Poland, pushing as far west as Cracow and capturing territory on both sides of the Vistula River. He revealed to us that he was working diligently to complete a new history of the Khazars which would shed an entirely new light on the history of European Jewry.

Dr. Schipper had always been a high-strung man; now, in the ghetto, his nerves were even more on edge. He was never without a cigarette between his lips and always carried in his coat pocket some tobacco and a gadget for stuffing it into cigarette papers. His lectures were among the most popular in the *Pedagogium* and were faithfully attended not only by his students but also by other faculty members and noted scholars who lived in the ghetto. His hoarse voice fluttered about the room like a captive bird straining toward freedom. He spoke in Polish, with much gesticulation. As he talked, he was in perpetual motion, pacing from one end of the classroom to the other. Yet all the time he seemed to be looking into the eyes of every person present. All this was entirely in character with his presentation, which was spell-binding.

Following his course on the Khazars, Dr. Schipper gave a series of lectures in Yiddish on "The Origins of Yiddish Folk Sayings." These lectures were not dry discourses but virtuoso performances. When he finished, we would crowd around him, reluctant to let him go, eager to hear more. In the informal discussions after his lectures, he would talk to us like an older brother, and we loved him very much.

One month before the mass deportations began, he delivered a talk entitled, "Let Us Laugh, For Who Knows Whether The World Will Last Another Thirty-six Days." The essence of this lecture was that we should enjoy every moment of living while we still could.

In 1943 I was to see Dr. Schipper again—in Camp No. 3 at Maidanek. We looked at each other in silence—he with the yellow Star of David on his tattered, filthy prison uniform, and I, his former student, wearing the red triangle identifying me as a Polish Gentile inmate—and then we parted, still without one word. By that time Dr. Schipper no longer looked like a human being. I took to watching him without his noticing it. He was working in the camp kitchen, peeling potatoes. One day the Kapo[25] caught him trying to hide a couple of potatoes on his person. For this crime the Kapo hit him savagely over the head, threw him to the ground and kicked him in the chest and stomach. Then he sent him off

---

25 "Trusty" or "overseer." Initially, Kapos were chosen from among German non-Jewish inmates imprisoned in the concentration camps on criminal charges, but in all-Jewish camps some Kapos were Jews. Kapos received special privileges, such as better food rations than the other inmates. While some Kapos were helpful to their fellow inmates, others were known and hated for their inhumanity.

to hard labor. From that day on, Dr. Schipper deteriorated rapidly. The last of his strength left him so that his legs could no longer carry him. The underworld characters who ran the camp made fun of the *"Herr Professor;"* they shoved him about, pulled down his pants and whipped his naked flesh. These tortures stripped him of the last vestige of human dignity. He dragged himself from barrack to barrack, begging for a little soup, and rummaging through garbage cans for scraps of food. He could be heard all day long alternately laughing and crying, mumbling incoherent phrases. He had become the camp madman. One night, after roll call, I stole into his barrack, tiptoed to his pallet and slipped half a ration of bread into his hand. He devoured it in one bite. I wanted to take him outside and show him a place where I could meet him every evening and bring him some soup and bread, but he would not go with me. He was afraid that I was trying to play a trick on him, for by that time he no longer recognized me—or anyone else, for that matter. A few days later, he was taken away to the camp infirmary, where he died. Thus ended the life of Ignatz Schipper, teacher, scholar, Zionist, man of wisdom and vision.

Also among the lecturers at the *Pedagogium* was Dr. Meir Tauber, the Bible scholar who before the war had been principal of the State Jewish Teachers' Seminary at 9 Gęsia Street in Warsaw. In the ghetto, Dr. Tauber was put in charge of the Hebrew section of the *Judenrat's* education department. He had a bad leg and therefore had to use a cane. Months of starvation had turned him into a grotesque figure; he was painfully thin, and his threadbare clothes further accentuated his tragicomic appearance. He always carried a Bible under his arm. Until the last moment of his life, he continued his studies with the same dedication that he had brought to his research in better days.

Then there was Dr. Moshe Alter, the former dean of the Tachkemoni Rabbinical Seminary. Every day he worked until noon as a building superintendent, but in the late afternoon and early evening hours he taught history at the *Pedagogium.*

The Talmudist at the *Pedagogium* was Rabbi Dr. Ephraim Sonnenschein, an outstanding Biblical and Talmudic scholar— quiet and easy-going but zealous in his endeavors to settle the age-old dispute between the schools of Hillel and Shammai.[26] He expounded the Talmud in Hebrew instead of the traditional Yiddish. Sometimes, after the ghetto police had made one of its mass roundups of slave laborers, Rabbi Sonnenschein might find only one single student in his class. But he would stay with that one student, and it often happened that the two would become so deeply immersed in their study that they continued beyond the curfew hour and had to spend the night together in the classroom.

Among the other educators in the Warsaw ghetto, I remember Zvi Rakowsky, a brillant Hebraist who had taught at one of the Jewish high schools before the war; Simon Rundstein, the young expert in the science of education, who had come to Warsaw from Lodz; and Dr. Nathan Eck, scholar, writer and active Zionist, one of the few ghetto teachers fortunate enough to survive the Holocaust.

Such were the Wise Men of the Warsaw ghetto who devoted their talents as teachers and scholars to the service of their fellow Jews, enriching the lives of their students and keeping up their courage until the end.

---

[26] Two distinct schools of Talmudic study, named after their founders, the first-century scholars Hillel and Shammai. The latter had a strict, conservative opproach to Jewish law, while the former was widely known for its lenient interpretation.

7
A Web of Blackmail

EARLY IN JANUARY, 1943, I went from Lwów to Bursztyn on underground business. In Bursztyn, I stayed at the home of my friend Tomek Ziemba. A year before, Tomek had made it possible for me to travel to Warsaw by providing me with the Aryan papers of the late Jan Krzus. This time, I was armed with another set of Aryan papers, the documents which I had received through Christina of the Falenty chicken farm, and which identified me as Pawel Kolodziejczyk, picture-frame salesman and pure Polish Aryan. Nevertheless, after only three days, Tomek urged me to leave Bursztyn as quickly as possible because every child in the district remembered me as Pinkhas Lazarovich Trepman, the teacher at the Polish school in Ludwikówka. Besides, Tomek told me that he himself was being shadowed by the Gestapo and the Ukrainian police who had begun to suspect him of being involved in underground activities.

I therefore decided to move on to Rohatyn the very next day. At four o'clock the next morning I took the train to Chodorów. Now it happened that the railroad station of Chodorów was one of the most dangerous spots in the entire area because a Nazi official named Wolff, accompanied by a hefty bloodhound, scoured the station day in and day out for Jews who tried to pass as Aryans, and it was known that he had managed to ferret out a number of such unfortunates every day. But the Lwów-Tarnopol train which stopped at Rohatyn was not due until that evening, and since it was a bitter cold day I decided to take my chances and stay inside the station building. I deliberately picked up a Polish girl and started a little romance with her. We looked like just another pair of lovers and it did not occur to anyone in the station, not even to Wolff, who kept pacing the waiting room with his bloodhound, that I was anything else but a true-blue Polish Aryan.

The train journey to Rohatyn—about 65 kilometers—flew by rapidly and uneventfully. The cars sped along the snowy expanse like so many black demons. Inside the train it was pitch dark, so that the passengers could not see each other, and I was safe.

In those days the ghetto of Rohatyn had not yet been sealed off. It was still simply the "Jewish quarter" of the city, and both Jews and Gentiles were free to move in and out as they pleased. I went to the home of the Felds, a family with whom I had been friendly during the days of the Russian occupation. But all that was left of the Feld family now was one daughter, and her husband and children, at whose home I had stayed for some time when they had still lived in Bursztyn. She told me that one of her brothers had died of a stroke, her brother-in-law had committed suicide, and two sisters had died of typhoid fever. I told her what I had been through and explained why I had come to her family: their home was the only place where I could safely stop for a few days. I warned her that no one in Rohatyn must find out who and what I really was.

While we were talking, the door opened, and in came Mondschein, the redhead, who had taught together with me at the Russian school in the Rohatyn district. I had always liked him; aside from his abilities as an educator, he had a fine sense of humor. We embraced like two long-lost brothers, and then we sat down to make plans.

The next day Mondschein took me to see Meir Weisbrojn, the chief of the Jewish community's police force who, according to all accounts, had proven to be a tower of strength to the Jews in the Rohatyn ghetto—and was an active member of the resistance movement. I found that it was safe for me to go about the town without a "Jewish armband," because very few of the Jews who had known me from the "Russian days" were still around. Most of them had died from starvation or disease, or else they had been shot by the Nazis. About 75 per cent of the ghetto's population now consisted of Jews who had been moved there from neighboring towns and villages. As a result, I rarely saw anyone I knew or who I thought would know my true identity. The rumor quickly spread that I was a friendly Polish Gentile who was able to get good "Aryan" documents for any Jew who wanted them.

When I first met Weisbrojn's wife, Clara, I thought she was an Ukrainian peasant woman who came into the ghetto each day to do housework for the Jewish police chief. She had typically Russian-Ukrainian features and a primitive peasant manner mixed with Ukrainian energy and temperament. Her accent, both in Polish and in Ukrainian, sounded so "native" that it would not have occurred even to a dozen Gestapo interrogators to suspect that she was Jewish. Because she looked and acted so much like a Gentile, her husband wanted to send her to Warsaw with as much money as he could scrape together, in the hope that she might be able to live there as an Aryan and so survive the war. As for himself, he told me, he was sure he would be killed, for he would not stand by idly if the ghetto were to be liquidated; he would make a last stand with his partisans and then hide out in the woods to continue the underground struggle against the enemy from there.

We sat until the wee hours of the morning—Mondschein, Weisbrojn, his wife and I—and finally decided that she should go with me to Warsaw, a journey of some 600 kilometers by train. She had already managed to obtain a Ukrainian birth certificate and passport. However, she said that she would need another two weeks to get ready. I agreed to stay in Rohatyn until she could leave.

During the night of February 15, 1943, Clara Weisbrojn and I left Rohatyn. I had slept all that day in preparation for our departure. A Ukrainian peasant, a friend of Weisbrojn's, had agreed to take us by sled to Przemyslany, a little town some 50 kilometers from Rohatyn, where we would board the train, for Clara was afraid to get on the train at Rohatyn, where many Gentiles and policemen knew her. At three o'clock in the morning, the peasant stole into

Weisbroin's house to call for us. After a tearful farewell to her husband and the rest of her family, Clara climbed into the sled with me and we started out. A Jewish policeman escorted us as far as the outskirts of the town. When we finally reached the highway, the horses raced ahead full speed to our destination. It was a clear, frosty night and the cold stung our faces. The highway was as smooth as a mirror. Not a soul was to be seen. Even the dogs were quiet. The huts along the highway stood silent and drowsy; the Ukrainians inside were sound asleep, safe and snug in the warmth of their downy featherbeds. A weird light shone all around us; the moon above, like a faithful guardian, accompanied our progress along the dangerously slick road.

The sun was rising as our sled glided into the railroad station of Przemyslany. We had completed the first lap of our journey without being stopped even once by the German police. Our faces were flushed and I could feel my heart hammering, but we had to pull ourselves together and act as natural and normal as any of the Gentiles on the train. Everything depended on that.

On the train there was a little trouble. A gypsy woman got a beating for stealing a chicken from the woman sitting beside her, and the peasants in our car raised a hue and cry because of what was happening to the produce they were taking to market in Lwów. The aisle of our car was a mess of spilled milk and broken eggs, and there was pushing and shoving everywhere. Yet not once did an inspector enter our car to see what the commotion was all about. Probably no inspector could have made his way through the crowd. It was a good thing for us, too.

We arrived in Lwów that evening. We spent the next twenty-four hours in a small room on Grodecka Street where I had stayed several times before. It was a modest, inconspicuous place and therefore relatively safe from police searches. Our hostess was a Mrs. Rykowski, who shared the room with her child. She had put up two additional folding cots for Clara Weisbrojn and me. Mrs. Rykowski was a simple, hospitable soul, a devout Catholic who hated the "Prussians" with all her heart. We sat around her rickety little table until after midnight, drinking tea with syrup and discussing the problems that were worrying the Poles at the time.

I made sure to kneel down and recite all the proper Christian prayers before going to bed, and our hostess was very pleased to see how pious I was. Then I lay down on my cot and fell into a deep sleep.

In the morning I went out to make a long-distance call to a Ukrainian secret agent in Rohatyn, who was in the employ of the Germans but was also a friend of Weisbrojn's. This man, who regularly brought small arms to Weisbrojn's house, had known of our journey and had agreed that we should call him from Lwow so that he could inform Weisbrojn of our safe arrival.

Afterwards I went to the station and bought two tickets for the night train to Warsaw. Again, everything went smoothly. But as I came out of the station, I saw a commotion in the street. Some Ukrainian agents had stopped an elegantly dressed woman whose platinum blonde hair added an aristocratic touch to her already impressive appearance. When the agents asked to see her identification papers, she opened her handbag, pulled out a little vial, swallowed its contents, and almost instantly slumped to the pavement, dead. It turned out that she had been Jewish, and that one of her good Gentile friends had recognized her and reported her to the police. I stood among the onlookers who watched unmoved, and tried to appear unconcerned. I did not mention the incident to Mrs. Weisbrojn.

Late that night, Mrs. Weisbrojn and I boarded the train for Warsaw. In return for a tip of 50 zlotys the conductor gave us two comfortable seats in a car marked "For Germans Only." Throughout the journey we sat in mortal fear of being caught. As Poles, we did not belong in a car reserved for the German overlords; as Jews, we were not supposed to be on the train at all. Clara Weisbrojn began to feel sorry that she had ever agreed to take the chance. Those were the days when the Germans in Poland stopped every train and carefully examined the papers of each passenger, when Poles by the thousands were taken off trains and dispatched to forced labor camps in Germany—if they were lucky. In most cases, they ended in Maidanek or Auschwitz.

Clara Weisbrojn and I purposely tried to sleep most of the time to avoid having to talk with the other passengers. The conductor came by several times and looked at our documents. When he saw the stamp on my papers identifying me as a Polish Aryan, he merely smiled. He never asked us what we were doing in a car reserved for Germans, because he was a Pole himself and felt a sense of solidarity with his countrymen. We were not the only Poles in the car. I do not think it even occurred to him that Mrs. Weisbrojn and I might be Jews.

Everything went well until we pulled into Zamość Junction. There, a fine-looking elderly man joined us. By this time the three of us were the only passengers left in the car. He offered us some cake, we reciprocated with cigarettes, and a pleasant conversation ensued. Then, shortly before we were due to arrive in Warsaw, he informed us in a conspiratorial whisper that he was a member of the underground, traveling on a very important mission. We did not react to his story. We no longer felt comfortable with him. We had not asked him any questions or told him anything about ourselves. Why, then, was he so eager to tell us all his secrets? He kept on talking, boasting about the exploits of his friends in the resistance movement. We tried to change the subject, but each time he turned the conversation back to his underground activities.

We were glad when our train finally entered Warsaw station, and we bade a cordial farewell to our strange fellow passenger. As we emerged onto Jerozolimskie Aleje, we saw a Polish policeman heading straight for us. He stopped us and demanded to see my identification card. I looked at him, pretending to be surprised, and produced the card with an air of nonchalance.

"So your name is Pawel Kolodziejczyk," the policeman growled. "But never mind your name—I know you're a Jew."

I pretended that this was all very ridiculous. I laughed out loud.

"Come with me!" the policeman said and led us into a nearby doorway. All this time he said not a word to Mrs. Weisbrojn. With her Gentile looks, he apparently took it for granted that my companion was not Jewish.

He tried to appeal to my common sense. "Look, I know you are a Jew," he said to me. "I've met plenty of people like you— Jews who try to pass as Aryans. Sure, you want to remain alive. Well, I want to survive, too. Look at it this way: you take care of me, and I'll let you go. We all have to live somehow, but I can't make ends meet on my salary. So, if you don't make it worth while for me, I'll simply have to turn you over to the Germans."

He talked on and on, but I stuck to my story that I was not a Jew but a Polish Aryan. I knew that if I were to admit he was right and attempt to pay him off, he would be at my throat all the time for increasingly larger gifts.

He took me to the nearest Polish police station. Mrs. Weisbrojn followed us into the office of the police commissioner. As I learned later, the commissioner, whose name was Shein, had been an ardent Polish patriot before the war, but after the Germans had marched in, he had donned the swastika emblem. Shein began to interrogate me; his questions were obviously designed to convince me that he, Shein, knew I was Jewish but that he would not turn me in if I took care of him properly. But I still stuck to my story. Finally, Shein lost his patience and produced his trump card. He ordered me to pull down my pants and, with a triumphant jeer, pointed to the physical proof that I was a Jew.

At this point all my bravado left me. I began to appeal to the conscience of my captors and to offer them money. Mrs. Weisbrojn sat quietly, in firm control of herself. Shein did his best to reassure me. "Nothing will happen to you. You can trust me. I sympathize with the Jews. You're very gifted people. All I ask is that you take good care of me and of Sobak here," he said, pointing to the policeman who had arrested me. "I know you have no place to go here in town. I think I can get Sobak to put you up at his house for tonight."

Of course this encounter upset all my plans. It was now out of the question for me to stay in Warsaw; the police would certainly shadow me day and night.

The four of us—Shein, Sobak, Mrs. Weisbrojn and I—got into a car and drove to Lucka Street, where Shein got out. Just before we parted, I slipped some crisp bank notes into Shein's hand. This was the price for my survival.

Mrs. Weisbrojn and I spent the night with a friend of Sobak's on Koszykowa Street. Before we went to bed, our hostess, a shrewd old Polish woman, demanded that we pay her 500 zlotys, which in those days was enough to support a family for a week on the Aryan side of town. We had no choice but to give her the money.

All the following day, we stayed at Sobak's house. His wife kept smiling at us while she told us the latest news of how "hidden" Jews in this place had been discovered and arrested by the Germans. In the meantime, Shein and the Sobaks had found out that Clara Weisbrojn was also Jewish. They said they felt sorry for us, terribly sorry, and demanded money from us for every little service. Commissioner Shein offered to put up Mrs. Weisbrojn at his home—in return for 15,000 zlotys per week. Clara would not hear of it; she was afraid that Shein and his people would take everything she had and then throw her out into the street or turn her over to the Nazis.

We sat in Sobak's living room in a fever of anxiety. We did not believe a word the three Poles were saying, and we expected the worst to happen at any moment. Sobak then informed us that the distinguished-looking gentleman who had engaged us in conversation on the train had pointed us out to him as Jews and told him to arrest us. Clara and I exchanged glances and quickly began to talk about something else. We gave Mrs. Sobak some money for the gas she had used to cook our lunch, put a bottle of brandy and other gifts on the living room table and promised the Sobaks to send them more goodies once we got to Galicia, Poland's bread-basket. We decided to go back to Rohatyn. Sobak simply threw us out into the street; he said he could not keep us in his home after that night because he did not want to endanger his whole family for the likes of us.

Early the next day Shein turned up again and squeezed another 5,000 zlotys out of us. Sobak's son then bought us two train tickets for Tarnopol and got 1,000 zlotys from us for his trouble. At nightfall we left Sobak's house to start on the next lap of our journey.

Much later, at Maidanek, I heard that Commissioner Shein had been shot to death by Polish partisan fighters. It seemed that he had acquired quite a reputation with the Gestapo for his ability to discover and apprehend members of the Polish underground movement.

In Warsaw's central railway station Clara and I elbowed our way to the train through the crowds among whom there were swindlers and informers aplenty, waiting to pounce on homeless, defenseless Jews like ourselves.

We bade Warsaw goodbye with fury in our hearts at the Poles. We Jews had lived among them for centuries, and helped them in their struggle for freedom, only to find that now, in our time of greatest need, they were totally indifferent to our tragedy.

8

The Death of a Jewish Community

JEWISH LIFE IN Galicia was in ruins. Trails of smoke from the burned-out ghettoes darkened the skies over the Jewish townlets and villages where the Germans had not yet come. Lwów was smoldering; Horodenka lay deserted, and death and destruction reigned supreme in Stanislawów. Boarded-up windows, shattered doors, broken furniture and other pitiful remnants of once-happy homes lay in the streets like refuse, like wreaths of thorns upon the mass grave of Polish Jewry.

Nearly all the ghettoes in the Chodorów district had been liquidated. The isolated few who had managed to escape a mass deportation or a pogrom by fleeing to another ghetto spread bloodcurdling tales which served only to heighten the terror in the hearts of the other Jews they encountered. Strong, brave men committed suicide. Almost every Jewish family arranged to procure vials of poison for themselves to use when the Nazis came. Jewish mothers tearfully begged Gentile neighbors to take their children, promising in return to sign over to them their houses or businesses, or to give them some other handsome reward once the good times would come back. The Jews who still survived in Galicia felt that their end was near.

The tension in the Rohatyn ghetto increased with each passing day. The women were still baking *bulbaniks* and all the other Galician delicacies, but swallowing the goodies had become a problem. The bunkers which the Jews had built for themselves were in good working order. After repeated drills the Jews had learned to move to their hideouts in an orderly, disciplined fashion and with maximum speed.

During those days I used to visit at the homes of various other families besides the Felds. Every now and then I took a quick trip to Lwów where I would do a little business and see Stach, the liaison officer between the Lwów and Warsaw units of our underground movement, to find out what was going on and to get his instructions for the immediate future. Stach was a wonderful man, a pure soul who took the same risks to help Jews as he did to help any of his fellow Poles. Stach knew very well that I was a Jew, a fact known to only one other Gentile: Tomek Ziemba of Bursztyn. At the time I was working for the underground buying silver objects from the Jews in the various towns and bringing them to Stach—whose real name was Jan Kaciura—in Lwów. Stach then arranged to have the silver smuggled into Hungary, from where we would receive weapons and ammunition in return. In Sokal, near the border, we made the acquaintance of a Hungarian officer who eventually became our "purveyor of arms." The weapons would be brought from the Hungarian border to their destination in peasants' wagons, well-concealed beneath bundles of farm produce. The wagons would make the trip during the night, using the sandy side-roads where they were not likely to be discovered and stopped.

Buying up silver from the Jews was a difficult and trying task. I found two young men in Rohatyn who agreed to work with me and threw themselves into the job with enthusiasm. We had to sweat blood to convince the Jews that we needed the silver because our resistance organization had to have guns, dynamite and rifles if we were not to be slaughtered like defenseless lambs. The Jews had hidden their gold and silver in holes they had dug into the ground and they would not part with it. But when the situation deteriorated even beyond the worst fears of the Jews in the ghetto, my two agents began to come to me each night with sacks full of silver. I brought the silver to the Aryan sector, to a retired stationmaster named Lewandowski, who allowed us to store the silver in a dark closet at his house until we could move it on to Lwów. At first Lewandowski, a man of sixty, had not wanted to take the risk, but the sight of some shining silver coins helped persuade him. After the ghetto of Rohatyn, Lewandowski's house became my second home base. Here, there was no one to suspect that I was anything but a Pole and an Aryan. Each day at nightfall, after a day's "purchasing mission" in the ghetto, I would stuff my pockets with the silver objects I had managed to buy that day, climb over the ghetto fence at a point near Feld's house and, with tottering legs, make my way to Lewandowski's place, praying only that I should not be caught before I got there.

Once each week a load of silver would be dispatched from Lewandowski's house in Rohatyn to Stach's place in Lwow. Whenever we heard that the trains were not overrun with German guards I would take the package to Lwów myself. But whenever we learned that the Germans were raiding the trains I would send a code telegram to Lwów, asking that a messenger be sent to me for the purpose of moving the "merchandise" to its destination. Almost all our messengers were Polish peasants who had been recruited by the underground. And our work went on, week in, week out, without any interruption.

Meanwhile, word had come to the Jews of Rohatyn—through clandestine channels—of the uprising in the Warsaw ghetto. Hearing the news, Meir Weisbrojn, the chief of the Rohatyn ghetto police, organized a group of courageous young men into an underground guerrilla unit. The first undertaking of this group was to build a huge bunker for 300 persons in the forest near the town. The planning and preparations alone took several weeks. As a first step, scouts were sent out to find a suitable site. The forests around Rohatyn were exceptionally dense; there were parts on which no human being had set foot for centuries. After the site had been chosen, a group was assigned to gather up tools and construction supplies and to bring them piecemeal under cover of darkness to the place, which was some ten kilometers outside the town. This meant that the men had to walk some twenty kilometers each night, back and forth, with fear as their unseen companion. But their iron determination to survive and to avenge the massacre of

103

their brethren in the Warsaw ghetto outweighed all other emotions.

For three weeks the young Jews of Rohatyn worked in three-day shifts to build a bunker in the heart of the forest where they and other ghetto fighters would be able to survive when the Nazis came. They had thought of everything: the bunker was equipped with bedrooms, a dining hall, a kitchen, lavatories, and a storeroom for arms. Perhaps the most ingenious feature of the shelter was the chimney: it was installed into the trunk of a tree, which had holes cut into it to allow the smoke to escape. The entrance to the bunker was about half a mile away from the bunker itself.

The work was completed before the first snows of winter began to fall. The group set about gathering food and medical supplies, beds and kitchen utensils. There was no time to lose; winter was fast approaching, and the Nazi vise was drawing closer and ever more tightly around the ghetto of Rohatyn.

One night, when the workers came to the bunker, they found the underground chambers in a state of disarray; obviously, someone had been there. As it turned out, the forest ranger, a young Ukrainian, had noticed footprints in the snow and traced them to the site. As a result, the whole shelter project, the product of so much work and planning, had to be abandoned.

A day or two later, the Ukrainian forester turned up at Weisbrojn's office and assured him that he need have no fear; he, the Ukrainian, would not tell anyone of his discovery. Weisbrojn pretended not to know what the forester was talking about. But from that time on the Ukrainian became a frequent visitor at Weisbrojn's headquarters, and before long he was performing various chores for the underground, particularly those related to the purchase and transport of weapons. He proved to be a man who could keep his mouth shut. If only he had known, he said over and over again, that the Jews had been building a bunker to hide out from the Nazis, he would not only have kept quiet about it but would even have lent them a hand. But Weisbrojn's closest associates, Lenek Engelberg and Munia Halpern, did not trust the Ukrainian entirely. Past experience had taught them to be careful. And so the bunker was never used; it remained only as a monument to the Jewish will to survive.

In the early days of my association with Weisbrojn, I had a feeling that he and his friends were very careful of what they said and did while I was with them. This distressed me not a little, for in my loneliness I was badly in need of friends. I wanted to know what was going on, and what plans they had, so that I should be able to offer them my help. But they felt they did not really know me and wanted to bide their time until they could feel sure of me. Eventually. I was able to overcome their suspicions and they drew me into their circle. "We have to be careful, you know," they later explained to me. "The Nazis are sending all kinds of agents into the ghetto to spy on us. There might even be some Jews who would inform on us to save their own skins."

After I had won the confidence of Weisbrojn and his coworkers, I was sent on various missions for the underground to places like Chodorów, Bukaczowce and Bolsczowce.

As the situation became increasingly precarious, the young Jews of the Rohatyn ghetto began to buy arms with which to fight the Nazis. Before long, Weisbrojn's partisan unit was besieged by hundreds of volunteers. Since, for strategic reasons, it would not have been safe to permit one unit to become too large, we decided to organize a second unit. This assignment was entrusted to me. It was a responsible and dangerous job. The Jews in the ghetto could not be allowed to know that I actually was one of their own; at the same time, on the Aryan side, death lay in wait for me at every step. I set about my task with the dedication of a priest preparing to perform a sacred rite.

My replacement as contact man with the other underground cells was a man named Katz who was known to be reliable in every respect. The attic in which he lived became the meeting place for our staff from which we sent out our orders. I would travel to neighboring towns and villages where I had been given addresses at which to get weapons. We paid for our weapons with gold or with American dollars. Most of our arms came from Ukrainians who had captured them from the Poles or the Russians.

Meanwhile, the Jews of Rohatyn were living in constant dread of what the next day might bring. The wealthier householders sent their wives and children to stay at the homes of peasants they knew; girls bleached their hair blonde to look "Aryan"; at night-time, many Jews slipped out of the ghetto and looked for a hiding place in field or forest, only to return a week or two later, crest-fallen and frustrated. They did not know what to do with themselves. The *Judenrat* tried to calm them down, the ghetto police sought to lift their sagging spirits, but the Jews of the ghetto no longer believed any of them.

Sergeant-Major Freitag, a Silesian German in the Rohatyn *Polizei Kommendatur,* came to the ghetto every day, escorted by a dozen or more German and Ukrainian policemen, and demanded his daily pound of flesh: ten, thirty or forty sick people, or old men and women.

"It's a pity to waste your bread and soup on them," he said. "The food could be used to better purpose by people who work for our *Wehrmacht.*" The Jews, not having any choice, let him have his way because he threatened that if they refused his demands the entire ghetto would be killed off. He personally took the victims to a place outside the town and shot them dead; he considered this his special, personal privilege. Later on, he started asking for healthy specimens as well. In addition, the Jewish ghetto police of Tarnopol would come to Rohatyn to seize Jews for the forced-labor camps where Rokita, the notorious Gestapo murderer, would rape the young Jewish women and then shoot them.

During the day the Jews in the ghetto could hardly wait for night to come: yet, when darkness fell they longed for the morning star to appear.

It was in this atmosphere of terror and living death that the underground unit of Rohatyn prepared to leave the ghetto to join the partisans in their battle against the Hitlerites.

Saturday, June 5, 1943 was such a gloriously sunny day that the Jews temporarily forgot about their troubles. Everybody went out-doors, strolling up and down the ghetto alleys and smiling at each other. Some even exchanged jokes as though nothing had ever been wrong in the world.

At midnight several members of our unit went down to the creek which ran along half the Jewish quarter, forming something of a natural boundary between the ghetto and the Aryan sector at this point. There, Ukrainians were waiting to hand over to them 25 Soviet guns and 35,000 bullets. The deal safely concluded, our "general staff" held a brief meeting and set the hour for our departure from the ghetto: our guerilla unit was to be ready to march the next evening—Sunday night, June 6. This meant that we had less than 24 hours in which to make our preparations. We parted and went to sleep; it was two o'clock in the morning.

The ghetto was deep in a weary, nervous slumber. Only the men on guard were awake, listening with hammering hearts for any suspicious noise. Completely exhausted, I had dropped like a heavy sack onto my iron cot; for the first time in many nights, I had taken off my clothes.

I was awakened by the crack of gunfire. In my first confusion, I could not grasp what was going on. My landlady shouted to me to hurry to the bunker of the house. Through the window I saw flashes of fire and running figures dressed only in their underwear. And above all the confusion I heard the wild shouts and curses of the Nazi beasts.

I pulled on my boots and clothes, emptied my pockets of everything except my Polish identity card, and ran outside. I was immediately enveloped by the moans of the wounded, by the screams of babies and their mothers being dragged away to an unknown fate. And through it all I heard the Germans commanding the ghetto Jews to surrender without putting up a fight.

The first attack on the ghetto lasted no longer than five minutes; yet it seemed very much longer as the Jews scurried about like driven cattle, the Nazi killers in their smart uniforms pursuing them like packs of hungry wolves.

It was still dark. I made for the ghetto gate, next to the house of my friends, the Felds. It was impossible to venture further because of the constant gunfire from the Aryan side. I entered the Felds' house. The rooms were empty, in wild disarray. I concluded that the Felds had taken shelter in their bunker. I found there was no way for me to leave the house again, for a Gestapo man was already keeping watch in the garden outside. Getting down on all fours, I crawled to the room directly over the cellar and stopped at the trapdoor; it was tightly in place. I knocked on it softly, whispering: "Frieda! Open up! It's your friend Pawel Kolodziej-czyk! Let me in!"

I had to keep up the knocking and whispering for a full minute before the cover was finally raised and I dropped into the cellar, a pit where living people had buried themselves in an effort to escape death. Eight human being were crammed into this cellar, which was barely big enough to accommodate two middle-sized individuals. Pressed close together like sardines in a flat tin can, scarcely able to breathe, we could hear the heavy tread of German boots above us, marching through the house and then out again. Each time the Germans came close we murmured *Shema Yisrael*,[27] certain that the angel of death was looking over our shoulders.

We could hear explosions outside. Apparently unwilling to search every house individually, the Germans were simply dynamiting the homes of the Jews wholesale.

Every hour or two we soundlessly lifted the trapdoor to let in some fresh air. Two of the women kept fainting; a third was groaning with cramps. We had to gag them so that they should not cry out and give us away.

We remained like that, crammed in the cellar, until evening. Then, toward nightfall, we heard the tramp of feet on our trapdoor and a voice—it sounded like a young man—shouting down to us:

"Come on out, Jews! Come out! Weisbrojn is dead! Amarant was shot! It's all over! Come out! Nothing'll happen to you!"

Our response was dead silence; we were determined not to move from the spot. But before long we heard the blows of an axe, harsh German commands, and then the trapdoor was yanked off. Hands reached down to pull us up, to the raucous laughter of the Germans above.

I immediately pulled my Polish identity card from my pocket, and walked up to one of the German officers. "Let me go," I told him. "I'm not a Jew. I'm a Pole, I just came to the ghetto to buy things from the Jews, and I got caught in this raid. Here are my

---

27 "Hear, O Israel, the Lord our God is One." Confession of faith recited by observant Jews each day, and also when death is near.

papers, see? If you don't believe me, call up Warsaw and they'll tell you."

The others from the bunker were led to the back of the house. One of the S.S. men stayed with me; he examined my papers in detail and then proceeded to search my pockets with slow thoroughness. With a triumphant grunt he pulled out a Russian compass which I had overlooked in my haste when I had emptied my pockets that morning. Now, this Russian compass was to save my life.

The S.S. man ordered me to take off my boots and struck me a blow on the back with his rifle butt—his way of telling me to do it fast. I did as I was told. Next, he tied my hands behind my back with a rope. Another blow sent me crashing to the floor, face down. I lay there for more than two hours. Every few minutes another German came by, kicked me and looked me over with contempt.

After a while, an S.S. man came along and began to question my guard, who had been standing over me all this time with his loaded gun pointed at my head.

"This one?" my guard replied. "He's a Pole, from Warsaw. They found him here with the Jews, in one of the bunkers. He had a Russian compass in his pocket. The Russians must have told him before they left to show the Jews how to shoot at our men."

"Well, if he was caught with the Jews, he'll get the same treatment as all the Jews around here!" the S.S. officer bellowed.

I came close to fainting, but I never lost consciousness. With every blow I received I groaned in Polish, "O Jesus, dear Jesus," like the Polish Aryan I was supposed to be.

Finally the top man himself, *Sturmbannfuehrer* [28] Oskar Brand, drove up in a military car. Brand, the "hangman of the Warsaw ghetto," had been placed in command of the Gestapo in Stanislawów. He gave me a kick with his boot. "We won't shoot this one," he told his henchmen. "We'll lock him up at our headquarters. There he'll sing soon enough and tell us who he is and whom he's working for."

---

[28] Equivalent to the rank of major in the regular army.

I felt weak from sheer relief. Let them question me to their hearts' content—anything, as long as they would not treat me as a Jew. If they ever suspected I was Jewish, that would have been the end for me. As long as they considered me a mere underground spy, there was still some hope.

They ordered me to get up and march. Four Storm Troopers escorted me to the Ukrainian police headquarters. To my right and left, in front and in back, there were other Nazis with guns at the ready, just in case I should attempt to make a getaway.

I was led through the market place. Off to the left, near the church, I saw what remained of the Jews of Rohatyn, waiting for their death sentence to be carried out. Barefooted and clutching their small bundles, they sat beneath the machine guns of the Nazis and looked at each other as they saw how Pawel Kolodziejczyk, the "good Polish Aryan," was being led away under heavy guard. So they got him, too, these unfortunates sighed. I gave them a mute look of farewell. A little while later, they all were taken to a hill near the graveyard, just outside the town, and shot.

The police kept me at headquarters for two days and one night, bound hand and foot, for "interrogation." An old Ukrainian, who had been locked up for theft, took pity on me and gave me a piece of corn bread. I lay on the right side of the prison chamber with the Aryan inmates. On the left side, I saw Jews who had been brought in after the raid on the ghetto. The Nazis took out the Jews, ten at a time, and we never saw them again.

Before long, the chamber was empty. The Jewish inmates had been taken away to be shot, and the Ukrainians had been set free. I was the only prisoner left.

In the middle of the night the commander of the German police entered the chamber, handcuffed me and pushed me out of the building and into a "Green Minna." [29] Guarded by two policemen, I was driven to the Gestapo prison in Stanislawów.

---

[29] German police wagon.

9

The Kingdom of
Oskar Brand

IT WAS ABOUT two-thirty in the morning when the "Green
Minna" arrived at Gestapo headquarters. One of the two policemen
who had sat in the car with me got out, marched up to the gate of the
building and rang the bell. A few moments later an armed guard
appeared, the policeman whispered something into his ear, the
heavy gate swung open, and we drove into a dark courtyard. The
car stopped and I was pushed out. Since it was pitchdark I could
not see my surroundings but I felt certain that the place to which
I had been brought was the Jewish cemetery of the town, and
that I would be shot in short order. I was sure Brand's directive
back in Rohatyn that I should not be shot because I would
eventually break down and "sing" had been a trick. All I could
think about was whether the bullets would hit me from the front
or from the back. However, it seemed they were not ready to kill
me, after all. The two policemen led me up some steps and into
a dimly-lit, not very large chamber. There, sprawled out on a
couch, lay a Gestapo man, almost naked. The policemen stalked
from the room and left me to his mercies. On the table beside
the couch I could see a gun.

The Gestapo man unlocked my handcuffs and set to work. His
face looked drowsy and his eyes were red-rimmed; obviously, we
had interrupted his sleep and he wasn't eager to waste too much
time on me. He questioned me in detail, carefully noting down

everything I told him—the life story of Pawel Kolodziejczyk, Polish Aryan:

"My father's name was Jan Kolodziejczyk. He died when I was twelve years old. My mother's name is Barbara. Her maiden name was Brochwicz; she's living in Warsaw at 5 Furmanska Street. I am a Roman Catholic. I've had some higher education. Prewar occupation: schoolteacher."

After taking down my recital, the Gestapo man called in a subordinate, who wore no insignia of rank and who ordered me to follow him. The fact that my "registration" had been accomplished so quickly without my getting beaten up worried me; it didn't seem normal for an interview with the Gestapo to proceed so smoothly. My escort never addressed a word to me. We passed a wall with a mound of sand at its foot. "This is where they'll finish me off," I thought. But the man did not tell me to stop. We walked on until we got to a flat, one-floor building. He produced a large key and unlocked the massive door. Inside, the corridor was dimly lit by small, green electric bulbs. He led me down a flight of steps into a cellar, which was divided into several chambers. We stopped at a door marked "10" which he unlocked. He gave me a shove and I fell sprawling to the ground. As I fell, I dragged some unseen object with me, and the next moment I was drenched with icy water. My first thought in the pitch darkness was that I had been pushed into a chamber filled with water and that I would be left there to drown. I had heard stories about the Gestapo disposing of their victims in that fashion. But I felt no more water, and the next morning I was to find out that the object over which I had tripped in the darkness had been a bucket full of dirty water in which the other prisoners had washed themselves.

I did not try to get up but quickly crawled across the floor until I was stopped by something big and soft. I was terrified, but when I reached out to touch the object, I understood. It was another prisoner.

"If you won't get off me this minute," the man yelled, "I'll knock your block off, you son of a bitch!"

"I'm freezing," I pleaded. "Let me have a piece of your blanket."

The whole cell exploded in raucous laughter. Curses and obscenities rained on me. Obviously, I had given the other prisoners
a good scare.

"It's not my fault the Prussaks shoved me in here," I said, in a
feeble effort to defend myself.

"Hey, Wacek, give him a rag so he'll shut up and go to sleep!"

"A new one, eh? Where did they get you?"

"In Rohatyn. I got caught in a raid on the ghetto," I said. "I'd
just bought a little diamond from a Jew woman there when the
whole ruckus started and they got me, too."

"Ha, ha, ha! You must have slept with one of those pretty Jew
women. They're ready nowadays to sell themselves for a piece of
bread. It's a shame. Somebody ought to do something for them.
But if you're a good-for-nothing, you'll stay here a long while—
a long, long while!"

"Enough talk," came another voice out of the darkness. "We
have to sleep. We can wait till tomorrow to get acquainted."

Somebody threw me a blanket and I covered myself, but I could
not sleep. I was busy figuring out how to act with my Polish cellmates so that I would not give myself away.

By the time the sky turned from black to blue, I was on my
feet. One by one, my cellmates woke up. I counted 34 of them;
I was Number 35, in a room which normally could not have held
more than ten, or twelve at the most. In one corner near the door
was the toilet. We were lucky, because we had a water closet. The
smell in our room was nothing compared to the stench in the
other cells which had only large, open pots, taken out only once
a day to be emptied into the prison latrine. Our toilet had an additional advantage: if you pulled the chain twice, the water over-
flowed so that you could put a bowl next to the toilet and get
some clean, cold water with which to wash yourself.

I got acquainted with my cellmates, one by one. They crowded
about me curiously and I had to tell them the whole story of my
arrest, with much time out for questions from the floor. I talked
slowly, careful with every word I said, because I knew the Gestapo trick of planting informers into prison cells to find out whatever details the Germans wanted to know.

113

The 34 Poles in Cell No. 10 represented a variety of human types. Most of them had been taken off trains and arrested because their papers had not been in order. As a rule, the Gestapo authorities would take about three weeks to investigate such cases. They would write to the mayor of the town from which the prisoner said he had come, and if the mayor replied that the man was known there and that he was a good and loyal citizen, he would be released the next morning. Others in our cell had a harder time. There was Travnitzky, who had been a businessman in Posen before the war. After the occupation, he had worked for the Germans in Stanislawów, but had been arrested because some Ukrainian had reported him to the Gestapo as being of Jewish descent. The fact that the accusation had been a pure figment of the Ukrainian's imagination made no difference. Another prisoner, Buczynski, told me he had been dragged from a train and arrested en route from Cracow, his home town, to visit a relative in Horodenka; he had been in prison five months now, but had not yet been called for interrogation. Biernacki, who hailed from Warsaw, also did not know why he had been brought to the prison. Two of my cellmates were railroad officials who had been accused of sabotage. Three weeks after their arrest, they still were covered with bruises. Zdziszek, who was only 17, had escaped from a forced-labor camp in Germany, returned to Poland and had managed to hide out for some time at the home of his parents and with various neighbors, until one of the neighbors, who had had a running feud with his parents, reported his whereabouts to the Gestapo. There also were some peasants in our cell, poor devils who had been charged with attempting to "rob" the German *Reich* because they had refused to turn over their entire wheat crop to the German "agricultural office" in their region.

Our cell had two small windows which admitted a little daylight, but not much, because most of the light was blocked by a huge pile of coal directly in front of the windows. The coal was used for fuel in the prison kitchen which was directly above us, on the street floor. The kitchen was presided over by two Ukrainians, also inmates of the prison. The story went that the two had been released, but had chosen of their own free will to stay in

114

prison permanently because of the good food they got in the course of their work. They prepared choice meals and fancy pastries for the prison staff, and every evening they sent huge baskets of food home to their wives in town. The baskets would be delivered by a Gestapo man who would come to their kitchen and be plied with delicacies in return for his services. The two cooks ran their kitchen on a lavish scale, but at the expense of the inmates. The daily menu of the prisoners consisted of black coffee and two pieces of black bread for breakfast, a bowlful of hot water with three or four cabbage leaves floating on top for lunch, and some more bitter black coffee for supper. This prison fare got us into such a weakened state that we could hardly stand on our legs. After drinking all this liquid we spent most of the night running to the toilet. One night I counted 22 "runs" as my personal record. So there was little chance for sleep at night, and just as little during the day, because sleeping in the daytime was considered a punishable offense. The guard posted outside near our window kept us under constant surveillance to make sure that no one tried to steal a nap. We would drag ourselves around our cell all day long as though we were drugged, exhausted from lack of sleep. If a man could not manage to keep his eyes open and lay down in a corner to catch forty winks, the armed guard would poke his gun through the window grating and order us to awaken the offender. A moment later the door of our cell would be thrown open, the guard would stride in and drag the offender out into the corridor. About half an hour later, the unfortunate would be flung back into the cell, with orders to have him lie still on his plank bed for a whole week, with one of us assigned to force-feed him. This order was hardly necessary, for as a rule the victim had been beaten up so savagely that he had neither the will nor the strength to move.

We had to get up at five o'clock each morning. The guard, a Slovak *Volksdeutscher,* made the rounds of the cells with a list of names in his hand for roll call. The "cell elder," an inmate appointed by the guard, had to make the report on behalf of his cellmates.

"Reporting Cell Number 10 for inspection, sir. Thirty-four prisoners, plus one additional newcomer, totalling thirty-five prisoners in all. All in good order, sir; nobody sick."

The tall guard slithered his way through the 35 prisoners, sniffing like a bloodhound for the smell of tobacco: inmates were not supposed to have cigarettes in their possession. At the same time he looked each prisoner up and down, inspecting shirts, pants and shoes. Following this personal inspection, he would turn his attention to the plank bed, noting whether the blankets were folded on the floor precisely according to regulations. Then he stretched himself full length on the ground, rubbing his back across the floor several times this way and that. The floor had to be shining clean; if he found any dirt or dust clinging to his spotless Nazi uniform when he got up, he put everyone through "punitive gymnastics": "Get up!" "Flat on the ground!" "Get up!" and so on for a full 30 minutes. These exercises were always accompanied by blows from his leather whip. Since "roll call" was held twice each day, our bodies were black and blue and our bones and muscles aching most of the time.

The morning roll call was followed by breakfast, which took only a few minutes. After breakfast came our daily "walk." That year the month of June happened to be unusually hot and the air inside our cell was steamy like in a sealed pressure cooker. We went about half naked, sweating like miners slaving in underground pits. Yet our daily "walk" around the cell was indispensable; since we sat or lay on the ground in cramped positions so much of the time, there was real danger that we might lose the use of our muscles. Because our cell was much too small for 35 prisoners to take their daily "walk" all at one time, we worked out an ingenious arrangement. We performed our "constitutional" in groups of six, three on the left side of the cell and three on the right. When the first group had completed its half-hour, the next six followed, and so forth, until all of us had had our daily exercise.

Meanwhile, those who had completed their walk sat in a semicircle near the window and performed the daily delousing ritual on their clothes and bodies. We had not bathed in weeks and only had a little cold water with which to wash ourselves and our shirts. Our pants, jackets and blankets served as bedclothes on the bare

116

floor at night, with the result that they made a fine breeding ground for lice. And so, in addition to the black and blue marks from countless blows of the Gestapo whips, our bodies were covered with bloody sores from constant scratching. Accordingly, we gladly followed the strict orders of our "cell elder," taking one full hour each day to pick the lice from our shirts and crush them between the nails of our two thumbs. New prisoners at first viewed this spectacle with disgust, but when the lice began to attack them also, they quickly mastered the method and at inspection time proudly displayed their clothing, clear and free of the little blood-sucking creatures.

As a rule, the delousing ritual took until lunchtime. We lined up in single file, waiting until the soup barrel was trundled over to us from Cell No. 9. by the two Ukrainian cooks, accompanied by a Gestapo man. Once again, the "cell elder" had to report the number of inmates in our cell while we stood silently at attention, soup bowls in hand. One flick of the ladle and we had our meal. The heat was stifling, and the sweat was pouring off our bodies, but we hungrily downed the boiling hot liquid.

After our meal we wanted a little smoke. Whenever a new inmate arrived, we "old-timers" would turn his pockets inside out, in the hope of finding at least a few grains of tobacco or a particle of cigarette dust there. If we were lucky enough to discover what we were looking for, we would gather up our "find" into a tiny piece of newspaper, and roll it into one small "cigarette" which then had to do for the entire cell. However, there were days on end when no newcomers arrived. Most of the time, therefore, we had to make do with tobacco dust scraped from a broom or an old cigarette stub. We would smoke the stuff avidly, never caring what it might do to our lungs.

Getting a light was also no easy task. Cigarettes were forbidden in the Gestapo prison, but the prohibition against owning matches was even stricter. Before a new inmate was brought down to the cellar, he was thoroughly searched for these contraband articles. But the desire for a smoke was all-powerful, especially once we had managed to roll a few bits of tobacco dust into a scrap of newspaper and all that was missing was a light. We would hunt

117

up two small sticks of wood and rub them together patiently. Many times we had to work for more than a quarter of an hour before we got a fire. We then enjoyed our smoke thoroughly, in the toilet, to avoid being seen by the guard outside.

I was greatly upset about the speed with which my beard was growing. My beard gave my face an unmistakably Jewish look, and, imprisoned as I was as a Pole among Poles, this could have been my undoing. My deliverance came from an unexpected source: one of my fellow inmates, Antoni Jemialkowski, former publisher of an anti-Semitic weekly in Katowice, who hated both Germans and Jews, had managed to smuggle a razor blade into our cell. The problem was that we had no razor into which to fit the blade. But this problem, too, was solved by one of the inmates, a railroad employee, who was an expert at making all sorts of tools. He cut a sliver of wood from the plank bed, split it lengthwise, fitted the blade into the slit, tied the pieces of wood together above and below the blade with a little thread, and the razor was ready for use. Since the blade was not too sharp, every shave left our faces raw and bleeding, but I figured it was safer for me to have a face covered with nicks and cuts than one framed in a distinctly Jewish-looking beard. With my beard gone, I had much more courage to look my cellmates in the eye without fear of being discovered.

Afternoons as a rule were spent in telling our life stories, trying to tell from a deck of cards we had somehow managed to "organize" [30] who would be the first to be called for interrogation, and exchanging spicy jokes to cheer us up a little. After our usual supper of black coffee, we made up our "beds." Each of us had a couple of scraps of blanket or the remains of a coat which we used as mattresses or covers. A few of the inmates found space on the shelves and benches, but most of us had to sleep on the floor. Since every inch of floor space was thus occupied, the darkness would be rent by shouts and groans whenever anyone had to go to the toilet because he would step on someone else's feet, head

---

[30] In prison camp language, to "organize" meant to take bits of food, pieces of clothing or other items wherever one could find them.

or stomach. Before going to sleep each of the men got down on his knees and said his prayers to Jesus. I also knelt in order not to be different, but the prayer I whispered to myself was the Hebrew *Shema Yisrael.*

After prayers, we would lie awake for some time, reciting patriotic poems or softly singing popular Polish marching songs about war, victory and freedom. Outside there was dead silence. The guard who had been posted outside our window all day long had gone off duty. All the prison gates had been locked and double-bolted for the night.

Such was a typical day in the kingdom of *Sturmbannfuehrer* Oskar Brand.

* * *

A few hundred yards away from our prison was a well-kept garden which was known as the "Gestapo Garden" because its fruit and vegetables were intended for the tables of Hitler's Storm Troopers. A sign at the entrance of the garden read: "Property of the S.S." Above the sign, swaying gently in the breeze, was a death's head. The garden was supervised by an *Untersturmfuehrer* [31] who spoke to us only in Polish. He was from Nadworne, in Galicia; as soon as the Germans had come there, he had declared himself a "German by nationality" and offered his services to the *Sicherheitsdienst.* [31] The Poles and Ukrainians who were working in the garden had been handpicked by the Nazi employment service for their loyalty to the Third Reich and were given preferential treatment.

When the fruit and vegetables were ripe, we, the prison inmates, were also assigned to work in the garden. But the privilege of working was bestowed only on those prisoners who had already spent a minimum of ten days in their cell and endured their share of cuffs and blows. All of us prisoners were eager to get assigned to the garden detail. Although a guard with gun at the ready stood beside each prisoner as he worked, the fresh air, an overripe apple

---

[31] Equivalent to the rank of second lieutenant in the regular army. Sichercheitsdienst—"Security Service." Nazi party intelligence service.

or turnip or a cigarette stub left lying unnoticed on the ground held untold charms for us. Those brief hours of "freedom," away from the stifling confines of our cell, made imprisonment easier to endure.

Every morning after breakfast the prison guard would come into our cell to select men for the day's work. Other guards were already waiting in the corridor with guns at the ready to escort us to our assigned place. The first day, I, along with two other Poles, was ordered to sweep the sidewalk and to weed the lawn in front of the Gestapo building. Two armed Gestapo men were stationed on the sidewalk to watch us and to make sure that we were not stealing glances at passers-by. By the end of the day our backs were breaking, but we liked the work because the grass always yielded cigarette stubs which Gestapo employes had thrown out the windows. We would wait until the two guards posted over us turned aside for a few seconds; then, quick as a wink, we would tuck our newly-discovered treasures into our shirts. All day long we looked forward to the evening when, back in our cells, we would be able to inhale a bit of the precious nicotine to calm our nerves a little. After the door of our cell had been locked behind us, all our "unemployed" cellmates would surround the three of us, eager to find out what we had been able to get that day. We took off our shirts, releasing a shower of cigarette stubs. Then one of the men, a specialist in the art of cigarette-rolling, rushed over, gathered up the stubs and tore them to free the tobacco. Sometimes there would be enough tobacco for him to roll into three full-size cigarettes. One such cigarette would have to do for twelve inmates. We sat around, hungrily watching as one after the other took a deep puff until, finally, our turn would come and we would get a drag from the communal cigarette, which by then had become stale and soggy. As soon as all the twelve inmates sharing one cigarette had had their draw, the process would be repeated, but we didn't inhale quite as deeply the second time around.

After I had worked at the front of the building every day for a week, I was transferred to the "Gestapo Garden." There, I was given a different assignment each day. I was glad whenever they sent me to the rabbit hutch. There I was locked in with the little creatures and ordered to clean the cages. I had to scrub the cement floor and feed the animals three times a day. I was given two baskets full of stale bread and a bucket of leftover soup to divide among the 60 rabbits, with the stern warning not to dare take so much as a single crumb of bread or a sip of the soup for myself. Since I was hungry all the time, I had difficulty controlling myself, but the Gestapo man threatened to shoot me on the spot if I would dare to rob his pets of any of their food. One day I gathered up my courage and took some of the bread crusts and potato scraps which the rabbits had left in the corners of their cages, and I enjoyed these morsels as though they had been the daintiest cakes. I prayed that luck should be with me and that I would be assigned to the rabbits again the next day. Unfortunately, just then the guard happened to come in and saw my jaws working. He took his rifle from his shoulder and hit me on the head with the rifle butt several times. Afterwards, he reported me to the gardener, who promptly assigned me to fourteen days' work at paving a path in the garden. This job involved lifting and carrying huge, sharp rocks with my bare hands.

The fourteen days seemed like an eternity. The sun burned down on our backs, and in this place we had no chance to "organize" a piece of bread or a cigarette stub. The guards, mostly Poles and Slovaks, drove and beat us mercilessly. Occasionally, we were called out to work in the courtyard of the prison, where we had to pull an enormous roller which smoothed the asphalt inside the courtyard, next to the section where the "criminals" were imprisoned. As distinguished from the members of our group, who were classed as "political prisoners," the "criminals" were privileged characters; they were permitted to receive food packages from their families. As we toiled in the courtyard, we enviously looked up at the windows of the "criminal" building where we could see jars of sparkling preserves, along with loaves of white bread and slabs of bacon drying in the sun.

The guards who kept watch over us, the "political prisoners," told us lurid tales of the scenes that had taken place in that courtyard the year before. All through that autumn, they said, hundreds of Jews had been crammed into this small space, forced to remain there all day and all night, sleeping out in the open even in the bitter cold and the driving rain. Once a day they would receive a little watery soup. Since there were no toilet facilities in the court-yard, the prisoners had had to relieve themselves on the ground, so that when night came, they had slept in their own filth.

"And you know," one guard, a *Polish-Volksdeutsche,* told us, some of those Jew women in that batch were really good-looking, and the commanding officer let us take home any one of them we wanted—to clean our rooms, you know. So we had a good time with them. And if any of them objected—well, we finished them off right then and there. Ha—ha—ha!"

"This went on all through the autumn months," he continued. "When winter came, we had a tough time with them. For five whole days we were busy carting these babes in sealed trucks to the Jewish cemetery. There we shot them and threw the bodies into big holes which we'd made their men dig for them before. You know—when we took them out to be shot they were singing! I don't get it..."

The guard who told us this story could have been no more than nineteen years old. He went on talking for two hours, relishing each grisly detail. It took all my will power not to show my horror. From that time on I trembled at the very sight of the courtyard. My fellow inmates working in the courtyard often managed to gather up bits of bread and butter which the "criminals" threw down to them from their windows, but I used every dodge possible to avoid having to work there; the ghosts of the Jews who had been tortured in that courtyard left me no peace.

Early one morning the guard came to our cell and ordered two of us—Buczynski and me—to come out with him. We were sure that our last hour was at hand. Other prisoners before us had been taken away in the same manner and we had never seen them again.

The man led us out into the garden, all the way to the other end, and stopped at a pretty little house.

"You are going to be in a wood-chopping detail here," he told us. "Do you know who lives in that house? Well, the Chief himself. So, better watch out and don't let me catch you at any funny business of I'll have to shoot you on the spot!"

He went away and, much to our surprise, he left us without a guard. We felt as if a ton of rocks had been lifted from our chests and we were able to breathe again.

The pretty little house was the home of *Sturmbannfuehrer* Oskar Brand, the Gestapo commander in Stanisławów. It was part of a group of dwellings occupied by Gestapo personnel who were operating in Stanisławów and neighboring areas.

Inside the villa, Brand's housekeeper took charge. She led us down into the basement where a pile of wood had been prepared for us to chop. We set to work with gusto; somehow, we felt safer here than anywhere else on the Gestapo grounds. No one would dare come to this place without permission; so, no beatings for us, at least not while we worked here, in the basement of Gestapo chief Oskar Brand. The housekeeper turned out to be a Polish woman whose son had been killed by the Germans in the invasion. She came down to us twice each day with three slices of bread spread with margarine, and a bowl of rich, thick soup. Toward evening she would bring us a bag full of cigarette stubs left by her employer and also a bucket of soup to take back to our cellmates. When our guard came to the house to escort us back to the prison, she asked him to let us take the bucket with us. Back in our cell, our friends fell on us with kisses when they saw the "gifts" we had brought them from the home of *Sturmbannfuehrer* Brand.

One day the housekeeper came down to us in the basement with a worried look on her face. It seemed that Brand's young son, Johann, was crying his eyes out; he had to have a helmet. He and his playmates, the sons of other Gestapo men living on the same street, were always playing games in which they were a troop of Gestapo men, carrying out "actions" against the Jews. Little Johann had been chosen commander of the unit. Now Johann already owned a wooden sword, but he still lacked a helmet and a gun, the kind his father took along with him whenever he went out to kill some Jews. And so he had been pestering his father's house-keeper until the poor woman was at her wits' end and decided to ask us, the prisoners, whether we could make a cardboard helmet and a wooden gun for little Johann.

Of course, Buczynski and I jumped at the chance. The housekeeper went upstairs and returned with some wood and cardboard, a large pair of scissors, a heavy needle and thread, and a sharp knife. Every few minutes little Johann himself would appear at the top of the stairs and toss us a piece of bread, a chunk of margarine or a few cigarettes. He never spoke a word to us; after all, he knew that we were criminals and enemies of the German Fatherland and that no decent person would talk to our kind. Two days later, we had the gun at the helmet ready. Johann was beside himself with joy. Before long the father of Johann's friends came to Johann's mother and asked her to have the two "Polish swines" make guns and helmets for their sons also. And so Oskar Brand's housekeeper brought us the glad tidings that we had perimission to go on making toys. The basement of Gestapo chief Oskar Brand had been converted temporarily into a toy workshop, and Johann's friends, whose fathers worked at killing Jews, would steal down to us one by one to bring us bread and cigarette stubs so that we would be inspired to make them the best and helmets ever.

Evenings, when we returned to the prison, our cellmates received us with open arms, eager to have us unpack the gifts we had received for our labors in Brand's basement and to divide them equally among the 35 inmates of Cell No. 10.

* * *

After I had worked in Brand's basement for nine full days, I was summoned for interrogation. Nineteen days had passed since I had first arrived at the Gestapo prison. A Gestapo man in civilian clothes called to me through the basement window that I should get myself ready and come with him to the office of the "political chief." He led me out into the street, across the prison courtyard, into the administration building and finally up to the second floor where the office of the "political chief" was located.

I realized full well that my life depended on the interview about to come. Quickly, I reviewed in my mind the answers I had rehearsed during sleepless nights in my prison cell.

As I entered the reception room in the "political section," I was struck a blow on the head and lost consciousness for some moments. The next thing I knew, I was being pulled up roughly from the floor and forced to stand with my face to the wall, with both arms raised to the ceiling. I had to remain in that position until the "political chief" had finished with the "customer" ahead of me. I felt as though my arms were about to drop off. After what seemed hours, I was grabbed from behind by a pair of strong arms and dragged into the adjoining room—the "political chief's" inner sanctum—where the door was padded and covered with leather. In addition to the "political chief," there were four other Gestapo officers in the room. One of them was Willy Mauer; he turned out to be the man who had knocked me to the floor in the antechamber. Formerly an officer in the Polish army, Mauer had switched his allegiance to the Gestapo at the proper time. The second man was Mauer's brother Hans. Both the Mauers were dreaded not only by the Jews in Stanislawów, but also by Poles whose loyalty to the German overlords was suspect. The third officer was named Adamski and, as I could tell from his accent, he was not a *Volksdeutscher* but a full-blooded Pole. Also present in the room was a young Ukrainian, who served as interpreter.

I was led to a chair and told to sit down. The "political chief" offered me a cigarette and held out a lighter to me. As soon as I began to inhale the smoke, Adamski pounced on me, tore the cigarette from between my lips and began to belabor me with a steel-tipped whip. "You Polish swine!" he shouted. "Smoking in the office of the political chief! You stinking son of a bitch!" Later, I learned that Adamski, who had been an inspector in the Polish police before the war, had acquired notoriety in the Gestapo as a hangman of the first water. In the end, Adamski was to be shot and killed in his own home by the Polish underground.

While Adamski was busy with me, the "political chief" sat quietly behind his desk, smiling at me in a good-natured, friendly way. After Adamski thought I had had enough, the "chief" whispered something into the ear of the interpreter, who then told me to give him the story of my life up to the moment of my arrest. I began to recite the life story I had composed for Pawel

125

Kolodziejczyk, pure Polish Aryan. In a sad but controlled tone of voice I told a tale of my youth as a Roman Catholic boy, how I had taught school before the war, and how the war had ruined my life because the Polish-language schools had been progressively eliminated, leaving me without employment and with no other means of support. I told the officers that I had an old, sick mother living in Warsaw (this part, or course, was still true at the time, except for what I did not tell: that she was living in the ghetto). In order to feed the two of us, I continued, I had taken to trading on the black market, although I knew that this was risky business. I said I had found out that trading with the Jews in the ghettoes was very profitable. Since Gentiles were not allowed to enter the Warsaw ghetto unless they had official business there, I had been "operating" in the ghettoes of Galicia, which were not entirely sealed off to non-Jews. There, the Jews had been selling me merchandise which I then sent on to Warsaw or Cracow for resale at a handsome profit. This, I said, was how I had happened to be in the Rohatyn ghetto when the Gestapo had come there to take the Jews off to the labor camps.

I dragged out my story for more than an hour. I had deliberately chosen to describe myself as a black market operator because I knew that the penalty for black marketeering was not so severe as that meted out for underground activities. I did not even dare contemplate what would await me if my captors were to find out that I was not even a Pole, but a Jew, traveling about with forged "Aryan" documents.

When I had completed my recital, the four Gestapo men in the room burst into loud laughter. The "political chief" turned to me and addressed me in German—directly, not through the interpreter, as he had done earlier in the interview. I pretended not to understand him and asked the interpeter to translate for me what the "chief" had said.

Again, there was loud laughter. "Don't give me that! It's not possible that a fellow like you shouldn't understand German. If you won't talk to us in German, you'll be shot at once!" the "political chief" said.

So they suspected me of being a Jew! For the first time, I came close to panicking. I decided to make one desperate gamble for my life.

"If you mean to say you think I'm a Jew," I calmly told the Gestapo men, "I can always let down my pants and let you see for yourselves that I'm not Jewish." Slowly and, I hoped, without showing a sign of the terror I felt, I opened the buckle of my belt, undid the buttons of my fly and let my trousers slide to my ankles. I was unbuttoning my underpants when the "political chief" motioned me to stop; it was not necessary for me to submit further proof. I had won the first stage of my battle with the Gestapo. They no longer suspected that I was a Jew. As long as they treated me as an Aryan, I told myself, nothing really terrible could happen to me.

After it had been decided that I was not a Jew, but "merely" a suspected underground member, the interpreter translated for me into Polish the "chief's" questions about my friends and acquaintances, the people with whom I associated in Warsaw, the underground movement and the "illegal" press. I was questioned about my political views—to what party I had belonged before the war, and what newspapers I had been in the habit of reading prior to the German occupation. Each question was fired at me as from a gun. My brains were reeling; I was given no time to think.

"I—I never belonged to any political party," I stammered. "Only to the Boy Scouts. The only friends I ever had were two fellows. They are now in Germany, working. I never had any other friends. I'm not interested in the illegal parties or in their newspapers because I have enough on my hands worrying about my mother."

I kept talking, telling the Gestapo men stories that I had rehearsed ever since my arrest. They asked me the same questions over and over again in hopes of tripping me up somewhere, but I stood the test. The "political chief" took down everything I said, on quadruplicate forms. Then he slowly rose from his chair and left the room, followed by the Mauers and the Ukrainian interpreter. Only Adamski remained behind with me. After the others had gone, Adamski tried to sweet-talk me into being a little more cooperative.

"As one Pole to another, let me give you a piece of good advice," he said. "Tell them everything you know about those young fools in the underground organization. Just talk, even if you have to make up some of the facts, because if you won't talk, they'll begin to torture you. They're giving you ten minutes. Think it over. Don't try to tell me stories. I'm sure you're working with the underground. But the hell with the Germans out there. Nobody will ever find out about what you said here, and you'll save your skin. It would be a shame for a young Pole like you to have to die. Besides, if they killed you, who'd look after your mother?"

"But I don't know anything," I insisted. "Believe me, if I would know something at all, I'd be glad to tell it to you and put an end to all this questioning."

Adamski left the room. A moment later he returned, bringing the whole Gestapo group back with him. Willy Mauer set to work on me with his whip. Meanwhile, Adamski pulled out from under the table a wooden press of the kind that bookbinders use and placed it in the center of the room. Willy Mauer raised the upper plate of the press a little and ordered me to put my two hands—palms down—on the lower plate. Slowly, he tightened the bolts and screws and the two plates came together. My hands were pressed like two sheets in a mangle. The pain was excruciating. I screamed, then fainted. I was promptly revived by a dash of cold water in my face.

"Will you talk now?"

"I swear by Jesus I don't know anything!" I moaned.

Mauer turned back to the torture press, placed a stool before it, pushed me onto the stool and ordered me to put both my feet between the plates. Again, the agonizing vise. The pain was beyond endurance. I screamed for mercy, even begged Mauer to shoot me. They kept my feet crushed in the press for fifteen minutes. But I told them nothing, and betrayed no one. In the end, the press was opened and I was free. But as I leaned against the wall in utter exhaustion, I felt Mauer's whip on my face and my body, and I slumped to the ground. Only then did the hangmen file out of the room. Again, I had stood my ground and survived unvanquished. I was left alone, unconscious, on the floor of the torture chamber.

I was brought back to life by a kick from Mauer, who grabbed me under the arms and dragged me back to my cell. As he pulled me along, he hummed a popular little German tune:

Everything passes, all things fade away,
Every December is followed by May...

My cellmates threw themselves at me and bombarded me with questions, but I could not utter one word, much less stand on my feet. I burst into tears and sobbed like a little child. My friends carried me to one of the plank beds. For three weeks, Travnitzky, the businessman from Posen who had been arrested as a suspected Jew, fed me like an infant because I was unable to move my hands. At night, I tossed from side to side in pain. But every morning, when I awoke, I murmured a prayer of thanks to God for having allowed me to live another day.

* * *

Early one morning we were awakened by a commotion in the courtyard outside our cell. We could hear the tramp of heavy boots up and down the corridor.

"Probably a transport," one of the two former railroad officials whispered. All week long a rumor had gone through the prison that a new transport of Jewish deportees was expected to arrive at the prison any day, and that we, the Polish prisoners, would probably be sent along with them to one of the death camps. Travnitzky awakened those who were still asleep. One of the men, Zdziszek, noticed that our view from the cell windows had been blocked on the outside with boards and crates. Our cell door creaked open and a guard came in.

"Anyone who looks out of those windows will be shot at once!" he shouted.

A few minutes later we heard voices speaking in German and the tramp, tramp, tramp of many feet. Through the cracks between the boxes and boards piled high outside our windows we saw a crowd of men, women and children.

"*Żydzi!* Jews!"

Zdziszek went to the door and listened for the approach of a guard. After he had made sure that none of the guards was about, we climbed onto the plank bed, one by one, and peered out the windows to see what was happening to the people in the courtyard. Curiosity, driven by fear for our own lives, spurred us on. Would we, the Poles, be made to share the fate of the unfortunate Jews outside?

The Jews had been lined up in four rows around the pile of coal that was kept there for the prison kitchen. We saw one of them, a tall, heavy-set, black-haired man, holding a huge red flag in his hand.[32] Gestapo men were running up and down between the four lines, beating the unfortunates with their whips. At a barked command, the Jews undressed and the men and women stood there together, naked, while Oskar Brand strolled about casually, lashing out to the right and to the left with his whip. One after the other, the Jews ran over to the coal pile, dropping their clothes and their last possessions—money, watches and whatever other small articles had not been taken from them at the time of their arrest. As they ran back to their places, the Gestapo men hurried them along with cuffs, blows and kicks. The faces of the helpless Jews were as white as chalk; all the blood seemed to have drained from them.

In our cell there was dead silence. We sat there as though we ourselves, too, had been condemned to die. Trawnitzky, who had little love for Jews, had tears in his eyes. I felt as if I had turned to stone. These were my own people, my brothers and sisters, about to go to their death. My mother had probably perished in the same way, in the Warsaw ghetto, along with my sister, and the rest of my family. Now, for the first time, I felt truly orphaned.

My thoughts were interrupted by the sound of heartrending sobs

---

32 This was obviously the Gestapo way of "demonstrating" that all Jews were Communists.

outside. From the window, I could see Brand and, facing him, pressed against the wall, one of the prisoners, a Jew of fine, cultured appearance, with a weeping little boy beside him.

"Herr Chef," we heard the man say to Brand in German, "let me go. I've served the Fatherland for so many years. In '14 I was a medical officer in the German army. I took good care of the soldiers; I saved the lives of thousands of them. I was always a peaceful citizen. I never mixed in politics but I was proud of my German Fatherland. This boy is my son. Back home in Kassel my boy had many friends—fine, true German boys. He played with them, ate with them, went on overnight hikes with them. Please don't kill us, sir. After all, you, too, have a son."

Brand answered with a whack of his whip, then turned his attention to another naked victim nearby. At last, the former army doctor's composure broke. "Down with Hitler!" he screamed. "Death to Nazism! Long live the Jewish people!" With that, he slumped to the ground. By the time Brand got back to him, he was dead. Perhaps he had taken poison. Cursing furiously, Brand kicked the corpse out of his way. We never learned what became of the dead man's son.

Several hours later, we heard the whine of truck motors. We could not see the trucks because they apparently stopped at the other side of our building, near the windows of the cells occupied by the Ukrainians and the female prisoners. When we looked out again some time later, we saw the Jews being marched away. Soon, we heard shots from somewhere in the distance—one shot after the other. The next morning, the Ukrainians in our labor detail told us what had happened. The Jews had been loaded onto the trucks, row upon row, first men, then women, then men again, thirty-six at a time, like so many living corpses, and driven to the Jewish cemetery which was not too far from the prison. There, they were shot to death. We figured out that at least 300 Jews must have been killed on that one day. Later, an old Pole who had been arrested that same day for having hidden a Jewish family in his home told us that this particular transport was the last that was left of Stanislawów's Jews. They had been rounded up at the railroad station, where they had been doing slave labor for the German army.

That morning, breakfast came two hours late. Afterwards, we were marched out into the prison courtyard and ordered to sort out the clothes which the Jews had left on the coal pile. As a reward for our trouble, each of us was given one pair of underpants from the loot. I accepted the "gift," fearful that if I did not, I might make myself suspect. I put on the shirt; as I did so, I felt as if my own body had become covered with the blood of the Jews of Stanislawów.

* * *

The number of prisoners in in our cell was growing smaller. Eight of the men who had been arrested because of trouble with their documents were released. But not long afterward, in the middle of the night, some new prisoners were shoved into our cell—three Poles, from Bursztyn. I immediately recognized one of them: he was Julian Kostecki, the town's postmaster, a quiet, honest man and ardent Polish patriot. He told me that his wife had been arrested along with him and had been put into the women's section of the prison. I had worked with Mrs. Kostecki for about a year while I taught at the Polish school in Ludwikowka, near Bursztyn. I often visited her when we had to work out class schedules. I would have long talks with her husband about politics and the chances of Poland's regaining her independence. We had also talked about Jewish personalities and Zionism, because he knew that I was Jewish. But when we came face to face in the Gestapo prison, he did not show a sign of recognition. I introduced myself to him as Pawel Kolodziejczyk, a Pole, from Warsaw. He made no comment. He and I stayed together most of the time, and we talked about many things, but he never said a word about the days when I had lived in Bursztyn under my proper Jewish name, Pinkhas Lazarovich Trepman. Now, in the Gestapo prison of Stanislawów, my life was in Kostecki's hands. One word from him about my true identity and I would have been finished. But Kostecki was still the fine, decent man he had been when I had first met him in Bursztyn, and he remained so until he died of typhus, in the death camp of Maidanek.

One day in August, 1943, after I had been in the Gestapo prison three months, we—75 men and women—were herded into big German trucks and driven out of Stanislawów, in the direction of Lwów. All along the highway, the countryside was covered with green and drenched in the dazzling sunshine of late summer. The people we passed looked at us in mute fear; the guns of the Gestapo cut us off from the free world.

That evening, we arrived at Lwów and were taken to Loncki Prison.

A few days later, I arrived in Maidanek.

PART THREE

10

The Sun Smiled Down on Maidanek

There never has been,
Nor will there ever be,
Anywhere on earth,
A sun like that which shines
Upon our Maidanek...

THUS WENT THE refrain of a song composed by an unknown Polish poet behind the barbed-wire fences of Maidanek. The words of the song were simple: they were full of yearning for nature, for the outdoors and for the sunshine with their unspoken message of freedom. No wonder that this song became the unofficial anthem of the camp inmates. We sang it everywhere we went, all day long: at work, at mealtime, before going to sleep, and even while we were kicked and beaten by our jailers. At night, as we lay on our bunks, our stomachs hollow, our spirits despairing, we would hum the "Maidanek Song" and see visions of fields and forests, towns and villages, visions of peace and contentment. And for a little while the heavy burden pressing on our hearts dissolved into healing tears of hope and yearning.

Many times I felt that the sun which shone down so brightly from the azure skies above Maidanek must be just as cruel as the Nazi hangmen who basked in its rays, for how else could it go on smiling when there was so much sorrow and weeping below?

But every time, on the heels of those rebellious thoughts, would come our song, and as we sang, we felt the powerful rays of sunshine warming our weary bones and reviving our faltering spirits.

This is the time to recall what happened on September 3, 1943, a golden autumn morning, beneath that selfsame sun as it smiled upon the valley near the village of Dziesiąta, not far from the city of Lublin, the valley which has entered history as Maidanek, the burial ground of tens of thousands from many lands and nations. On that September day, all the Jews in Maidanek, Lipowa [33] and Camp Piasky were done to death—except one: Pinkhas Lazarovitch Trepman, alias Pawel Kolodziejczyk. Perhaps Providence intended that I, with my false "Aryan" identity and non-Jewish appearance, should be spared from that slaughter so that I alone, having witnessed it, should live to record this one event which otherwise might have been omitted from mankind's testimony against Adolf Hitler.

Two weeks before, Maidanek's commanding officer, *Sturmbannfuehrer* Weiss, had gone on furlough, leaving behind as his substitute the diabolical Anton Tuman. No sooner had Weiss gone, leaving Tuman in sole charge, than all five sections of the huge camp were declared quarantined. Maidanek was divided into five distinct sections or "fields," which were separated by barbed-wire fences charged with electricity. Camp One was for female inmates; it also had several barracks set aside for children. Camp Two was reserved exclusively for Russian prisoners of war. Camps Three and Four held the many thousands of inmates who made up the pool of slave laborers; it was from these two camps that the daily labor details were drawn. In Camp Five, which was directly adjacent to the crematorium, were the courtyard, the camp clinic and infirmary, and, on the right-hand side, the walled-in quadrangle where the executions took place.

The reason for the quarantine was that a typhus epidemic had broken out at Maidanek. Since the courtyard in Camp Five was

---

[33] The Jews of Lipowa were the last remnant of the Lublin ghetto.

already crowded with sick inmates, camp headquarters ordered four barracks in Camp Three to be sectioned off with barbed wire and assigned to serve as a special "typhus area."

The day the quarantine was declared, all five camps were sealed off and no inmates were permitted to go out on daily labor details. Specially appointed "sanitation details" went about the camp, boarding up all the barracks and sealing all cracks in the barrack walls with long strips of paper, which kept out the fresh air. After all the barracks had been sealed off in this manner, the "medicos" sprayed a special chemical through minute openings in each barrack to kill the lice and bedbugs that infested the wooden bunks and the straw mattresses. During that time we had to spend the night outdoors, sleeping under the open sky. After three days of "disinfection" the barracks were opened again and the clean-up details were given brooms to sweep out the piles of dead vermin that had accumulated inside.

During the quarantine period, we suffered even more from hunger than before. Under "normal" conditions, we had two fairly reliable sources of food. The labor details that were sent to work in the city or in other places outside the camp almost always managed to bring back with them some bread or a few potatoes. The punishment for anyone caught smuggling food into the camp was 75 lashes on the bare skin, and sometimes even death, but the pangs of hunger had a way of overcoming fear. Also the plumbers, electricians, drivers and bricklayers from the outside who were employed on construction projects in the camp would bring in foodstuffs which they sold to the inmates for gold, jewelry, or huge sums of money. But when the quarantine was declared, both these sources were cut off, increasing the sufferings of the inmates whom starvation had already turned into shivering bags of bones.

Every day, from six o'clock in the morning until nightfall, the inmates in their thousands stood in military formations according to their barracks, hunting for lice in their underwear. Every two hours or so an S.S. delousing detail fell upon the inmates with blows and kicks, demanding to see how many lice they had found. Whoever had no lice of his own to show would borrow a few from the inmate beside him in order to be able prove that he,

139

or she, had been obeying orders. Twice each day we had to take showers. In the meantime, our clothes were taken away and disinfected in the same chambers where dozens of Jewish transports had been gassed. Oddly, after each "disinfection" there seemed to be more lice on our clothes than before.

All through this quarantine period, Maidanek seemed dead. Because no workers from the outside, not even sewage employees, were permitted in the camp during that time, we had no water. The camp post office was closed; therefore the food packages that arrived for Polish, Czech and French inmates remained outside the camp, unclaimed. Palates became bone-dry; legs, too weak to support even emaciated bodies. Thefts of bread reached epidemic proportions among the inmates, and fistfights became commonplace even among the closest friends.

We were haunted by fears and phobias. We took to observing the moods and movements of every Nazi officer in sight, straining to read in each face what the next day might hold in store for us. Our efforts were fruitless; the expressions of the S.S. men were inscrutable. But we noticed that the Nazis laughed and joked a great deal among themselves and appeared to be having a particularly good time together.

Then the report spread like wildfire over the camp grapevine that the quarantine would be lifted on September 3. The news was rapidly passed from inmate to inmate, and everyone eagerly awaited the official announcement that "Operation Hygiene" had come to an end. The report proved to be true, but little did we know what else Anton Tuman, the deputy commander of Maidanek, had planned for that day.

The day began like any other, but somehow the mood was different. Roll call had been completed, but the Camp Elder [34] had not yet given the usual order for the labor details to line up.

Why this deviation from the regular camp routine? All sorts of conjectures were whispered up and down the countless rows

---

[34] The inmate in charge of all the camp quarters. This position was held by a hardened criminal who had been in concentration camps for a number of years.

140

of inmates standing at attention. Suddenly we became aware that we were surrounded by a cordon of S.S. men, their loaded rifles pointed at the inmates, ready to shoot. This was odd. Ordinarily, the S.S. men did not follow that practice. On "normal" days they promptly withdrew after roll call. Obviously, something out of the ordinary was about to happen.

And then the charged silence was broken by the Camp Elder's sharp command: "All Jews report at once to the camp office!"

What followed can only be described as chaos. The massed rows of inmates arranged according to barracks split into two, three and four separate parts. Jews poured out of the kitchens and infirmaries; typhus patients, half dead, were carried on stretchers and loaded onto wagons. As loudspeakers blared forth the strains of a popular German song: "Rosamunde, Give Me a Kiss and Your Heart," the wagons moved off in the direction of Camp Five. Some of the Jews panicked and fled into their barraks, only to be dragged out again, bruised and bleeding, by the pursuing S.S. men. Non-Jewish inmates had been ordered to the rear section of the camp. All the Jewish inmates had crowded into the camp's front section next to the gates and the offices.

That day I was on duty at the camp post office, along with eight Poles and three Jews. The Jews in our group were taken away immediately. It did not occur to the murderers to take me, for the letter "P" on my prison uniform identified me as a Pole. The rooms housing the post office were off to one side, away from the barracks. They thus offered a good vantage point from which I was able to see what was happening to my fellow Jews.

Deathly pale, like living corpses, the Jews stood massed in front of the camp office. Every few moments they were joined by other Jews who had been pulled out from their stations in the office, in the "political division" and in the camp commander's suite. There were to be no "exceptions," no "privileged characters;" all these people, no matter what their special skills or work classification, were Jews and therefore had been marked for death.

On the other side of our barbed wire fence, in the far part of our camp, was Maidanek's main road. Lined up in a double row along the full length of that road were members of the "death's-head squad" who comprised the "Jew extermination detail." As these men and their dogs stood at attention, waiting for the action to begin, Jewish women appeared on the thoroughfare, marching toward Camp Five and the ovens.

I felt as if my head were about to fall from my shoulders; my heart stood still as I watched these women—my sisters from Warsaw, Lódz, Vilno, Paris, Vienna, Budapest and Bratislava—march up the road, to their death, separated from me only by a quirk of fate. They walked quietly, their heads lowered, accompanied by obscenities, guffaws and blows from their torturers. The loudspeakers contined to belt out their merry song and the sun shone more brightly than ever as the procession moved on.

Shortly thereafter, the men began to march: young men, strong men, stooped and broken men; boys, youths and grandfathers; distinguished personages who had managed to keep their dignity even in Maidanek, and tragic figures who had been eating filth and garbage in their struggle to survive. And all the while, the loudspeakers kept on playing "Rosamunde."

The Poles with me stood paralyzed, afraid to move so much as an eyelid. Henryk Kozlowski, an underworld character from Lwów, was crying bitterly. "The rotten sons of bitches! They'll pay for this!" he hissed to the man beside him. The socialist Stanislaw Zelent, an educated, cultured man, ground his teeth and muttered: "We'll avenge them!"

In the afternoon the time came for the Jews from our own camp to leave. Quietly and with dignity, they passed through the wide-open gate. They walked proudly, their heads high; some of them even managed to smile and to raise an arm in farewell to their non-Jewish fellow inmates. Thus they moved out of our sight, forever.

The death march and mass slaughter of Jews on September 3, 1943 was the largest single operation of its kind at Maidanek. It began at seven o'clock in the morning and continued without pause until six o'clock that evening. All that day we saw Jews march away to a place from which there was no return. It was a breathtakingly beautiful day on God's earth but we did not see the beauty. We only saw that the sun was beaming merrily from a large patch of blue sky while thousands of Jews below were being taken to their death as the German loudspeakers played "Rosamunde, Give Me a Kiss. . ."

The next morning the chimney of the crematorium began to belch smoke. It smoked for a long time, scattering the ashes of 22,000 Jewish men, women and children across the face of the smiling golden sun and the cloudless blue sky so that both sun and sky turned black.

11
Bubi,
the Boy Executioner

How CAN ONE TELL the story of a child of one's own people, a child whose name must remain a curse forever on the lips of all who ever heard of him? This is the incredible tale of Bubi, the Jewish boy who became a beast among beasts. Bubi, whose coalblack, gypsy-like curls hung above his brilliant black eyes as he calmly watched the bodies of his own father and mother swinging on the gallows. Bubi, who with his own two hands had tightened the noose about the necks of his parents. Bubi, the boy executioner, age sixteen.

Bubi had put the noose first around the neck of his father and then around the neck of his mother. His mission accomplished, he trotted over to his friend Peter, the Camp Elder, like a child who runs to his teacher to find out whether he has passed his test.

Peter stood there, his hair disheveled, sleeves rolled up, breathing hard with drunken pleasure. The little Jew devil certainly knew how to please him! Not in all the fifteen years that he, Peter, had spent behind the barbed wires of concentration camps, sleeping with young Polish boys had he felt such a surge of gratitude to any of his lovers as he had to this little fellow who instinctively seemed to know what would please him most.

Bubi had just proved that his love for Peter knew no bounds and that he, Bubi, could no longer live without him. Peter had become the center of Bubi's life. It must be so, Peter told himself, for as proof of his love, Bubi had hanged his own father and mother just because he, Peter, had wished it.

Still basking in Peter's approving smile, Bubi pulled the dead bodies of his parents free of the nooses and dragged them off to Block No. 22, where many other bodies, the hangman's harvest of the day, were already awaiting the arrival of the *Leichenkommando*—the "dead bodies' detail"—whose job it was to cart them away to the Maidanek crematorium. Bubi was too busy to do much thinking, yet he could not help wondering: why had he done this thing? After all, he had loved his father very much. And his mother—why, she had always given him half of her own bread ration in the ghetto. This he knew, although she had always tried to keep it from him. More than once he had been on the point of giving it back to her instead of eating it himself because he was afraid that she might die of starvation. Why, then, had he now put her to death with his own hands?

But he quickly pushed these thought out of his mind. There was no time for weakness. Bubi wanted to live, to survive until the war was over, and this, he felt, was much more important than the life of his mother or his father. And for Bubi, living, really living, meant to be able to go into Peter's bedroom, to take off his clothes and to snuggle up to him under a warm blanket. . . . Anyway, his parents had been old, at least forty-five, and they had been very weak. They would have lived another two or three months at the most. So, in a way, he had actually done them a favor for which they would no doubt have thanked him now, had they been able to speak.

Having satisfied himself that he really had done no wrong, Bubi hurried to Block No. 1. Half the building was taken up by the camp office; the other half, by roomy, comfortable quarters for the *Kapos* [35] and the Camp Elder.

---

[35] *Kapo*: "Trusty" or overseer in charge of labor details or various departments in a concentration camp. *Kapos* were camp inmates appointed by the SS officers in charge to carry out their orders. Some Kapos were German non-Jewish inmates, but in all-Jewish camps there were also Jewish Kapos. Kapos enjoyed special privilages, including better food rations than the other inmates. Some Kapos helped the inmates in their charge, but many of them were hated and feared for their cruelty.

Outdoors, all was quiet again. Only a cough or a yawn was heard occasionally from one of the sentries posted on the watchtowers, guarding the prisoners with their machine guns. But inside the barracks, 50,000 pairs of eyes remained wide open, unable to rest.

* * *

Little Bubi had come to Maidanek with his parents in a transport that had been brought in from Kolo or Konin—no one was quite sure which. As a rule, Jewish children were promptly weeded out and sent directly to the crematorium. But Bubi had so enchanted one of the S.S. men in the "political division" that the Nazi wrote on Bubi's card *"Ins Lager"*—"Into the Camp"— meaning that the little boy should be given various light jobs to do on the camp premises.

A velvety tan complexion, eyes black as coals, pearly white teeth, regular features in an innocent-looking face, and a sturdy little body—this was Bubi when he first arrived at Maidanek. His parents were plain people, but Bubi was beautiful. When Bubi was herded into the public shower house with the others and stood there naked as the day on which he was born, the sight of his body dazzled some of the Nazis on the scene who had certain sexual preferences. They began to ask him all sorts of questions, and finally one of the German non-Jewish inmates who held an important position in the camp took Bubi by the hand and led him and his parents to Camp Three. That was how Bubi fell into the hands of Peter, the Camp Elder.

Peter, the Elder of Camp Three, was a German non-Jew who had been put into concentration camp because he had been a Communist. Before his arrest, he had been a violinist by profession. In the camps where he had been imprisoned he had acquired notoriety as a homosexual and a ruthless executioner of his fellow inmates. Although Peter was, in fact, a prisoner like all the other inmates, his position as Camp Elder earned him the privilege of giving orders carrying no less authority than those of Anton Tuman, the temporary camp commander. Peter had

147

been assigned quarters in two attractive rooms in Block No. 1, and it was there that he now brought his new friend, Bubi. Meanwhile, Bubi's parents had to sleep in the open, in the coal field. Officially, Bubi was the personal servant of the Camp Elder, whose tasks included such chores as cleaning Peter's rooms, shining his boots and preparing his coffee. But in fact, everyone in the camp knew that Bubi was Peter's new "pretty boy." The very next day after he had moved into Peter's quarters, Bubi received a pair of fine, new boots, new pants, a light brown jacket and a special cap such as was worn by the "privileged characters" in the camp. A day or two later Bubi sported on his sleeve a green silk armband with the black inscription: "Junior Camp Elder." To the best of anyone's knowledge, this was the only time in the annals of Nazi concentration camps that a boy of sixteen had been given unlimited power over thousands of inmates. It was a sadistic idea on the part of Peter, the Camp Elder, who derived a perverse pleasure from watching Bubi torture people much older than himself and use his whip not only on Jews but also on inmates of other ethnic origins.

Once in a great while Bubi would go to see his mother and father and bring them a little margarine or a piece of bread. That was all that Bubi did for his parents, who had already shriveled to bare skeletons and were scarcely able to stand on their feet. Bubi could have done a great deal to help them. One word from him to the Elder would have been enough to get his parents easier work, bigger bread rations or a pair of decent shoes. But Bubi did not even attempt to talk with Peter about his parents' plight; he was afraid Peter would be angry that he, Bubi, should still be thinking about his father and mother.

Bubi exploited his power to the full. He never had to stand in formation for roll call or wait in line for his food ration. He was excused from all work, from the daily delousing operations and from going to the public shower house. He always carried his whip in his hand. The thick, braided whip with its leaden tips became part and parcel of his equipment as "Junior Camp Elder." Bubi strutted around the camp with an air of smug arrogance, cheerfully flicking his whip against his gleaming boots. The

148

sharp crack of the whip brought fear and trembling to every "Muselmann" [36] within hearing.

"Don't you see who's standing here in front of you?" he would demand. "Why don't you take off your cap, you stinking carcass?"

"Oh, please, Mr. Junior Camp Elder, sir, I, didn't see you... Excuse me, please," the offender would plead in terror.

Jewish inmates watching Bubi at work wept tears of shame and indignation. I, Pawel Kolodziejczyk, could have wept, too, but I could not afford to show my emotions because I was supposed to be a Polish Aryan, not a Jew.

Whenever Bubi entered one of the barracks, the "Block Elder" in charge had to leap to his feet and shout "Attention!" as he would for any S.S. officer or for the Camp Elder himself, until Bubi granted him permission to stand "at ease." Bubi would inspect the bunks to see whether they were neat and whether the blankets were folded according to camp regulations. If Bubi found a bunk not up to his standard, the man who slept there had to kneel down before the boy and endure the cutting lashes of Bubi's lead-tipped whip.

One day Bubi visited our own barrack, Block No. 14. During his stroll of inspection, he came upon an aged priest so broken and bent that he could no longer stand up straight. Bubi dragged him to the front of the barrack and ordered him to get to his knees. As the old, sick man knelt at his feet, the boy shouted:

"Where do you think you are, you loathsome old pimp? In a rest home or at some fancy hotel? This is the place where people come to die! Understand, shit-bag?"

The whip of the "Junior Camp Elder" began to dance across the broken body of the old priest who, as all of us, including Bubi, knew, had been brought to Maidanek for the crime of having tried to save Jews by supplying them with "Aryan" documents. Bubi whipped him so long and so hard that he finally collapsed, unconscious. Thereupon the young monster spit on

---

36 *Muselmann*: Lit.: "Mussulman." Concentration camp nickname for prisoners whom tortures and starvation had turned into "zombies."

him and kicked him before striding out of the barrack. A few days later, the priest was dead.

Bubi was hated by the Polish inmates, but most of all he was despised by his fellow Jews, particularly those who had known his family in their home town. For the boy made no distinction between Jew and non-Jew, between friend and stranger, and the non-Jewish inmates whom Bubi beat up always vented their rage on their Jewish fellow prisoners.

As the weeks and months went by, Bubi's crimes multiplied until that night when he hanged his mother and father with his own hands.

*   *   *

And then, one cold winter morning, the word spread around Maidanek that Peter, the Camp Elder, had been shot. Later it turned out that his death had come as the result of a dirty money deal in which he had been involved. It seems that, in his capacity of Camp Elder, Peter had received a large transport of Jewish deportees. A body search of the prisoners yielded a great deal of money, gold and jewelry. Peter formed a partnership of sorts with the S.S. officers who had guarded the transport and witnessed the search. Peter had given the S.S. men what he considered their fair share of the loot and thought that this was the end of the affair. But his "partners" thought otherwise and continued to press for a larger share. Peter claimed that he could not give them any more because somebody had stolen the money from him, but nobody believed his story. One night, two S.S. men entered his quarters, called him outside on a pretext, and shot him dead.

Now that his patron was dead, Bubi was quickly demoted from his exalted rank. The green silk armband vanished from his sleeve, and he had to give up his lead-tipped whip. Now, at last, Bubi was a full-fledged orphan. The prisoners all heaved a mighty sigh of relief. Some of them would have liked to finish him off, but they were afraid of the camp authorities.

Suddenly, Bubi became very quiet. He was glad to be left alone.

He crept about the camp, seeking out the Polish inmates who had been friends of Peter's, and some of them gave him a piece of bread or a bowl of soup. He tried to get into the good graces of the inmates with sugary smiles and sweet talk, but they all hated him, just the same.

In the mass slaughter of all the Jewish inmates in Maidanek, Bubi, the boy executioner, also met his death.

And our own Block Elder, a burly Pole, said as he saw Bubi march off to the crematorium in a long line of other Jewish inmates:

"You aren't even worthy of dying together with them, you little whelp . . . ."

151

12

"La Piconera"

AFTER THE HEROIC RESISTANCE of the Greek people had been crushed by the Nazi juggernaut, the first Greek Jews began to appear in the German death camps. There, for the first time, the Jews of Eastern and Western Europe came face to face with fellow Jews of whom they had known heretofore only by hearsay or from books.

On the face of it, the Greek Jews whom we met in the concentration camp seemed to have little in common with their brethren from Poland, Hungary, Czechoslovakia, or France. Their hair, eyebrows and eyelashes were black, like those of Mulattos, and their skin was the color of light chocolate. They were tough and stubborn, and they talked very fast. They spoke to each other in Greek, and sometimes also in French, Spanish, Italian or even Hebrew, but they knew neither Yiddish nor German. As a result, Jewish inmates who wanted to talk to them had to do it through a Jewish fellow prisoner who happened to speak both Hebrew and Yiddish; the non-Jewish Poles, Czechs, Hungarians or Ukrainians had to rely on the help of Ukrainians who knew French or of Czechs who knew Italian.

Their inability to speak or even to acquire the rudiments of the German language brought the unfortunate Greek Jews a lot of grief. When an S.S. man or a Kapo barked an order at a Greek Jew he might just as well have shouted at a deafmute because the poor Greek understood not a word of what he was saying. So the German had to call on one of the linguists among the inmates to act as interpreter. But until the "interpreter" arrived on the scene, the Nazi or Kapo would belabor the hapless "African"—the Nazi name for such Greeks—with cuffs and blows because the *Dummkopf* was obviously too stupid to know German.

The Greek Jews stuck together like brothers. They never stole from one another, and took it for granted that each would help the other in every possible way. At work, the younger inmates would help the older men, although that was tantamount to courting death at the hands of the Nazi taskmasters. They washed one another, lent each other their bowls and spoons, and even gave each other pieces of bread. They had in their group a cobbler, who made it his business to repair the shoes of all the others, and a tailor, who patched up the pants of the others and made them vests from paper concrete-sacks to protect their backs from the biting Lublin winds. If one of them was put to work in the garden, he would "organize" some of the produce to share with his countrymen; those who were assigned to the clothing center or the store room saw to it that all the other "Greeks" should have decent clothes and shoes to wear. When a Pole, or some other non-Greek, got into a fight with one of the Greek Jews, all the other "Greeks" came to the aid of the victim.

The others in the camp respected the Greek Jews not only for their strong fists but also for their devotion to each other and for their ability to maintain their dignity as Jews and as human beings even amidst the surrounding inhumanity in the concentration camp. When Jewish inmates from other groups quarreled or started a fight, there always would be someone to separate the parties and to admonish them: "Look at the way the Greeks act with each other! We could all learn from them how to stick together!" And if a non-Jewish inmate happened to see a Jewish Kapo mistreat one of the Jewish prisoners, he would look at him with contempt and say: "Your people from Greece would never do that."

The Nazis, however, had anything but admiration for the Jewish inmates from Greece. In fact, they hated them even more than

154

they despised the other Jewish prisoners because they knew of the dogged resistance which the Greek Jews had put up when Greece had been invaded. The Kapos had secret orders to finish off the Greek Jews as quickly as possible. Thus, before long, only a few dozen of the hundreds of Greek inmates were left alive. But they all maintained their courage until the end. No Greek Jew was ever seen weeping, or begging an S.S. man to have mercy, and no Greek Jew ever stooped to pick up a cigarette stub discarded by some Nazi—despite the fact that the "Grecos" were all avid smokers, willing to give up a day's bread ration in exchange for one cigarette.

Quietly but relentlessly, this proud group of Jews waged their own war against the Germans, counting as their enemies not only the Nazi camp authorities but also the non-Jewish Germans among the inmates at Maidanek.

When I first came to Maidanek in the late summer of 1943, I saw no Greek Jews there. But several months later, toward the end of the year, after the entire Jewish population of the camp had been exterminated, a new transport was brought in from Auschwitz—sick people suffering from various contagious diseases. It was said that they had been sent to Maidanek for "a cure."

We had not seen a Jew in Maidanek for over two months. It seemed that the massacre had been followed by a definite improvement in our condition. We were getting more bread than before, the soup was thicker, and the portions of marmalade larger. Some of the jokers in our barrack—even in the worst of times there always were a few who did not lose their sense of humor—began to refer to Maidanek as a "first-class health resort."

It was following that idyllic interval, when our stomachs were "satisfied" and our minds filled with dreams of liberty and freedom, that the "sick transport" arrived from Auschwitz. Fully half of the new arrivals were Jewish. Almost at once we noticed among them a type of Jew we had not seen before; these were the Greek Jews. All told, there were only 14 in a total of 105 Jews, but their influence on the others was obvious; they were looked upon as the leaders of the whole group.

Needless to say, the S.S. men gave the Jews the usual welcome of cuffs, kicks and obscenities. The Block Elders were instructed to see to it that the Jews slept apart from the "Aryan" inmates, near the barrack toilets, and that no one should talk to them.

It so happened that my bunk was not far from the "Jewish corner" of my barrack. As a result I could hear almost everything that the newcomers from Auschwitz were saying to each other as they lay on their bunks at night. The Greek Jews talked among each other in Greek and Hebrew; the others conversed mostly in Yiddish. I was careful not to show that I understood Yiddish and Hebrew. They talked freely because they were sure that none of the Aryans in the barrack understood what they were saying. Most of the talk was about their homes, their families, and their experiences since their deportation. The Greeks had only praise for their Gentile countrymen, but they had little good to say about the Germans, the Poles and the Ukrainians. They took a wry view of what the future might have in store for them. "Let's eat up all our bread today," they would tell each other, "for who knows—tomorrow we might be smoldering in the crematorium."

That first night, after the talk had quieted down, two voices out of the darkness began to sing; they were two men from the Greek contingent. It was the first time we had ever heard such a strangely intimate style of singing; it went straight to our hearts like the words of a mother, a sister or a sweetheart. As if at a signal, 300 bony bodies sat up in their bunks, very still, scarcely breathing, listening intently. Even the noisiest, the meanest and the most quarrelsome men in the barrack remained quiet, their faces gone oddly soft with nostalgia. When the song ended, everyone heaved a great sigh. Although we could not understand the words, the melody had stirred us to the inmost depths of our hearts.

No one was able to think of sleep now. As if drawn by a magnet, we climbed down from our bunks, one by one. The Block Elder had one of our men stand near the barrack door to make sure that no guard was near. And then all of us, clad in concentration camp shirts, or in undervests, or in nothing at all, crept up close to the "Jewish corner" from where the singing came. For all of us miserable humans, from all over Europe, the song of the two Greek Jews came like a call to prayer and to renewed hope, like a

156

signal for new courage and solidarity. Slaves reduced to walking skeletons, we crowded around the bunk in that dark corner where two other skeletons sat, singing. One of them had a wild look about him, the look of a human being almost stripped of his humanity; the second of the pair was little more than a reflection of the first. But as we pressed around them, their eyes lit up; obviously, they were pleased with our response to their singing.

We gave them no peace that night. Although it was late, and any disruption of the camp schedule was subject to severe punishment, we made the two Greeks go on singing. Even the Block Elder forgot his duty and begged them to continue. And since any request from the Block Elder was a command, the two Greeks settled themselves a little more comfortably on the bunk and lifted up their voices, The one, whose lyric tenor seemed to recall the weeping of a child, led in the melodies; the other, a basso profundo, accompanied the main theme. Together, their voices blended into one harmonious whole, one heart-rending plea.

They sang in a language we did not understand, but there was no need for us to follow the words; it was the music that moved us. Most of all, we responded to a song they called "La Piconera." Perhaps the lyrics of this song were trite words on an overworked theme of unrequited love, but the melody was so touching, heartbreaking and healing at the same time that we begged the two men to sing it over and over again. That one evening, they sang "La Piconera" at least a dozen times over, and each time, work-blistered hands brushed away bitter tears.

It was long past midnight when we finally decided to go to sleep. But before that, we showed our gratitude to the performers with gifts of bread or soup which we had saved for the next day, or a piece of our horsemeat sausage rations which we received only once a week. Never had any singer, not even the most renowned in the world, received more precious rewards than these. The two Greeks actually wept with joy. From my bunk I watched them divide their gifts among their fellow Jews in the "Jewish corner" of our barrack. While they were busy dividing the food, and eating some of it, two of the non-Jewish inmates, men with a good knowledge of music, sat down beside them on the bunk and began to talk to them. I can still hear the two Greeks, in a broken mixture of German, French and Italian, quietly telling us the story of their lives:

"We are from Salonika. We are singers. Sang in the synagogue choir. You good comrades; you gave us bread. Block Elder is also good man; he has a good heart. We will not live long, but still we sing much before we die. Germans no good. The Greeks fight the Germans. We also fight. Papa, mama, *kaput.* All the Jews *kaput.* But in the end, all Germans go *kaput,* too."

They sat for some time, quietly talking, and the Poles kept asking them whether they were really Jews. They knew that they would not be able to talk with the "Grecos" during the day because conversations between Aryan and Jewish inmates was strictly forbidden. Finally, with great reluctance, we returned to our bunks and went to sleep.

The next day the two Greek singers were the sensation of the camp. As they stood in formation for the morning roll call, the inmates of Camp Three cast furtive looks toward the place where our little group stood in line; they wanted to catch a glimpse of the "Grecos." Later, even some of the S.S. men came to our barrack to ask about the two Greeks.

All of us had been yearning for a change in our camp routine, something to stir our souls. Singing was strictly forbidden at Maidanek, at least during working hours and after nine o'clock at night. I do not mean the songs which we had to sing as we marched to our work assignments; those were marching songs which we had been commanded by our taskmasters to sing; they were designed to strike terror into our hearts, not to give us consolation or new hope. We had forgotten what it was like to sing of our own accord, to sing from the depths of our hearts. It was no wonder, therefore, that all the inmates were overjoyed at the opportunity to hear some good singing, although it was virtually at the risk of our necks, and that even the worst anti-Semites among the non-Jewish inmates did not mind that the two singers happened to be Jews.

One of the two Greeks dropped a remark that he and his companion would be able to do much better if they had a guitar with which to accompany their singing. Lo and behold, the next morning a guitar turned up; no one knew, or even wanted to know, where the instrument had come from, or who had found it. Our Block Elder took charge of the guitar, hiding it in the morning before we went off to work, bringing it out from its hiding place only after supper and evening roll call, when we were back in our barrack and ready for our nightly concert.

The two Greeks were kept busy singing every night, not only in our barrack but in many others as well. The all-time favorite number was "La Piconera." After the evening's performance the two would return to our own barrack with their "wages"—the buckets of soup and pieces of bread which they had received from inmates all over the camp, and which they happily divided among the other residents of the "Jewish corner."

These concerts continued for several weeks. But eventually, the entire camp was evacuated to Gross-Rosen and only a few dozen of the Jews who had survived the massacre remained in Maidanek. Later, we learned that these Jews had been murdered and cremated by the Germans just before the Russian army had captured the city of Lublin. Among those who died were also the two Jewish singers from Salonika.

13

A Tale of Two Brothers

No ONE KNEW FROM where the two brothers had come. What made us notice these two human skeletons in particular was that nothing—bad or good—seemed to move them, and that they clung together like a pair of Siamese twins.

They never cried and never complained. They also never smiled, not even when the announcement came one evening that, starting with the next day, all the inmates would receive half a teaspoon of marmalade along with their daily bread rations. It was as though they could not have cared less. They were utterly indifferent to the other inmates, the barbed wire, the lice and the crematorium. It seemed they had made up their minds that nothing was really worth caring about since they would never come out of Maidanek alive, anyway.

One day we saw a Kapo—Herbert, an Austrian political prisoner who had a reputation for particular cruelty—wreaking his wrath upon the two brothers, alternately slapping them with his massive hands and thrashing them with his whip, kicking them and pulling their hair. And all the while the two wretches made not a sound, not even a grimace. When Herbert had finally had enough and had walked away with the air of a warrior after a major victory, the two brothers quietly rose from the ground and scraped the mud from their prison uniforms as though it had all been no more than a little mishap.

They were always together. When one of them squatted on the ground to pick the lice from his underwear, the other would squat down beside him and follow suit. When one of them went to the latrine, the other inevitably went along. They ate, slept and worked together, and they also received their beatings together. One has to remember that it was well-nigh impossible in a concentration camp for two people to stay together all the time. Work assignments, barrack arrangements and transfers from one unit or camp to the other invariably tended to separate friends and families in Maidanek. Yet these two brothers, these human wraiths who never spoke, had managed the feat; it seemed that no power on earth would be able to part them.

One day the Kapo responsible for a certain subterranean work project seized hold of one of the brothers and began to beat him. It was a Sunday afternoon; there was no work to do and time was hanging heavy on the Kapo's hands. So he decided to while away an hour or so with a little experiment: to beat up one of the "Siamese twins" just to see how the other would react. The Kapo did not have to wait very long. When the other man saw what was happening to his brother, he rushed up to him and tried to shield him with his own body. This brought a roar of laughter from the others, including the Block Elder, who in the meantime had gathered round to watch the proceedings. Thereupon the Kapo began to beat the other brother as well. But now both brothers had fallen back into their usual apathy; they made not a sound, reacting neither to the blows of the Kapo nor to the jeering and guffawing of the men who stood around them like spectators at a cockfight.

The pair were a natural target for all kinds of tricks and indignities, not only from the savage Kapo but also from the inmates, from the Block Elder down to the lowliest prisoner. At night someone would pour a bucketful of water on the bunk they shared or smear the two with mud and excrement while they slept. They would have their bread rations stolen more often than any of the other inmates. Their pants or the straw sack on their bunk would disappear mysteriously. They would be commanded to play servants to the other prisoners. In the face of all this, the two broth-

162

ers remained as they had always been—silent, docile, seemingly totally indifferent to the brutality of the others. They remained thus for many months until, one day, the dam burst and they became the chief protagonists in a real-life drama that shocked the entire camp and separated the two brothers for all eternity.

The never-ending, nagging pains of hunger had led to the gradual development of primitive, harsh rules that rigidly controlled the distribution of the daily food rations. In those days the daily bread ration—one quarter or one sixth of a loaf of German *Kommisbrot* [37]—was the basic sustenance of the concentration camp inmates. It was not the daily quart of watery soup, nor the sausage which contained more water than meat, nor the rancid dab of margarine, nor the drop of *ersatz* marmalade that kept the prisoners on their feet; it was only the bread, the sour, black, frequently underbaked bread that provided us for a few hours with enough energy to carry on somehow until the next bread ration would be distributed. Bread at the concentration camp was more precious than jewels. As a result, like gold and silver, bread in Maidanek became the cause of crime and tragedy.

This is not the time to trace the mysterious detours and byways through which our bread had to travel between the bakery, where it was made, and the distribution center, where it was handed to the inmates. Much of the bread was stolen en route. S.S. men bought the best cognac, and the best women, with the bread that was supposed to go to hundreds of starving prisoners. The result was that the daily bread ration, which originally had been one loaf for four men, was eventually reduced to one loaf for six, and finally to one loaf for eight.

After the bread had passed the camp officers, it had to go through the hands of the Block Elder and his orderlies, who divided it in such a way that they always had extra rations left for themselves, to exchange for liquor and bacon. Sometimes they would cut out the soft inside part of the loaf for their own rations, and then slice the remaining crusts into four or six meager portions. It was very obvious to the inmates what was happening to

---

[37] Loaf of German army bread.

their rations, but no one dared protest because informing on a Block Elder or on an orderly was a sure way of losing one's life. Only when conditions had truly became intolerable, or on one of the rare occasions when Red Cross committees came to inspect the camp and the Nazi authorities wanted to show the visitors how well the prisoners were being treated, did some of the inmates muster the courage to toss anonymous notes into the camp office, telling the administration about what the Block Elders were doing. Miraculously, the complaints had some effect; one day, the Block Elders were told that they could no longer divide up the loaves of bread with their own hands but had to call on groups of four inmates ("bread partners," we came to call these groups) to divide each loaf among themselves.

The inmates evolved various systems of their own to make sure that bread rations were distributed equally. Some constructed primitive little scales from bits of wood and cord to weigh out the portions. In some cases, a group of four "bread partners" would appoint one of their group as "caller." The "caller's" job was to stand with his back turned and his eyes shut, while another man of the group cut the loaf into four equal parts. The man who did the cutting would then point to each quarter in turn and ask, "For whom is this one to be?" Thereupon the "caller," his eyes still tightly closed and his back still turned, would call out the name of one of the four "partners," who would then step forward and receive his ration. In order to make sure that the "caller" would not be tempted to steal a sidelong glimpse at the bread quarters and thus short-change one of his group, another member might stand beside the "caller" and cover his closed eyes with his hands. In the beginning, this elaborate ritual seemed silly, but in time it was adopted all through Maidanek as the most foolproof method of ensuring an equal share of the bread ration for everyone.

Relatives, friends, or neighbors from the same home town would seek, if possible, to form their own "bread foursomes." Inmates devised all sorts of novel schemes. For instance, one in a "foursome" might undertake to pass up his daily quarter-loaf ration for three consecutive days so that, on the fourth day, he might get a whole loaf for himself alone. In this way he could savor the bliss of a full stomach at least once in four days, even if it meant starving on the other three.

Like the other inmates, the two silent brothers also belonged to such a foursome. Together, the two would go without bread for two consecutive days, and on the third day they would receive a whole loaf, which they halved between themselves. In the course of several weeks they had managed to save up enough unused portions from their rations to exchange for an extra whole loaf, a "spare," which they guarded zealously for such eventualities as a camp quarantine period, when no bread might be available, or a move to another camp, when one day's ration might have to do for several days of travel. In order not to be left with a loaf of moldy bread on their hands, they kept exchanging the "spare" loaf for a fresh one every few days. When they got the fresh loaf, they would place it into a little bag which they always kept hidden behind the coat of the one or the other. The other inmates cast hungry looks on the little bread-bag, but no one ever attempted to lay hands on the bag because they all knew that the two brothers, silent though they were in the face of every other provocation, would fight to the death for their hard-won treasure.

One morning in the late fall of 1943, Block 14 of Camp Three was awakened by wild screams. The men who ran to the bunk from which the screams came saw a grisly scene. One of the two brothers lay sprawled on the bunk. The other was bent over him, both bony hands around the throat of the prostrate figure. By the time the others realized what was going on, the brother on the bunk was already dead, and the surviving brother sat beside the body, gulping down what remained of the "spare" loaf of bread the two had owned together. The other men began to hit him, and the Block Elder struck him with his whip, but the man remained silent, clutched his piece of bread in his hands and continued to eat. Neither the knowledge that he had killed his brother with his own hands, nor the fact that his barrack mates were probably about to kill him, too, seemed to disturb him. He just sat there beside his brother's body, like a statue of stone, only his lips and jaws alive, chewing the bread.

Later, we were able to reconstruct what had happened: On the night of the murder, the "spare" loaf had been in the custody of the man who had been killed. As the first rays of light had begun to filter into the barrack that morning, he had awakened, grabbed hold of the loaf, and started to tear out great chunks of the bread, devouring them hungrily, hurrying to finish before his brother, or anyone else in the barrack, awakened. Suddenly, his brother awoke and saw the other greedily gobbling up the treasure which had been intended to keep both of them alive some day. Blind with fury, he could think of only one thing: by taking for himself all the food that had been meant for both of them, his brother had wanted to kill him. And so he fell upon him and, pressing the fingers of both his hands tightly on his throat, he put an end to his brother's life. He did not seem to feel any remorse at what he had done. His brother had been willing to abandon him to a slow torturous death by starvation; he, on the other hand, had been kind and finished him off quickly. He never said a word, but his eyes told us what he must have been thinking.

The Block Elder stopped beating him, motioned to one of the orderlies, and they both withdrew.

Having finished his bread, the surviving brother got up and went to his work, quietly, as always. Quietly, too, he returned to the barrack at the end of the day, drank his bowl of soup and lay down on the bunk to sleep. He had more room there now than he had had the night before. . . .

The next morning he was found dead in his bunk. No one ever could decide which of the two brothers had, in fact, been the murderer and which the victim.

14

Anton Tuman, the Beast of Maidanek

"TUMAN IS COMING!"

Those three words were enough to freeze the blood in our veins. The way to the gas chamber took only five minutes; asphyxiation, no more than 120 seconds. Other deaths—from typhus or dysentery—took longer, but at least you were able to stay on your bunk and rest your bones until the end came. The coming of Anton Tuman, acting commander at Maidanek, on the other hand, foretold the most extreme and long-drawn tortures ever to be devised by human cruelty.

Tuman always carried himself proudly, with the arrogance of the Prussian *Junker* caste from which he had come. His favorite pose was that of Napoleon at the height of his career—one hand at his side, the other on his chest. He held his head high, his lips tightly shut, and his entire body taut like a wild beast about to pounce on its prey. He was always followed by four S.S. men, two armed with braided whips, the other two carrying a "flogging bench" built of sturdy oak and shaped to fit the curves of the victims' bodies. At each end the bench had screws to pin down the victim's hands and feet.

Whenever this procession was seen approaching a barrack we knew that within moments, human bodies would be writhing in agony under the ministrations of Tuman and his henchmen. But the flogging bench was only one of Tuman's many means of "keeping order" in Maidanek.

Anton Tuman hailed from Silesia. According to some of the S.S. men, Tuman's great-grandfather had been a Pole and had even fought against the Prussians for Poland's independence. But all this had happened long ago, and the only remnant from that period in the family's history was the fact that the Tumans were able to speak Polish. In every other respect, they had become true-blue Germans. Anton had attended German schools, studied law at the University of Berlin and had received many commendations for acts of German patriotism. When Hitler came to power, Tuman had joined the Nazi party and, before long, had risen to the rank of *Sturmbannfuehrer* in the S.S.

Eventually, Tuman landed in Poland. His knowledge of the Polish language seemed to qualify him eminently for the task to which he was assigned: the execution of tens of thousands of Poles, and the extermination of Polish Jewry.

Before starting his "work" in Poland, Anton Tuman had helped build the concentration camp of Gross-Rosen, in his own native Silesia. When I arrived in Gross-Rosen after the evacuation of Maidanek, I learned something of how Tuman had gone about setting up that death camp, which was not far from Breslau.

He had made it his practice several times each day to climb to the top of the mountain where prisoners were uprooting great rocks with their bare hands. Tuman would then dislodge a rock himself and roll it down the mountainside. As it hurtled toward the prisoners below, the rock would dislodge dozens of other rocks. and within seconds, dozens of slave laborers would be crushed by the resulting avalanche.

Apparently Tuman carried out his job to the complete satisfaction of the S.S. command, because huge transports of Russian prisoners of war began to arrive at Gross-Rosen. The Russians did not last long there. Within six months, Anton Tuman had killed off 65,000 Russian prisoners. This is how he had done it: He had them fed with special "soups" consisting entirely of grass, water, and great amounts of salt. After drinking this brew, the prisoners got so thirsty that they drank huge quantities of cold water. The result was that before long they contracted dysentery and died like flies.

Another trick of Tuman's was to awaken the occupants of the "Russian" barracks in the middle of the night, drive them half naked out into the icy wind and keep them outdoors for two or three hours, depending on his mood, to do "gymnastics"—rolling on the ground, running, jumping and the like. Meanwhile he himself watched, with a smirk on his face, to see that his commands were faithfully carried out. If any one of the prisoners could not keep up with his orders, Tuman rushed over to him, dragged him out of line and beat him so long and hard with his little bamboo cane that thereafter the wretch was fit only for the crematorium.

Eventually, Tuman was transferred to Maidanek. When I first arrived in Maidanek, Tuman was already there. As acting commander, he had the fate of tens of thousands in his hands. All the gassings, the hangings, the interrogations, the roll calls, the delousing inspections, and the "welcoming ceremonies" for new arrivals had to be carried out under Tuman's personal supervision, not because all this could not have been done without him but because he derived an exquisite pleasure from watching other human beings suffer. When he was seen riding on his horse toward the crematorium, everyone in Maidanek knew that he would soon be followed by a load of human fuel for the ovens. It never failed. Minutes after he had passed by astride his horse or on his motorcycle, huge sealed trucks would come rolling up to the crematorium and disgorge their load of Jews. Tuman would always return from these "exercises" with a very satisfied look on his face.

Tuman had about him an air of relaxation, even indolence; he seemed to have worked out his torture methods with cold-blooded, mathematical precision.

One day a female prisoner committed an "unforgivable crime." As she marched off to work with her labor detail, she saw her husband in the men's section and called out a few words to him, although it was strictly forbidden for men and women in the camp to communicate with each other, no matter what their relationship. Now this woman had not noticed Tuman, but Tuman had noticed her. He immediately ordered her column to halt and pulled the woman out. He ordered her to stand beside the "live" barbed wire and to remain there until the evening. At evening roll call, the men were commanded to form one huge square, with ample space in the middle, as if they were about to be shown a performance of some sort. Into this space Tuman's men placed the notorious flogging bench. Next, the woman was brought there and ordered to take off her clothes, while Tuman stood by, his arms folded across his chest, the usual smirk on his face. At a signal from him, two S.S. men seized her, bound her to the bench and began to flog her naked flesh, until she could no longer stand the pain and lost control of her bowels. At the sight, Tuman broke into loud, raucous laughter. When the show was over, he personally untied her, kicked her with the pointed toe of his boot, and ordered her to gather up her filth with her own hands because, after all, the camp had to be kept clean.

Tuman's eyes seemed to be everywhere at the same time. He could see when prisoners dared pause for a moment in their work. He could tell at a glance when a prisoner had a piece of bread hidden in his shirt or in his pocket, or wore two shirts or two pairs of underpants, or had smuggled in some "contraband" from a day's work outside the camp.

Every evening, when the "outside" labor details returned to Maidanek, Tuman would stand at the camp entrance and watch the marching columns of slave laborers pass. If he saw a man dragging his feet, Tuman promptly turned him over to the Kapo in charge of the crematorium. We were expected to move briskly, with our arms swinging in time to the beat of the march played over the loudspeakers, our heads turned smartly toward the S.S. men who stood to one side, counting the marching prisoners. Tuman never missed such an inspection, and he never failed to strike out at the men with his cane, or to pull someone out of line and have him flogged until he bled. He always had some pretext: the prisoner had dared to lag behind the others, or he had been hiding a piece of bread on his person, or perhaps he had cigarette smoke on his breath. For this latter offense, the culprit would be flogged so cruelly that as a rule he would be permanently out of the "labor force."

170

One night a battalion of slave laborers returned to the camp, bringing back with them the bodies of six men who had been beaten to death during the day. This happened shortly after the Kapos had been given to understand that the camp commander would not take it amiss if each one of them were to beat a couple of Jewish prisoners to death every day. When the column was about to pass through the camp entrance, Tuman commanded them to halt and ordered them to uncover the six corpses. When the clothes were pulled from the dead bodies, some loaves of bread, onions, garlic and a piece of butter came tumbling out. Some of the inmates had bought these treasures from Polish civilians during the day outside the camp, and had hidden their loot in the clothes of the dead men. But Tuman had found them out. He ordered all the prisoners in the column to strip naked and began to lecture them:

"You have committed a great sin. You pigs have desecrated the bodies of your own dead brothers. You have exploited their death for your own profit, to smuggle food into the camp. Where are your morals, your sacred teachings, you children of the Bible?"

The entire group had to stand naked in the biting cold, without a morsel of food, for three days and three nights. At the end of the three days, Tuman ordered the camp pool to be filled up with water. After this had been done, he drove the "criminals"—twenty-six men in all—into the freezing water for "a bath." They jumped in, naked, prodded by blows and kicks from Tuman and his men. They froze to death almost at once. Meanwhile, Tuman, bundled in a warm fur coat, stood at the edge of the pool, pushing the heads of the prisoners under the water with a long pole. When all the heads had vanished from sight, he called over the Camp Elder and ordered him to "clean the filth out of the pool and drain off all that crappy water."

On another occasion Tuman stopped a returning labor battalion at the camp entrance and commanded all the men to open their mouths wide. He then proceeded to smell the breaths of 120 "shit-bags," as he generally called the prisoners, for traces of tobacco, liquor, onion or garlic. Onions and garlic were highly prized by the inmates because it was believed that they helped blood circulation, cleansed the system in general and particularly cured the boils brought on by filth and hunger. To be stricken with boils amounted to a death sentence, a quick trip to the crematorium. As a result, inmates would give away their bread and soup rations for an onion, or a clove or two of garlic. But onions and garlic were "contraband" foods on Tuman's list and so he sniffed at mouth after mouth for traces of the forbidden vegetables. Finally, when he reached the last prisoner, a Russian named Sasha, Tuman found what he had been looking for: the unmistakable smell of onion! Calmly and seemingly without much effort, Tuman kicked Sasha in the stomach with such force that the man fell to the ground. Next, he began to beat him with his notorious little bamboo cane, with special attention to Sasha's face. How long all this took, none of us knew, for we were not permitted to have watches in the camp and so we had lost all our sense of time. When Tuman finally stopped, Sasha's face had turned into a swollen, bloody pulp.

But all this was nothing compared to Tuman's way with the Jewish inmates. His joy was never greater than when he had an opportunity to stand over a Jew who was close to collapse. Tuman would proceed to beat his victim, and then pause for a while. When the wraith caught his breath, Tuman would start beating him again until blood streamed from the Jew, and perhaps excrement as well, the by-product of dysentery and sheer terror. On more than one occasion, Tuman would then order his victim to take off his pants and to stretch out on the ground with his face down. Then Tuman would take a stick and shove it into the man's rectum, "to stop the stink," as he explained.

Such was Anton Tuman—graduate of the University of Berlin, able lawyer, brave soldier and loyal representative of the "master race," the would-be molders of Adolf Hitler's New Order.

15

The Fate of
Kapo August

WHEN KAPO AUGUST CAME TO Maidanek, he was already
a veteran of several concentration camps. He was a "green" Kapo;
the green triangular identifying badge on the left front of his prison
jacket identified him as a "regular" criminal. Long before Hitler
had come to power, August had served terms at various prisons
in Germany. When Hitler instituted the concentration camps,
August was taken from the prison where he happened to be at the
time and transferred to Dachau, where he was given a measure of
freedom and permitted to help torture the German Jews who had
been brought there.

Despite the fact that his fatherland had deprived him of his
liberty and his rights as a pure Aryan citizen of the Reich,
August remained an ardent patriot, loyal to whatever regime
happened to be in power, regardless of its political credo. He
had much the same passionate feeling for his profession, which
was crime. Born in the Berlin underworld, August had played
leading roles in a long list of robberies, thefts and murders.
Whenever he reminisced about his early escapades in Berlin, his
eyes took on a dreamy, far-away look like those of an old man
recalling his happy youth. Whenever he had some free time on
his hands in Maidanek, August would gather his friends together
and hold forth on the sensational bank robberies, burglaries and
train robberies in which he had "cleaned out the fat cats."

"Ah, the booze, the women, the money, and the shootouts with the police. . . those were the days," he would sigh. "When will they ever come again?"

August was a man of medium height, but his hands were out of all proportion to his build; they were three times the normal size, the hands of a true thief. His face was covered with scars, souvenirs of stab wounds, of fights with the police and with rival gangs. His walk was like that of a bear, and his eyes were like those of a fox. His voice was thick and gruff; his words seemed to be squeezed out from between the two rows of gold teeth that filled his mouth. When August spoke, it reminded you of a dull saw cutting through wet wood.

August ranked somewhat above the other Kapos. The low number on the green triangle badge sewn on his jacket showed that he had been one of the first to be transferred by the S.S. command from some other prison camp to help build up the "model" concentration camp that was Maidanek. These "pioneers" were selected from among the "aristocrats" of the convict world, men of German birth, with proper ideas of what a concentration camp should be like. Putting up a new concentration camp, especially a death camp like Maidanek, involved building barracks, paving roads and, above all, building gas chambers and a crematorium. It also included stealing food from the first inmates to arrive at the camp.

August had early acquired a reputation for his fanatical hatred of Jews and Poles. He was therefore a logical choice to superinted the entire "pioneer" project at Maidanek. He was put in charge of the largest labor details because everyone knew that, with Kapo August as "boss," none of the inmates in the unit would remain alive for more than a day or two. He was assigned to direct also the most dangerous jobs, because under his supervision, none of the slave laborers would dare lag behind in the work. And he played a prominent role in all the official mass extermination projects; when August himself laid hands on an inmate, the unfortunate was not likely to survive.

When Maidanek already bore the look typical of all concentration camps, August used to boast that he knew every barrack, every rock, every bit of soil in the place. He would proudly recall that, while building this barrack or that, he had finished off 80 Jews; while putting up the barbed wire fences he had polished off 200 men, and while setting up Camp Three he had dispatched 2,000 inmates.

"But the crematorium—that's where I made my record. There I laid out 7,000 shit-bags," he would trumpet, and laugh until he sputtered and coughed. It had taken him six months, he would say, to build the crematorium, and he was not sure how many slave laborers he had managed to kill in setting up that project, but he thought it had been about 7,000.

August would make the rounds of Maidanek for all the world like the manager of a huge factory who knew every last nail and screw in the place. He really loved everything about the camp because he regarded it all as visible evidence of his own devotion to his fatherland. He was a big shot at Maidanek, but his career of murder and torture did not end there. He was destined to journey also to other death camps, leaving a trail of blood wherever he went.

The prisoners at Maidanek breathed a fervent sigh of relief when the word spread that August was leaving. He had been appointed Kapo in charge of a special unit that was to be transferred to Auschwitz. The sunken, wizened faces of the inmates managed only faint smiles, but they felt indescribable joy. Could there be any greater happiness than to be rid of August, the greatest murderer of them all? Some of us even considered this development as a sign from God that the end of our sufferings was at hand.

It was a clear winter morning when 300 "specialists," who had been selected from among the most skilled slave laborers in the camp, fell into line in rows of five and awaited further orders. A moment later, Kapo August appeared, followed by 80 S.S. men who surrounded the "specialists." Some last commands, a few final cuffs and blows, and the "specialists' battalion," with August at its head, moved off.

In Auschwitz, August continued his work as only he knew how; his exploits were recounted far and wide. For no obvious reason, he would pounce on inmates and strangle them. He cheated Polish, French and Belgian prisoners out of the food packages their families had sent them. If he caught a Jew not busy at work, he killed him on the spot. He beat to death hundreds of Russian prisoners and then mutilated their bodies. And so Kapo August became well known in all the Nazi concentration camps, from the biggest to the smallest, until, at last, his own star began to decline.

Early in 1945, when the Red Army was approaching the German sector of Poland from the east, the Germans began to evacuate all the concentration camps on Polish soil. Thus, the inmates of Auschwitz were moved west into camps within Germany proper. Kapo August landed in Ellrich, a small camp in the Harz mountains, which had "only" 7,000 inmates. The inmates of Ellrich had been forced to dig deep caves into the mountainside. Thousands of slave laborers died while working on this stupendous project, which took fourteen months to complete. By the beginning of 1945, the huge tunnels had already been put to use as munitions plants to turn out secret weapons, probably the "robot bombs" on which Germany counted so desperately to save her from final defeat during the last months of the war. Because these hidden munitions plants were set up deep within the Harz mountains, the Allied bombers could not destroy them, and they therefore continued in operation practically until the last day of the war.

Of all the concentration camps I personally experienced—Maidanek, Gross-Rosen, Sachsenhausen, Retzow, Ellrich and Bergen-Belsen—Ellrich was the most horrible. People died there like flies. We got no bread at all. The soup was made from water and half-rotten, unpeeled mashed potatoes. Even when the weather was ice cold, we went about half-naked because our prison uniforms had been worn to shreds and new uniforms were not available. Ellrich had no crematorium; the bodies of the dead were piled up in huge funeral pyres and burned. The lice were so abundant that we were convinced they had come from all over the world to Ellrich just to torture us. Ellrich was small and almost unknown but far more gruesome than the larger notorious death

176

camps that have become bywords in the history of human bar-
barism.

When August arrived in Ellrich, he no doubt understood at
once that if he did not want to starve to death he would have to
use even more of his peculiar brand of imagination than he had
used in any of the other concentration camps he had known. His
reputation for zeal in his work brought him an assignment as Kapo
over an all-Jewish unit of inmates. But he did himself out of that
job very soon, for after just one week of August's ministrations,
the entire unit—170 inmates—had been wiped out. August had
finished them off, every last one, without wasting any time.

He was then put in charge of a group of 250 Polish inmates who
had been taken captive in the Polish uprising in Warsaw late in
1944, and sent off to concentration camps. The majority of these
prisoners were professional people—doctors, pharmacists, teachers,
accountants. Within two weeks, August, with his trusty whip and
his two huge hands, had done away with all of them. Many of
these Poles had, in fact, been Jews who had managed to "pass"
as Aryans.

Early in March, 1945, about seven or eight weeks before the liberation, Ellrich was sealed off. The labor details no longer went to
the underground munitions plant. Instead, the thousands of inmates simply lay on their lice-infested bunks. slowly starving to
death. The camp rations, meager to begin with, had been reduced
even more, and the prisoners longed to die. During those days
August would go from barrack to barrack, calmly taking the little
bit of soup that had been doled out to the half-dead inmates. This
was the only nourishment to be had at Ellrich now, and August
did not hesitate to kill so that he could have a bowlful of the thin,
foul-smelling stuff. He had developed a procedure all of his own: he
would approach one of the bunks, hit the inmate over the head,
and then sit down on the bunk beside the lifeless body and calmly
drink up the soup intended for his victim.

August went on in this manner until the end of the month, when
the camp authorities divided the inmates into two big transports
for transfer to North Germany, away from the swiftly advancing
Russian forces. The transport to which I had been assigned was

taken to Bergen-Belsen, and its guardian angel was none other than Kapo August.

For six days our train, consisting of forty-some cars, dragged nearly 4,000 prisoners along a route which could normally be covered within seven hours. One hundred and thirty persons were crammed into each car, pressed together like sardines in a can and reeking like rotten garbage. One S.S. man and one Kapo were assigned to each car to keep these pigsties in order. A tiny window, heavily barred, let in a miserly bit of fresh air. No one was allowed to get off the train at any of the stops, and there was no place for the prisoners to relieve themselves. If a passenger finally lost control of his bladder or bowels, the Nazi overseers would beat him till he bled and toss him from the moving train, and the S.S. man would fire a bullet after him to make sure he died.

But now we very much wanted to live. With liberation so close at hand, everyone hung on to life by his fingernails. Most of us, therefore, mustered the last of our strength to control ourselves despite the discomfort which quickly turned to excruciating pain. We were given no food; all we got was beatings. Our legs had grown numb from lying huddled together in one place so long without being able to move. The car smelled like an untended lavatory.

Every time the train made a stop, Kapo August inspected all the cars. As chief of the Kapos in our transport, he was making the entire trip in a special car where the food was kept. It was he who had talked the leaders of the transport into not distributing any of the food among the prisoners. "After all," he explained, "you never know what'll happen tomorrow." Each Kapo got half a loaf of bread every day; the prisoners got nothing.

When the horror train finally turned off into the Bergen-Belsen siding and the S.S. men and Kapos started driving the prisoners out of the cars with their whips, more than half the prisoners were unable to stand up; their feet and legs seemed paralyzed. Those of us who managed to leave the car did not walk; we staggered. We were terrified that if we would be unable to move fast enough to please the S.S. men, we would have our brains blown out on the spot. So we forced our legs into whatever motions we could and, with a superhuman effort, we followed the uniformed guards. Those who could not keep up with the rest of us, those who faltered on the way, were gunned down at once. The road from the railroad siding to the camp was littered with dead bodies.

We entered the camp and were herded into military barracks. There we found tens of thousands of earlier arrivals who, like ourselves, had been brought to Bergen-Belsen from other concentration camps and were now waiting to be assigned to their "permanent" barracks. From them, we learned that Kapo August had been appointed Camp Elder in charge of the entire area. We took the news as a bad omen. It could only mean, we felt, that we did not have long to live, because August had become the very symbol of death. True, the Allies were no longer far away, but we knew that the Germans were capable of mowing us all down even five minutes before our liberators could arrive.

The S.S. were having a hard time of it, too. Making arrangements for so many thousands of prisoners in true "concentration camp style" was no small task. But it provided August's evil genius for murder with the ideal setting, and he went to work with a will. Accompanied by his "aides," the Kapos from the German underworld, he rushed from barrack to barrack, killing and maiming prisoners to the right and the left, robbing the helpless of their last bit of food and hastening the death of the sick. On his sleeve he sported an armband identifying him as the "Camp Elder."

This was the climax of August's career of crime. During those final weeks before liberation. he managed to murder hundreds of inmates. We longed to hurl ourselves at him but the German soldiers who moved about the camp, armed to the teeth, held us back. So August was able to carry on to his heart's desire until April, 1945, when the first British troops entered Bergen-Belsen.

When Bergen-Belsen's great expanse of barbed wire was torn down at last, when thousands of prisoners mobbed the British liberators and covered the armor of the British tanks with ecstatic kisses, Kapo August was nowhere to be seen. He had vanished. His heady adventure had come to an end, and he knew what would be in store for him now.

179

During the first day or two that followed our liberation, no one gave August a thought. But after we had calmed down somewhat, when the joyous shock of deliverance had worn off, we remembered Kapo August and began to search for him. The most persevering prisoners in this search were the Jews and the Russians, who had suffered the most from August's excesses of "patriotism." They combed cellars and attics, taverns and latrines, gardens and forests.

Finally, one afternoon, the word spread that Kapo August had been found. Two of the Russian prisoners had discovered him right there in the camp, hiding out in a potato cellar. Immediately, a mob of humanity rushed to that cellar. But his two Russian captors would not let anyone lay a hand on their precious find. Instead, they led him into their barrack—No. 69. There, they politely asked him to strip. When he stood there stark naked, with thousands of eyes piercing his body, his face took on a waxen hue, and his hands began to shake. The foxy little eyes had become humble and pleading. That was the way we had always wanted to see August, and the sight was balm to our eyes.

One of the Russians ordered him to lie down on the floor. August obeyed without a word. Then, first the Russians and, after them, all others, began to pelt him with rocks and stones. No one tried to beat him, or to kick him; they simply threw stones at him until the blood spurted from his nose and mouth. It was an act of primitive justice—Kapo August was stoned to death by men who had been sustained by one desire; to take revenge for their dead comrades and for their own shattered lives.

The British soldiers who watched the scene said not a word. They had already learned all there was to know about Kapo August.

16

A Gallery of
Holocaust Portraits

*T*HE ELEVEN BRIEF *sketches that follow depict a miscellany of men and women whose paths briefly crossed mine during the era of Nazi terror. This "gallery of holocaust portraits" includes heroes and victims, martyrs and fighters, and a few tragic figures whose minds and souls were maimed by the cruelty of men and circumstances.*

Yanka The Redhead

The entire Grzybów neighborhood in Warsaw knew her, or rather, her chestnut hair which framed her pretty little face like a shimmering halo. When she walked down the street in the long-ago days before the war, people would turn around to look at her and say: "There goes Yanka the Redhead." She lived with her mother and brother in a small apartment on Miedziana Street. They were in modest circumstances; Yanka's father had died and left his family very little to live on. The sole breadwinner was Yanka's brother, but he could not make much money because he was still hardly more than a child.

Yanka was pleasant, quiet and unassuming. She was beautiful but not vain; she did not flirt with the young men who courted her. She spent her free time with a group of friends, going to the movies or to dances at the Adria or Paradise Clubs. In the summertime, they would all go rowing on the Vistula River. She used to tell us that men would follow her in the streets and try to strike up a friendship with her. We knew that she was not trying to show off. She was telling us the truth. She attracted attention wherever she went, because there was no girl quite like her. Yanka's shining hair, her pretty figure, long, aristocratic hands and shapely legs robbed many a man, young and old, of his peace of mind.

But Yanka was not impressed. Deep in her heart she cherished dreams of marriage someday in the far-off future to a man whom she would be able to love and who would help her take care of her mother and brother. There was no lack of candidates, but Yanka always insisted that she was not ready yet. She would have to finish school first, she would say. Some of us predicted a great career for her: she would go to Hollywood and become a famous movie star. Meanwhile, her swains kept giving her yearning looks and had their hearts broken.

And then the war came, robbed us of our dreams and of our youth, and scattered us far and wide. One of my friends was killed in an air raid; some fled east to Russia. and some remained in Warsaw. I spent almost two years in the Ukraine, and then returned to German-occupied Poland with a set of forged "Aryan" papers. From time to time, I would enter the Warsaw ghetto to visit my mother, who was living with several relatives in one single room on Gnójna Street.

One day, when I got to the corner of Dzielna at Karmelicka, I saw an elegant young lady strolling slowly down the street. Her heavily made-up face was topped with a mass of strikingly beautiful copper-red hair. She was dressed in the latest fashion and carried a fine leather handbag. To me, she seemed painfully out of place amidst the misery and squalor of the ghetto. Here she was, smiling, obviously well-fed, the picture of beauty and radiant good health in the midst of all that hunger, those rags, bare feet and starved bodies. I looked at her and could not turn my eyes away. Despite the makeup, her face seemed somehow familiar, and that hair. . . . I kept telling myself that I must be mistaken. Yet that coppery hair, the girl's figure and her walk were those of Yanka the Red-head. I wanted to stop her and say something to her, but I re-

strained myself. This couldn't possibly be Yanka, strolling down
the street, looking for men. Not our modest, demure little Yanka!
But my eyes had not deceived me; it was Yanka, all right, still
beautiful—the same hair, the same saucy little nose, the same large,
dreamy eyes. She did not notice me. I decided to stop for a while
and watch her, to make sure one way or another. She was walking
up and down Karmelicka Street; she seemed a little tired, but otherwise proud and erect. I saw her stop a couple of good-looking
men, and she did it in a strangely refined, lady-like manner. Some
beggars passed by; she turned to them to drop a few coins into
their hands and to murmur some encouraging words. Now I was
sure that it was Yanka.

I stepped out from the shadow of the entranceway where I had
been standing all this time, watching her, and she walked toward
me. She did not recognize me. I must have changed a great deal,
I thought. She smiled at me and murmured: "Shall we go?" She
took hold of my arm and walked along with me, apparently
pleased that I had not shaken off her hand. My heart was hammering, my mouth dry. Yet I felt I would have to say something to her so that she might recognize me. I had to know what
had brought her so low—our lovely Lady Yanka.... Finally, I
swallowed and said in a choked voice: "Don't you know me,
Yanka?" She stopped as if I had struck her, stared into my face and
screamed; "Pawel! Pawelek!" Then she burst into tears. "Let's
go away from here," she sobbed. "Let's go to my place. Oh, Pawel.
it's been so long!"

She took me to her place at 21 Dzielna Street. She unlocked
the door, threw herself on her bed, buried her head in the pillow
and cried bitterly. I sat down on the edge of the bed beside her,
stroking her shining hair, but I could not calm her. Finally I asked
her for a drink of water. This worked. She got up, dried her tears
and assumed the role of the perfect hostess: she brought me not
only a glass of water but also cigarettes and some bread and
butter. Then she hugged and kissed me, tenderly, as if I had
been her father, and whispered: "Thank you for bringing me back
my youth, a little happiness from old times."

She opened the door to the adjoining room. There, on a bed,

lay a man. "This is my husband," she said. The man remained motionless and barely acknowledged my greeting. Yanka and I went back to the other room, and she began to talk.

Yanka's life since September 1, 1939 had been one long chain of tragedies. Her mother had been killed when a bomb hit the cellar where she had taken cover at the first wail of the air raid sirens. Her brother had gone off with the Polish army and never returned; she did not know what had happened to him. She herself had married a young man who had been of great help to her during the siege of Warsaw, and the young couple had moved in with his parents. But then a bomb scored a direct hit on the house, the parents were both killed, and the two young people survived with nothing but the clothes on their backs. They were desperate and close to starvation. All day long, they begged in the streets; at night, they slept on doorsteps like stray dogs. Finally, Yanka's husband, a gentle, refined young man, came down with typhus. He had not died, but the illness had left him paralyzed. Yanka made no effort to find work because she knew that whatever she might be able to earn would not be enough to support herself, let alone both of them. Nothing mattered to her anymore; life had lost all its meaning for her. She had no more strength left to stay home and watch her husband suffer. And so she had begun to go out into the street. Her heart might be bleeding, but she had to wear a smile on the outside. "When we'll be free, my husband will forgive me," she wept. "After all, I'm doing it only for him, for bread—to keep him alive."

I sat beside Yanka, listening to her story, unable to utter a word. There was nothing I could do to help her then, except to sit there with my own heart aching, while she unburdened herself to me.

When I finally left her, it was already quite dark outside. The streets were empty, the street lamps unlit. Here and there I saw a Jew scurrying by like a shadow, hurrying to get home before the curfew...

Fat Kuba

The first time I saw him again in the ghetto, shuffling through the street with his sister, I could not believe my eyes. I would not even have recognized him, if a friend had not told me that this walking skeleton was Kuba Steineisen, and the girl with him, his sister Bella. I hurried over to them, called out Kuba's name and stretched out my hand in greeting. Kuba stopped and remained standing, stock still. His face expressed utter amazement, as if to say: "Is there really anyone left who will talk to me?" He said nothing more, but began to cry, as if he felt he had done something to offend me. His face was unshaven, covered with scratches, and incredibly caked with dirt. His eyes stared out at me like the eyes of a wounded animal. He was covered with rags. At first I did not notice that his feet were bare because they were coal black with filth. His sister Bella seemed to be in even worse shape; she did not look like anything human. And both of them gave off a terrible, nauseating stench.

Let me tell you what Kuba and his sister had been like before the war.

Their parents had been plain people, but very well-to-do. The father had been known as the "Fishmonger King" of Hale Mirowskie and the family lived in an elegant apartment at 8 Skórzanna Street, which had a large front balcony. On Sabbath afternoons during the summer months the four Steineisens would sit on that balcony, relaxing and munching various goodies. All the boys in the neighborhood wanted to be friends with Kuba because he owned a bicycle. It was the only bicycle in the two streets where we children lived with our families, and every now and then Kuba would allow his "best friend" to take a spin on it. Then, too, Kuba's pockets were always filled with candy which he would generously share with us. He often invited us to his house, and occasionally he would even treat one of us to a movie. It was quite an experience for us youngsters to be invited to a home where there were so many expensive things around. Mrs. Steineisen would offer us oranges, bananas, pineapples, candy—delicacies which some of us saw in our own homes only on holidays and which many of us, in fact, could only admire from a distance in fancy window displays. It was therefore only natural that we should envy Kuba. We also envied the boy who happened to be Kuba's "best friend" of the moment, for it was not all that easy to become Kuba Steineisen's "best friend." Kuba was our leader, our uncrowned king. When he joined the Strzelec youth group, a para-military organization for boys in those days, the rest of us joined, too. Of course this does not mean that Kuba had no enemies. He did, and they called him "Fat Kuba" because, like his father, Kuba was grossly overweight.

Kuba's sister Bella had never been pretty, but she had always been a friendly, good-hearted child, and was therefore quite popular. Whenever her mother gave her some fruit or a piece of cake, she never failed to share it with her friends. She never considered herself any better than those of us who were not as wealthy as her own family. Later, she was unlucky enough to come down with meningitis. It cost her parents a fortune. Bella survived, but she had somehow changed. She was still gentle and good, but she had become high-strung and sometimes she did not talk sense.

As we got older, we drifted apart a little because we began to develop different interests. Kuba devoted much of his free time to athletic activities. He joined the boxing section of the Warsaw branch of Maccabi, the Jewish athletic club. Eventually, he became Maccabi's heavyweight champion. We would see his name on posters advertising boxing bouts between Maccabi and other athletic organizations. He became very popular and acquired a host of admirers who had full faith in the prowess of his fists and who kept laying heavy bets that he would win over this or that opponent. So Kuba Steineisen became a star in the sports world of our Jewish community, and there was no lack of young people who considered it a privilege to be able to spend some time in his company.

Then the war broke out. The Steineisens' home was burned to the ground in an air raid. Kuba's parents lost everything they owned, but they were glad that they and their children had been spared. Eventually, however, Mr. Steineisen died of starvation in the ghetto; his wife died soon thereafter. Kuba and Bella had been spoiled and petted all their lives; now they were left with nothing to call their own except the clothes they wore. They had no friends in the ghetto. Everyone was too busy with his own troubles to recall Kuba's past exploits in the boxing ring, or to remember the fine home from which he and Bella had come. And so these two young people, who had never before lacked for anything, were reduced to begging in the streets of the Warsaw ghetto. That was where I came upon them. By this time, thanks to my "Aryan" papers and my various underground pursuits, I was in a position to help them. I asked them what I could do for them. Bella wept piteously, and begged me to buy them a loaf of bread. As for Kuba, all he wanted was a couple of puffs from my cigarette.

Isaac Kohn, Ghetto Policeman

Isaac Kohn lived in Warsaw at 19 Prosta Street. His father, who dealt in lumber, was a devout Jew, but not a fanatic. He believed in the basic virtues of justice, integrity and loving kindness. He made a good living for his wife and his two children, a son and a daughter. Isaac, the son, had already gone "modern." He no longer wore the traditional black hat of the Polish hasidim. He was always well dressed, his shoes were polished till they shone, his neckties were of the latest style and adjusted with military precision. Slender, blond, with a fair complexion, Isaac Kohn was a pleasant, attractive young man.

When the war broke out, Isaac was close to 20 and still living at home with his parents. He had shown no interest in finding a job or learning a trade. He had dropped out of high school, explaining that he wanted to go to Palestine as a pioneer. He would sleep until noon each day. In the evening, he would go to the Betar clubhouse, a Zionist youth organization in which he was one of the leaders. Isaac's parents did not approve of his way of life. His father would sigh and scold, and his mother would cry, but Isaac insisted that helping build a homeland for the Jewish people in Palestine was far more important than getting an education or a good job.

So, Isaac was a problem to his parents and most likely to himself as well. But he had many lovable qualities which made him popular with the other boys. He was a good friend, eager to help others and to do favors. He was cheerful, easy-going and blessed with a fine sense of humor. His parents were always glad to have his friends at their home, and it was by no means unusual for a dozen or more of them to sit down at the Sabbath table with the Kohn family to enjoy a bowful of rich, fragrant *cholent*.

The day after I first arrived in the Warsaw ghetto to visit my mother, I went to see my friend Isaac. The Kohns were still living in the same apartment, but they had only one of the rooms for themselves; the other rooms were occupied by strangers whom they had been forced to take in. Isaac's parents were delighted to see me and we spent some time talking about what we had gone through since the outbreak of the war. Mr. Kohn was no longer working, and the family kept going by selling their clothes, piece by piece. In addition, the Kohns were among the fortunates in the ghetto who received extra supplies of food and other necessities free of charge. Their good fortune stemmed from the fact that Isaac had a job at last: he was a member of the ghetto police force.

It was two o'clock in the afternoon but Isaac was still asleep, having been on duty all the night before. On the table I saw his officer's cap; next to his bed were a pair of shiny officer's boots and a pair of breeches, a wide leather belt and a uniform jacket with copper buttons.

While his parents and I were talking, Isaac awoke and we had a grand reunion. But then, in the midst of the jubilation, I pointed to his officer's cap on the table and asked him: "Tell me, Isaac, how in the world did you get this job?"

His mood changed at once, and I sensed a sudden chill between us. I immediately regretted having asked him this painful question, but now it was too late. Yet, I was anxious to find out why Isaac had joined the ghetto police force. People in the ghetto did not have much good to say about this police force, which consisted entirely of Jews. And so I believed that, rather than keep my feelings of mistrust bottled up inside, it would be far better to have it out with Isaac now, even if the truth would hurt.

At first Isaac appeared ill at ease, but as he talked, he seemed to regain his self-assurance.

"I know that people are saying all sorts of bad things about the ghetto police force," he told me, "and I am afraid a lot of the talk is founded on fact—at least in my opinion. But on the whole, the ghetto police is not the unmitigated disaster than some make it out to be. If we Jews here in the ghetto had not organized our own police force, the Germans would have done it for us, and it isn't very hard to imagine what kind of characters *they* would have recruited. And as for the idea of having the Germans do the policing themselves—just picture what that would be like. We wouldn't be able to exist. You can always, somehow, cope with even the lowest type of Jewish official, but never with a German.

"Sure, we have some shady characters who used all kinds of tricks to get into the police force; they are the ones to blame for our bad reputation. But then, tell me, Pawel, what organization does not have its share of shady characters nowadays? You will find them everywhere, also in our ghetto institutions. The damned Germans have a way of cultivating the worst types, especially among us Jews.

"But on the whole, we aren't nearly as bad as we look. Much of the talk against the ghetto police force is simple envy. People envy us because we can walk about freely even during the raids, when other Jews are rounded up to be sent off to labor camps. They envy us because the wives and children of our policemen are not forced to do hard labor and because, as policemen, we get supplementary rations of food and other essentials. This bonus is probably one of the main reasons—if not the main reason—why they hate us so. And it's not so hard to understand why. Nowadays anyone who walks down a street in the ghetto with a bagful of food will pass plenty of hungry people who'd murder him if looks could kill. It is taken for granted that anyone in the ghetto who has enough to eat must be doing something illegal, such as spying on other Jews for the Gestapo. You think he's got to be a crook, a 'fixer,' a smuggler or some other kind of vermin. That's what the Germans have done to us. Nowadays, when people talk about Adam Cherniakow, the head of our *Judenrat,* they don't talk about what he has been able to accomplish for the people in the ghetto but only about the fact that he always seems to have enough bread and soup in his house. They talk the same way about all the other decent people in our *Judenrat,* in our soup kitchens and in the stores where we buy rationed goods. Go into the soup kitchen sometime and you'll hear how everybody curses the servers, the cooks and the supervisor. Go into one of the grocery stores and you'll hear how everybody calls the salespeople thieves, cut-throats, robbers and Gestapo stooges.

"Do you really believe that there are no more decent people left in the ghetto? You know that isn't true. There are many wonderful people who hold responsible jobs in our community, but even they are accused of the worst crimes all the time. We have to remember that the ones who are making up those accusations aren't normal. How can we be normal in these ghetto conditions? They are sick, starved, broken in body and spirit; they've lost their faith in mankind and in their fellow Jews. That's why they are so quick to pass judgment on others. When a theft is discovered at one of the institutions, they jump to the conclusion that everybody who works in any of those places must be a thief. Catch one thief and the people here in the ghetto immediately spread the word that all the teachers, social workers, policemen and other officials appointed by the *Judenrat* are crooks. Oh, it's true that some of our policemen really act as if they were a law unto themselves, but for every one of those I could name tens of ghetto policemen who are good and clean and loyal, and a credit to the Jewish people.

"The only bad thing you could say about many of us is that we joined the ghetto police force in order to get extra rations and to be able to protect our families and ourselves. You may call us egotists, but then everybody in the ghetto has become an egotist, one way or the other, because we all want to survive. Serving on the ghetto police force can help us survive. Therefore, if everyone in the ghetto could join us, they certainly would. . . .

"If you think about it objectively, you will also understand that the Jewish ghetto police isn't doing anything to help the Germans. On the contrary, we're doing our best to make things easier for the Jews who are doomed to die. We are all doomed to die, you know. . . .

"So, if any future historians will condemn our ghetto police force, they'll do it only because they themselves did not experience the hunger and the torture of the ghetto. No outsider will ever be able to understand. . . ."

Isaac fell silent. I sat there, unable to take my eyes from his face, searching into the depths of his soul. This is my last memory of Isaac Kohn, because he died in the holocaust. To this day his words ring in my ears as a last will and testament uttered in his own behalf and for all the other men on the police force of the Warsaw ghetto who served their fellow Jews until the end. Was Isaac Kohn right or wrong?—who can judge!

Mira Jakubowicz, Playground Superviser of the Ghetto

Before the war, Mira Jakubowitz directed the work of the EVA women's organization, which devoted itself to cultural and athletic activities, to the training of young Jewish women for participation in the social and civic life of their community. In other words, the members of EVA believed that women did not belong only in the kitchen but had a role to play also in the world outside. EVA girls were much admired by the rest of Warsaw's Jewish community for their proficiency in sports, their social skills and their cultural attainments. Any girl who belonged to EVA was definitely considered to be a "better type" of young person.

Mira Jakubowicz was the spiritual mother, the driving force behind EVA. She was cultured and tactful, clean of body and mind, and she had a wonderful talent for making friends. In addition, she was blessed with outstanding leadership abilities and boundless energy. Whenever she had a new idea, she insisted on translating it into action at once and on doing it all by herself even when there were others willing to assist her.

I cannot remember ever having seen Mira laugh before the war. It almost seemed as if she did not know how to laugh. Her graceful, athletic figure, her stern, almost masculine features, and her commanding voice inspired awe rather than love. Yet Mira was a gentle, compassionate woman who loved children so much that

191

she devoted half her life to the physical training of Jewish boys and girls. Before the war, she had taught physical education at several schools and athletic clubs and had published a number of booklets on games and gymnastics for children.

When the Germans herded the Jews of Warsaw into the ghetto, Mira Jakubowicz continued her work there, for the *Judenrat* was deeply concerned about the welfare of the ghetto children. Schools were set up where the boys and girls received not only an education, but affection and care. As a matter of fact, the ghetto schools became a second home to many children, a place where they got milk, hot meals, and from time to time, a pair of new shoes. The *Judenrat* even established orphanages for those children whose parents had been murdered, killed by disease or starvation, or deported to concentration camps. The teachers at the schools and the counselors at the orphanages were forever thinking up new ways of making these children smile and of providing them with all the other things that boys and girls need besides food and clothing.

One of the things the children missed in the ghetto was a park or a playground in which to play and enjoy the good air. Trees, shrubs and grass were a rare sight in the Warsaw ghetto. The boys and girls would longingly peek through the cracks and holes in the ghetto walls to get a glimpse of the trees and flowers that grew on the "other side," where the "Aryans" lived. The educators in the ghetto, aided and encouraged by Adam Cherniakow, head of the *Judenrat,* were determined that their children should have a playground. They cleared away the debris of three houses that had been completely destroyed in the air raids at the beginning of the war and converted the site into a small park. They set out paths, planted flower beds, and installed playground equipment, including a swimming pool complete with diving boards. There was also a dining room for the children, and an office and living quarters for the playground supervisor. The construction work was done by German Jews who had fled to Poland only to be overtaken by Hitler and locked into the ghetto. The project turned out so well that educators from "outside" actually came to the ghetto to study the layout and the arrangements.

Eventually, the Warsaw ghetto boasted three such recreation grounds—one at 21 Grzybowska Street, another on Nalewski Street and the third on Nowolipki Street. The recreation programs were coordinated with the teaching schedules of the ghetto schools and orphanages so that every class could visit one of the three "Gardens of Eden" twice a week. The playground staffs included counselors who taught singing, games, calisthenics and supervised the children at play. The playground was the one place where the children were able to laugh and sing, to enjoy their birthright of happiness. They used the swings and see-saws, played basketball and soccer, and bathed in the swimming pools which, in fact, were the only places in the ghetto where one could bathe. For a few short hours, in the midst of a world doomed to die, the little ones could forget the fears which they felt no less than their elders, and be children again.

The mind—and the heart—behind all this was Mira Jakubowicz. It was under her direction that the playgrounds had been built and the recreation programs drawn up. She herself kept a watchful eye on the swimming pools, and personally saw to it that the grounds and the toilets were clean. She sang songs with the children and held meetings with the counselors. Sometimes it seemed as if Mira existed in triplicate so she could be on duty on all three playgrounds at the same time. She was always the first to arrive at a playground in the morning and the last to leave, just before the curfew.

Mira, whom I had never known to laugh before the war, was smiling and laughing almost all the time she was with the children, and she expected her staff of counselors to do likewise. "Laugh! Laugh!" she would shout at them. "We have to bathe our children in laughter!"

Mira looked like a pure-bred Polish Aryan. She spoke a pure, cultured Polish, without the faintest trace of a Yiddish accent. In fact, she did not even know Yiddish, for she came of an assimilated family. She could easily have passed as an Aryan, but she refused to leave the ghetto. Other Jews envied her Aryan looks and could not understand why she did not take advantage of her appearance to save herself. Once I, too, asked Mira about that.

193

"I consider it my duty to remain here in the ghetto," she told me. "For many years I was far away from Jewish tradition, from the Jewish way of life that is so full of trials and sorrows. But the suffering which has come to our people now has only strengthened me in my resolve never to abandon our Jewish children. Don't you see how much they need love and care and laughter? They have so little time left..."

And so Mira Jakubowicz remained with "her" children in the Warsaw ghetto until the very end.

The Good Doctor: Janusz Korczak

Every child and teen-ager in our neighborhood knew that, not far away from us, there lived a kindly old doctor who had written wonderful stories for children and who had devoted his entire life to the care of Jewish orphans. When we were children we would stop whenever we passed the orphanage, and whisper to each other in awed tones: "This is where the Doctor lives." When we became a little older, we would devour his stories about Jewish and Polish boys and girls very much like ourselves. We would see Dr. Korczak's boys and girls in their school uniforms at various Jewish gatherings and celebrations, arriving together, sitting together, and leaving together to return to the orphanage. "These are the Korczak kids," the others in the audience would say with a proud, proprietary air. Years later, when I was close to twenty, I would meet young people my own age who had graduated from Dr. Korczak's orphanage long ago but who still considered themselves loyal "Korczakites." At Dr. Janusz Korczak's orphanage, they had received a good education, and expert guidance in choosing the vocation best suited to their interests and aptitudes. Many of the teachers, nurses, clerks and artisans, respected members of Warsaw's Jewish community, had been raised at Dr. Korczak's orphanage.

I had never met the Doctor himself before the war. Not until we both were in the Warsaw ghetto did our paths cross, and then I came to know him very well indeed. During my brief visits to the ghetto, I would help out at the Grzybowska Street playground where the children of Dr. Korczak's orphanage came twice each week.

The "Korczakites" were different from all the other children who would come to our "Paradise." They laughed easily and often, they were playful and mischievous, but at the same time they were orderly and well-disciplined. We never had a moment's trouble with them; in fact, they seemed to brighten up the place whenever they came. They would come marching in—one of the teachers in the lead and the troop of youngsters behind him or her in an orderly procession. Dr. Korczak himself, leaning on a cane, would bring up the rear; it was typical of the old man's devotion to his children. The boys and girls would start in immediately on the games and sports, while the Doctor sat on a bench somewhere on the side, watching them with obvious pleasure. Every few minutes another youngster would dash over to him, tell him about some little exploit at play, plant a resounding kiss on his wrinkled cheek, and then run back to the others. Dr. Korczak usually had with him on the bench a few youngsters who were unable to join the others in their games—there might be one who was blind, another with only one leg, and a few who were recuperating from an illness. To work off their surplus energy, they would climb all over the Doctor, and he took it with a good-natured smile. He would put on a show for them, making funny faces, mooing like a cow, and jumping up and down on all fours like a rabbit, painful though this must have been for his aging joints. The children were delighted and we—Mira Jakubowicz and the other teachers and playground helpers—marveled at the boundless love this man had for children. What else, if not love, could have got this earnest old gentleman to forget all about his age and his dignity, just to make his little charges laugh? But knowing how much the children loved him in return, we understood that the Doctor must have felt richly rewarded.

One day I told Dr. Korczak how close I had come to feel to him, how much I admired him and how grateful I was for the privilege of talking with him and watching him at his work.

The old gentleman smiled and put his arm around my shoulders.

"Mr. Trepman," he said, "you look like a young man of about

twenty, but to me you seem just like a little boy talking a lot of foolishness. It's not right for a teacher like yourself to be so modest. Look, your Dr. Korczak is just an ordinary human being, no different from anybody else—except that maybe I'm a little older and have a little more experience."

With that, he gave my hand a warm squeeze and went back to our children.

Dr. Korczak had grown very pale and thin in the ghetto, but he had not lost the aura of genuine simplicity, warmth and inner grace which had always drawn people to him. He was goodness personified, a true friend who gave new strength and courage to all who came into contact with him.

I had known for some time that Dr. Janusz Korczak—his real name was Henryk Goldschmidt—could have had a brilliant medical career, and I had never been able to understand why he should have spurned it in order to devote his life to the care of Jewish orphans. Only when I began to come to him with my own personal problems did I realize that what I had considered to be a "sacrifice" on his part had been to him merely a matter of course, and would have been so even if there never had been a Hitler in Germany or a ghetto in Warsaw.

Dr. Korczak could very easily have left the ghetto and passed as an Aryan; he looked more like a benign elderly Polish noble-man than like a tired old Jew. His perfect Polish speech and man-ners would have defied even the most expert "race detectives" to suspect him of being anything but a full-bred Pole. Moreover, he had many Gentile friends who literally begged him to let them save his life, who sent messengers to guide him out of the ghetto to the safety of the "Aryan" sector. In short, a combination of upbringing and good fortune offered him a priceless passport to survival.

But Dr. Korczak would not hear of it. He would not abandon "his children," particularly not when they were in such great danger. It was perfectly logical and natural for him to follow the road that led him from Krochmalna Street, where his orphanage had been before the war, to the cramped quarters on Śliska Street, where he had been forced to move when the ghetto was set up, and finally to the *Umschlagplatz,* the transfer station on Stawki Street which led straight to the death camp of Treblinka. To Janusz Korczak, it was very simple: Through all the years, he had lived with his children and had never left them, not even for tempting offers of lucrative medical practices in the larger world; so, now, too, he would not leave them, not even for the chance that he might survive. Thus he accompanied his boys and girls to Treblinka and remained with them until the end.

Mordecai Anielewicz, Hero of the Ghetto uprising

Mordecai Anielewicz—or Motek, as he was known in the days before the war—had grown up in the poverty-stricken Solec neighborhood on the outskirts of Warsaw. Like the other Jewish children in this part of town, he had been beaten up by Gentile rowdies, and hit by the rocks of Polish hoodlums. Yet, again like the other Jewish children in his neighborhood, he remained quick, alert and undaunted, looking out at the world with two wide-open eyes and absorbing everything.

Motek was born and raised on Dobra Street, in the heart of the Gentile slum district, among the burly half-drunk Vistula bullies who pawed through the sands of the river for their sustenance. Among his other neighbors were Polish bricklayers, stevedores and laborers, and a couple of dozen Jewish families. His father, who wore the beard and the dark hat and coat of the old-style Polish Jews, owned a grocery store on Dobra Street and worked very hard to support his wife and two children.

Motek played in the street with Jewish and Gentile boys. Later, he went to the Tarbut school, where he was a star pupil and learned to speak Hebrew fluently. By that time he no longer played with the Gentile boys in the neighborhood but became a member of Betar,[38] the militant Revisionist Zionist youth organi-

---

[38] Betar, B'rit Trumpeldor, which was founded in the 1920's, early began to protest against the Nazi persecution of Jews in Germany and British anti-Zionist policies in Palestine. It followed the Revisionist doctrines set forth by Vladimir Jabotinsky and his disciples: a more aggressive

zation, at whose clubhouse he spent his evenings. He was preparing for the day when he would be able to leave Dobra Street and the Vistula River behind him and go to Palestine to fight for the Jewish Homeland.

After graduating from Tarbut, he was given a scholarship to the Laor Gymnasium, a Jewish high school. During the years that followed, he devoted his days to his studies and his evenings to meetings of Betar, where he drank in the teachings of Jabotinsky that Jews had to fight for their rights as a nation in a land of their own.

As Motek grew older, he began to feel that, in addition to fighting for the Jewish Homeland, he wanted to help wipe out the social evils that were causing so much poverty among the Jews in Solec, and to make sure that the same social wrongs would not be transplanted into Palestine. But his friends in Betar concentrated all their energies on the political and military struggle for the Jewish Homeland and seemed to feel that other problems would have to wait until the main objective—a free Jewish state in Palestine—had been attained. As a result, Motek quit Betar and joined the left-wing HaShomer HaTzair which, while just as deeply committed as Betar to the upbuilding of the Jewish Homeland, had taken up the cause of socialism. Motek made this change sometime in 1936, three years before the outbreak of the war.

Motek became just as active and popular in HaShomer HaTzair as he had been in Betar. But he never openly criticized Betar because, as he always stressed, his years there had taught him much that was worthy of respect and emulation. In fact, the training he had received in Betar was to stand him in good stead later on—in the Warsaw ghetto.

---

policy toward the British mandatory government in Palestine; mass immigration, and the systematic training of young Jews for self-defense against Arab terrorism. Politically, Betar and the Revisionists (the Herut party in Israel today) have pursued a right-wing line and stress private enterprise and individual initiative in the development of the Jewish State.

I saw him in the ghetto only once—in the children's recreation ground on Grzybowska Street. He had come there with a group of other young men for a game of basketball. After they finished their game, they went off to a corner of the garden and began a quiet discussion. It looked like a typical discussion group of HaShomer HaTzair: the boys sat in a circle, with Motek acting as the leader. But I could not hear what they were talking about.

Mordecai was very happy to see me. After all, we had spent a good deal of time together before the war. I had taken the role of "big brother," helping him prepare for his entrance examinations to the Laor Gymnasium. Of course Motek had changed a lot since I had seen him last. The delicate, smiling face of the boy had matured; he looked, talked and acted like the man he had become. I told him what I had been doing since the outbreak of the war and he asked me what plans I had for the future. He told me very little about himself, and nothing at all about his activities in the ghetto, although by that time he must have been deeply involved in the plans for the uprising which was to take place in the spring of 1943. He apparently felt uneasy about discussing these things even with me, whom he regarded as a trusted friend, for even in the Warsaw ghetto, where all the Jews, regardless of party affiliation, were pitted against a common enemy, there were individuals whom suffering and sheer terror had turned into potential collaborators and informers. This was the reason why Mordecai Anielewicz and his friends had chosen the playground as their secret meeting place. There, amidst the noise and commotion of young children at play, they felt they would be able to lay their plans without running the risk of being overheard.

Much later, when I first learned of the part which Mordecai Anielewicz had played as commander of the uprising of the Warsaw ghetto, I was filled with pride and with admiration for the young hero who had been my friend. I had watched him grow up as a child of the Jewish slums, where he had learned to shoot, to fight, and finally to die for his people. When the challenge came, Mordecai Anielewicz had been ready, and earned himself everlasting honor and fame as the Judah Maccabee of his generation.

The Peasant Girl in the Ghetto

Marusia was born in a little village near Bursztyn—somewhere between Halicz and Rohatyn. Her father, Petro Havriluk, was a well-to-do Ukrainian peasant who tilled his twelve acres of soil, punctiliously attended church, sent expensive gifts to the priest, and had raised two daughters and five sons. Marusia, his youngest child, was the one great joy of his life. He was utterly devoted to her. She was his comfort when he returned home from a hard day's toil under the burning sun, and all his thoughts were of her when he drove his team to the market to buy gifts for his family. In short, Marusia was the queen of Petro Havriluk's household.

As a matter of fact, Marusia was the pride and joy of the whole village. Her beauty had become a legend in the villages round about, and many a young man spent sleepless nights on her account. Whenever the peasants' sons met in the market place and the conversation turned to girls, most of their talk was about Marusia Havriluk.

Marusia was choosy about the company she kept. As a rule, she was quiet, pensive and withdrawn. Instead of going to the places where other Ukrainians young people gathered, she would sit for hours on end, gazing misty-eyed at the house of her father's nextdoor neighbors. These neighbors were the only Jewish family in the village. Like the Havriluks, Yekkele the Jew, too, was a wheat farmer, who diligently tilled the rich Ukrainian soil. Yekkele had an only son, Gedaliah, who won out over all the other young men in the village—not because of sheer physical vigor or special acts of manly courage, but because he was breaking Marusia's heart into little pieces. She would not look at any of the other young men but waited all day long for a glimpse of Gedaliah—in secret, of course, for she knew that her devout father, though he loved her to distraction, would surely beat her to death if she were to show an interest in the Jewish boy next door.

Gedaliah, too, kept looking at her. His eyes told her all that he might have said to her with his lips during long walks through the woods, making plans and exchanging lovers' vows. While he was saddling his father's horses, pitching hay into the hayloft, or cleaning the barn, his eyes would meet the eyes of Marusia and conduct a mute dialogue of passionate kisses and declarations of eternal love. But the two lovers never met as other lovers do, and never put into words what they felt in their hearts. At most, he would ask her, "How are you, Marusia?" or she might say, "How are things, Gedaliah?" But anything beyond these casual exchanges was too fearful for either of them even to contemplate.

Years passed. Marusia had grown to ripe young womanhood, but the ache in her heart for Gedaliah had not abated. On the contrary, it kept on growing and growing, filling all her days and nights.

The same thing was happening to Gedaliah. He had lost all interest in his work, in his parents' home and eventually in life itself.

Marusia was losing her youthful radiance, keeping to herself even more than in the past, and speaking crossly to her beloved father. Petro Havriluk got worried and talked to the parish priest, who urged him to marry her off as soon as possible. And so, one sunny autumn Sunday the thing that Marusia had feared all those years came to pass: she was taken in a flower-bedecked wagon to the village church to be married to the man her father had picked for her—the son of a substantial Ukrainian landowner.

So Marusia was gone, and Gedaliah grieved for her, even though in spirit she was with him all the time. A cloud of sadness settled over his features and life lost its meaning for him. When Marusia bore her husband a child, and then another, Gedaliah could no longer abide the village and began to spend weeks on end in the nearby town.

Marusia, too, hated her life. Her husband often complained to her father that she was forever daydreaming instead of attending to her children and to her household duties, and that her thoughts seemed far away from her husband and her home.

One day the village was stunned by the incredible news that Marusia had left her husband, her children and all that she owned, and had disappeared.

This happened just at the time when the Germans invaded Galicia and herded the Jews into ghettoes. The Nazis had rounded up all

201

the Jews in the district and taken them to Rohatyn, where they had to live in the Jewish quarter, strictly segregated from the Gentiles of the town. The Nazis had found even Yekkele, although he was the only Jew in his village. Together with his wife and his son Gedaliah, he had to say farewell to his beloved soil, his cattle, and everything else he had, and, taking with them only the few small possessions permitted by the Nazis, the family moved into a small room in the ghetto of Rohatyn.

From that time on, Marusia could no longer stay in her own home, for she realized that Gedaliah was in dire peril. Knowing that the Germans would kill him along with the rest of his people, she could neither rest nor sleep. After weeks of struggling with her conscience, she rose at dawn one day, left her home and the village where she had lived all her life, and went to the ghetto in Rohatyn to join Gedaliah. She had thought it all out carefully and come to the conclusion that her place was beside the man she loved, to help him live through the tragedy of his people and, by her presence, to ease his own sufferings.

Gedaliah's parents greeted her warmly but did not understand why she had come. "It's different for us," Yekkele said to her. "We have no choice. But why should you, Marusia, want to accept our burden out of your own free will?" Only then did Gedaliah's father and mother learn what had been going on between their son and their neighbor's daughter all those years. Yekkele understood and did not condemn his son, because Marusia's act had made it clear to him that the love between her and Gedaliah was not just a cheap affair. Nevertheless, Yekkele and his wife, and even Gedaliah, tried to persuade Marusia to return to her village, and to her husband and children. But Marusia refused to listen. She settled in the ghetto, and set about doing the household chores in the little ghetto room of Gedaliah and his parents with a zeal she had never applied at her own house back in the village.

Every morning Marusia got up at sunrise, stole out of the ghetto and went to some nearby village where the people did not know her, to buy a piece of butter, some eggs, bread and milk. Each day she went to a different village, carefully avoiding the village in which she had grown up. When she returned to the ghetto at the end of the day, she quickly put on her "Jewish armband" again and triumphantly strode into the room where Gedaliah and his parents were waiting. If she happened to meet a peasant outside the ghetto who stopped to talk and to shake his head in pity and bewilderment over the lot she had chosen, she would answer with a radiant look. She was happy to devote her life to her beloved Gedaliah and his people.

At first, the other Jews in the ghetto were terrified about Marusia's presence in their midst. They feared that her father would inform the Germans that the Jews were keeping a Ukrainian girl in the ghetto, and then they would all be murdered at once. Marusia understood their fears, and she did what she could to reassure them and to help them. She began to bring food for them also; whenever she returned from one of her "shopping expeditions," the neighbors knew that she always had some milk, butter or corn flour for them, too.

When the Germans marched all the Jews of the Rohatyn ghetto to the old cemetery and shot them down, Marusia was among the martyrs. Together with her beloved Gedaliah, his parents and their fellow Jews, she went upon her last journey, prodded by the rifles of the storm troopers.

Today, whenever Jews speak of the Rohatyn ghetto, they talk also of Marusia, the Ukrainian girl who cast her lot with the Jews in the day of their destruction. Marusia, the village beauty for whom all the young men of the province had pined in vain.

"Diadia Misha" of Maidanek

Before being captured by the Germans, "Diadia Misha," a short, broad-shouldered man, had been a sergeant in the Red Army. In Maidanek he was given an important position—chief of the potato peeling detail in the kitchen of Camp Three. He lived in Barrack No. 11, which was the residence of the camp cooks. This block became a mecca of sorts for countless other prisoners, who would come there in the evening in hopes that one of the cooks would give them an extra bowl of soup, a couple of potatoes, a spoonful of preserves, or perhaps even a piece of bread. Barrack No. 11 was a lively place, for the cooks were the only inmates who got enough to eat and had clean clothes and underwear. They seemed to have a good time together, laughing and joking constantly among themselves. Their visitors, eager for a handout, put on forced smiles and attempted to tell an off-color joke, sing a bawdy song, or make up some story about the latest news from the battle front—anything to entertain the cooks and gain their favor.

"Diadia Misha" was a prominent figure in Barrack No. 11. It was considered very unusual for a Russian prisoner of war to get such an important position as that of chief potato peeler, because the Germans ordinarily did not assign Russians to chores which were relatively easy and which would put them in a position to "organize" extra food for themselves and their friends among the other prisoners. Rumor had it that Misha had not been an ordinary soldier in the Red Army, but had served in military intelligence and had been a spy. Some even claimed that he had been ordered by the Russians to let himself be captured and brought to Maidanek, so that, after the war, he would be able to act as a witness against the Nazi war criminals and also to report on how his own Russian compatriots had behaved as prisoners of war in the death camp.

No one was sure that these rumors were true, but it seemed to us that this man had occupied some important position not only in the Red Army but also in the Communist party hierarchy, because many of the Russian inmates had known him from before the war and because he acted as the "conscience" of all his Russian fellow prisoners. Whenever two Russians fought over a piece of bread or a few spoonfuls of soup and were unable to come to an understanding, they would go to Misha, and accept his judgment as final. It may be said that Misha had life-and-death powers over his fellow inmates. When Misha saw another Russian prisoner barely able to stand on his feet and hence a sure candidate for an early trip to the ovens, Misha would tell him to report to Barrack No. 11 immediately after evening roll call. At the barrack, Misha would feed him four or five bowlfuls of soup at a clip, and continue this treatment every evening until the man seemed to be out of immediate danger.

Conversely, if one of the Russians stole the bread ration of another Russian prisoner, that man would be found dead the next morning, strangled sometime during the night by one of Misha's men, on direct orders from Misha himself.

Misha loved the Russian people, the cities and the countryside of his Motherland, and his leader, Josef Stalin. His faith in Communism was based on idealism pure and simple. But he also loved other people, including anti-Communists. In this respect he was different from the fanatical Communists we had known and for this reason all the prisoners in Maidanek held him in high esteem. The Poles even forgave him his Communism because they saw in him a noble human being who remained human even in Maidanek, where men were likely to turn into beasts in order to be able to survive another day. The Jewish prisoners idolized him. On more than one occasion, he shielded Jewish prisoners from the blows of an angry Kapo, and he pretended not to see when Jewish potato peelers in his detail hid some of the potatoes from the kitchen in their clothes for future use. One day he even beat up a Polish block elder for flogging a fellow Pole. "Beating up your own people, you son of a bitch—that's even worse than stealing," he muttered.

Misha had his hands full trying to preserve law and order among his Russian "brothers." The Russian prisoners of war in Maidanek were the biggest thieves in the camp, past masters at snatching a bowl of soup from under the nose of another inmate, and at pulling blankets, shirts, coats and even underwear from other prisoners while they slept. The one excuse for these outrages was that, after the Jews, the Russian prisoners of war were the hungriest and the most ill-treated. So, in order to survive, they stole what they could from each other, even in broad daylight, grabbing food and clothing packages that had been sent to Czech and Polish prisoners by their families.

"Diadia Misha" considered it his sacred duty to keep his Russian compatriots in line and to improve the bad image which they had acquired in the minds of the other prisoners at Maidanek. And in this he succeeded to a considerable degree. "Diadia Misha" was a good man, even in Maidanek.

Stanislaw Zelent, the Angel of Maidanek

Stanislaw Zelent was an engineer by profession and a Socialist by conviction. He had been arrested for underground activities against the Germans and brought to Maidanek as a political prisoner. He never lost his courage or his dignity. When an S.S. man beat him, Zelent stood proudly erect; he never begged for mercy, never cried out, never allowed himself to grimace in pain. Even the Germans came to accord him a grudging measure of respect. Zygmunt Meller, the block elder, who was not generally known as a respecter of human beings, did not dare to lay his hand on Zelent. Everyone addressed him by his Polish academic title, "Mr. Engineer," an unusual mark of courtesy at a time and place where people had little heart for social forms. If a Polish prisoner was near collapse, Zelent came to his aid. If a Jewish inmate was in need of help, Zelent was also there. The Jews blessed him and called him "the Angel of Maidanek." He had a smile for everybody, even for the Germans, though there his smile was a little bitter, I suppose. His face radiated kindness and compassion; more than one of us confessed to an impulse to kiss him, as one would a gentle, loving father. Stanislaw Zelent, or Stasiek, as we called him, brought a ray of hope and sunshine to hundreds of sick, broken spirits in the living hell that was Maidanek.

Stasiek was the foreman of an *Innenkommando,* a labor battalion assigned to various chores inside the camp. He was in charge of all the work that had to be done on barracks, sewers and electrical installations, and he also supervised the carpentry and locksmith shops. It was thanks to Stasiek that Maidanek got a sewage system at a very early date; in this way, epidemics were largely prevented and probably thousands of lives saved. Most of the chores assigned to Stasiek's supervision were comparatively easy and uncomplicated, requiring no more than 20 men at a time, but Staszek always requested authorization to draft 120 prisoners. He would then select his crew from among those Poles, Russians and Jews who seemed to him the weakest and therefore unlikely to survive in the battalions that did hard labor outside the camp under the clubs and whips of the Kapos.

Zelent had been given a small hut to use as a toolshed. We privately called the hut "Zelent's Sanatorium," for whenever he saw a prisoner who looked especially bad, or one who was recovering from an illness, Zelent would assign him to the toolshed, officially for the purpose of cleaning the shovels, spades and picks used by the rest of the crew. At least that was the notation entered in the camp's work records. In fact, however, the only work that the prisoner would be asked to do was to light the oven in the toolshed while Zelent went to the kitchen to "organize" some *ersatz* coffee, potatoes, or dried peas. When Zelent returned with his loot, the prisoner would prepare soup and coffee to share with fellow inmates who would come in from the biting cold outside when the guards were not looking. In this way, again, Stasiek saved dozens of human lives.

There were other things, too, going on in Stasiek's toolshed. The better elements among the inmates, those who had still maintained a reputation for decency and clean behavior, would gather in the hut for clandestine lectures on Polish history or discussions of the situation on the battlefront, particularly the chances for a speedy German defeat. One of the "Zelenites"—as the group was informally known—would be posted outside the hut as a lookout. He would pretend to be digging, or performing some other work, but in reality he was watching out for S.S. men or for informers from among the inmates. Zelent knew very well that what he was doing could cost him his life, but he willingly assumed that risk.

People in the camp said that Zelent could have become a rich man in Maidanek because he had free access to the "clothing magazine" in Camp Five, where the clothes of the cremated prisoners were sorted. But Zelent could not bring himself or any member of his crew to rummage through the clothing of the Jews who had gone to their death in the ovens. He would make all kinds of excuses to avoid having anything to do with this work. He was terribly shaken by the fate of the Jews in Maidanek.

Whenever he saw the Germans driving what they termed "another transport of firewood" to the furnaces, Zelent's face would be flaming, his eyes red and his whole body shaking. "All of them together are not worth the shit of one single Jew!" he would mutter through clenched teeth.

All the inmates of Maidanek who knew Stasiek loved him for his honesty and goodness. They respected him, too, for his unswerving, outspoken Polish patriotism. Many of his fellow inmates secretly envied him for the inner discipline that enabled him to withstand the corrupting influences of concentration camp existence and to keep his hands clean. Through the long months and years of imprisonment, Stanislaw Zelent kept alive in thought and in deed those human values which the Nazis vainly sought to destroy. He waged his own private war against Maidanek and emerged victorious.

After we were liberated in Bergen-Belsen, Stasiek told me that he would go back to Poland as soon as possible to help translate his Socialist ideals into reality. He urged me to come with him. In the new Poland that was about to emerge, he said, Jews and Gentiles would work hand in hand to build a better society, based on freedom and equality for all, regardless of descent or creed. But I could not see myself returning to a land which had become a vast cemetery for my people, and so I parted from Stasiek. We both were near tears as we bade each other farewell.

Today Stanislaw Zelent is maybe a high official in the Polish government. Perhaps, some day, when all the world will be truly free, we will meet again.

Professor Michalowicz, Tower of Strength

Professor Michalowicz had spent nearly all his adult life teaching at the University of Warsaw. In addition, he had been active in the Polish Democratic Party, of which he had been chairman for many years. As the leader of Poland's middle-of-the-road liberals, he had often come under violent attack from the ultra-conservative and reactionary forces that had ruled Poland prior to World War II. What particularly annoyed these circles was the fact that this professor had dared speak up for the civil rights of his Jewish fellow citizens. It may be that one of his Polish enemies had helped send him on his way to Maidanek by reporting him to the Nazi occupation authorities as a "Jew-lover."

When Professor Michalowicz came to Maidanek, he was already an elderly man, close to 70. Therefore the Polish inmates who had acquired some influence with the camp authorities saw to it that he was given only light chores to perform. He was assigned to the "clothing magazine," to sort the clothes left behind by the Jewish inmates who had been killed. Before long, this barack became a gathering place for the other Polish prisoners. Dozens of them would come in to visit with "the old man," to get a piece of good advice or a few words of encouragement, or to bring him some morsels from the food packages they had received from home.

On the initiative of Professor Michalowicz, a group of Poles in the camp, including myself, organized secret gatherings that took place every Sunday afternoon. On Sundays we worked only until noon; officially, we had the rest of the day off. To be sure, the Germans did not permit us to go entirely free even on Sunday afternoons. They assigned us "voluntary" work such as delousing sessions, cleaning the barracks and bunks, and picking up trash and refuse on the camp grounds, with S.S. men watching to make sure we did not lie down on the job. Nevertheless, thanks to a few decent Polish block elders, our group of Polish inmates managed to escape these Sunday afternoon chores. We were therefore able to spend our Sunday afternoons with the professor.

Our meetings were held in a different barrack each week, for the sake of secrecy. One of the participants would stand guard at the door of the barrack to look out for unwelcome guests. The actual proceedings took place in a rear corner of the barrack, but some of the men stayed in the front section so that, in case an S.S. man appeared before our lookout could sound the alarm, they would be able to divert his attention and keep him from discovering the rest of us.

Usually, we had some 20 men at such a meeting. Not all of them were members of the professor's party; there were Socialists, a few Catholics (including two priests) and even a lawyer from

Cracow who before the war had been a member of the anti-Semitic "Endek" party. What all the men in the group had in common was a fierce hatred of the Germans and a passionate love for Poland. They had no reason to suspect that I was Jewish and assumed that I was just another one of the many Polish Catholics in the camp.

Our group was more than just a clandestine discussion circle: its intent was to serve as a leadership cadre of sorts among the Polish prisoners. Our aim was two-fold: to prepare ourselves morally and psychologically for the liberation which we felt was sure to come, and to give moral and material help to fellow inmates. Our discussions covered a wide range of subjects, such as Polish history, literature and culture, along with current political events, giving special attention to Nazi Germany and her designs for world conquest. Although the members of our group took turns as chairmen of the meetings, the leading spirit behind our sessions was always Professor Michalowicz. To us, his word was law. We sought his advice and guidance in all our problems and disputes, and we accepted his verdicts without questioning because we loved him, just as he, too, loved us all, even those who were his fiercest political opponents. We did what we could to strengthen the morale of Polish prisoners whose spirits were sagging, and dealt appropriately with inmates who had forgotten that they had to behave like human beings, even in Maidanek. We were anxious to help those of our Polish fellow prisoners who did not receive packages from home. After much effort, we finally succeeded in establishing contact with a legitimate organization in the world outside that was in a position to help us. This organization was the *Rada Główna Opiekuńcza* (Central Welfare Council) in Lublin, which the Germans had permitted to function in Poland after the liquidation of the Polish Red Cross. The Council supported children's homes and free soup kitchens in many Polish towns and cities and, what was most important for our purposes, sent gift packages to Poles held in prisons and concentration camps within the German sector of Poland. Through our contact man, an electrician from the outside who worked on the camp premises, we sent the Council the names of Polish inmates in need of assistance. Early in 1944, the Council managed to obtain a permit from the S.S. command in Lublin which enabled them to bring to every Polish prisoner in Maidanek twice each week a quart of good soup, a whole loaf of bread, some onions and garlic, two apples and ten cigarettes. On every Polish national holiday the Council sent us packages containing 4 kilos—almost 9 pounds—of special holiday delicacies. Needless to say, the Poles gladly shared these gifts with inmates of other nationality groups. There were no Jews in Maidanek at the time, for the last contingent had been murdered in the massacre of September 3, 1943.

When the Russian armies got dangerously close, the Germans evacuated Maidanek and shipped all the inmates west to concentration camps located in Germany proper. As it happened, I was assigned to the same transport as Professor Michalowicz. We ended up at Camp Gross-Rosen, in Silesia. This camp had been built by slave labor and thousands had died in the process. Life in Gross-Rosen consisted of hard labor at stone-breaking, a diet composed almost entirely of grass, and a steady routine of murderous beatings from S.S. men. Here, inmates were not shot to death but were killed with special injections. To my dying day I will remember the three young Frenchmen whom I myself saw being led away to the "surgery" adjoining the crematorium. The block elder in charge of their barrack had informed them that morning that they were not to go to work but to report at ten o'clock for injections. With a calm smile on their lips and a wave of the hand, the three men walked away to their death with a tragic dignity that was enough to make the very heavens weep.

We spent our first two months at Gross-Rosen in quarantine. These were eight weeks of sheer horror, during which we did not even enjoy the status of "normal" inmates. The inmates at this camp had evolved a hierarchy of their own. At the top of the ladder were the "camp officials," who had been appointed to various administrative jobs by the German authorities. On the rung directly below were the "upper crust." Next came the "old-timers." We, the newcomers, were at the very bottom, fair game for torture and exploitation not only by the Germans but by all the inmates who had come to Gross-Rosen before us.

211

Yet, even there, a miracle came to pass. The gift packages from the Central Welfare Council of Lublin which had reached Maidanek after we had been evacuated were forwarded to us in Gross-Rosen! One bright sunny afternoon a team of prisoners pulled into our fenced-off "newcomers' section" the wagons which carried the food packages that had been sent to Maidanek for us by the Welfare Council and by the families of the prisoners. There was no end to our joy. The distribution of the packages was supervised by an S.S. man of Silesian origin who spoke Polish quite well. One of the inmates who worked in the camp office called out each prisoner's number in turn. Then the S.S. man handed over the packages, each of which had already been opened and inspected to make sure it contained no illicit items. There was a package also for Professor Michalowicz, but he was standing very far in the back and did not hear when his number was called out. When he did not step forward, inmates further toward the front began to call out: "Professor, Sir, there's a package for you! Hey, fellows, send the professor up front!"

Apparently the respectful manner in which the men called the professor was too much for the S.S. officer, for he flew into a towering rage. He stopped giving out the packages and motioned to the old man to come closer.

"So you're a professor, are you?" the Nazi demanded. "A professor of whores and pimps, of Polish swine and criminals, no doubt? Well, let me tell you—we don't have any *Herr Professors* in this place. Here you're all the same, you're all criminals. You won't live to see your university again, you old gangster. Get down on your knees! On your knees, I said! Look, shit-bags! How do you like your precious professor now, down on his knees before me, a plain old locksmith? Ha, ha, ha!"

With that, he began to beat the professor savagely with his whip until the old man collapsed and lost control of his bowels.

The S.S. officer howled with laughter. "Take your stinking professor away from here," he bellowed, "or I'll kill him on the spot!"

Slowly, ever so slowly, Professor Michalowicz, barely breathing, raised himself from the ground and, clutching his package, staggered away. The 600 other prisoners in the "newcomers' section" watched in silence, not daring to utter a word of protest.

When our group was evacuated further westward the professor remained behind in Gross-Rosen. At first, I thought that he had died there, but eventually I learned that he lived to be liberated and had returned to his beloved Poland, where he died several years later. I will always remember him as a great spirit who through months of torture and degradation not only remained unbroken himself but also helped many others retain their sanity and their human dignity.

Carl Jantzen of Norway

Still was the night
When the γak shells burst.
They're coming again,
The British flyers—
Air raid alarm
Over Berlin!

In Sachsenhausen
Things were fairly calm,
With everyone happy
Enjoying himself.

Still was the night
When the flak shells burst.
They're here again at last,
The British flyers—
Air raid alarm
Over Berlin!

This was the song we sang in Sachsenhausen, where we had been brought when the Russian armies got too close to Gross-Rosen to suit the Germans. Sachsenhausen, the most dreaded of all the extermination camps, was just a few kilometers away from Berlin.

We stayed in Sachsenhausen only seven days. Then we were

213

transferred to the Heinckel Aircraft Works, 9 kilometers away, where we had to help build the heavy bombers known as H-177. Some 8,000 concentration camp inmates from many lands were herded together in barracks on the grounds of this factory. Many of the barracks had already been reduced to rubble by British bombs. The target of the RAF was, of course, the aircraft plant, but now and then stray bombs hit the prisoners' barracks, killing the men inside. Horrible though this was, we were happy whenever the air raid alarm went off in the middle of the night because to us the wail of the sirens sounded like a trumpet call heralding the victory of the forces of civilized mankind.

The days were more difficult to live through. The back-breaking work, the vicious beatings from the Kapos and the German plant foremen, our dread of being classed as "expendable" if our production fell below the required output, and, above all, the gnawing pain of hunger, had reduced us to walking shadows. Prisoners were collapsing in increasing numbers. The portions of soup we received could be swallowed in one gulp, and our daily bread rations could do little more than remind us that there was still such a thing as bread in this world. There was nothing at the Heinckel Works for us to "organize" because the only movable supplies on hand were screws, tools and aluminum bars—nothing edible. To top it all, our German foremen would parade in front of us with slices of buttered bread in their hands, eating with gusto.

One of the prisoners started pulling up blades of grass from the ground, cutting them into small pieces and dropping them into his soup to make it thicker. At first, we thought the very idea was nauseating. We upbraided the man for his lack of self-control, for acting like an animal instead of endeavoring to keep up his human image until the end. But eventually, alas, we, too, forgot about our human image and started adding grass to our soup also. We did not care that we had to run to the latrine all night long and that our bodies were covered with pus-filled blisters; all that mattered was that the grass made our bowl of soup more filling. We stuffed ourselves with the sharp green liquid and, in fact, grew so accustomed to eating quantities of grass each day that we worried

214

what would happen if we would still be there at the end of the summer, when the grass would wither and die.

But then, suddenly, good fortune smiled on me. Together with two other Polish prisoners from the Gross-Rosen transport I was put to work at the Fuerstenstelle, where the blueprints for various parts of the H-177 were drawn up. There, in the engineering department of the Heinckel Aircraft Works, I quite literally came back to life. We sat in a comfortably-heated hall at a desk laden with books, typewriters and sheets of figures, and did nothing but make calculations all day long. The deafening roar of the machines at the other end of the hall sometimes made it difficult to concentrate, but this did not really trouble me. Imagine the extraordinary luck of being allowed to sit at a desk all day long instead of having to do slave labor out in the cold and on an empty stomach! After only a few days in my new job my swollen legs began to look normal again, and my stomach also received its due at long last. The man to whom I owed this was a concentration camp inmate named Carl Jantzen, from the city of Trondheim, in Norway.

Jantzen sat directly opposite me, doing precisely the same work as I. He had been in that job for over a year, and even the Germans seemed to respect him because he had become something of an expert at the work. From the very outset, he did all he could to help me, teaching me shortcuts and generally giving me hints on how to get my job done with greater dispatch and efficiency. From time to time he would whisper into my ear: "Keep up your courage, man. It won't be long now. We'll be free soon." I looked at him in shocked amazement; how dared he say such things here, in the very nerve center of the Nazi extermination machine?

Carl Jantzen was the type of man with whom women fall in love at first sight. He was tall and well-built and had a face from which it was hard to turn one's eyes away. His blond hair shone like pure gold. I should add here that the other Norwegians in our group were also strikingly handsome. We liked and respected them because of their fine character traits which remained unchanged even in the concentration camp. They were meticulously neat and clean, tactful, calm and refined, with iron will and hearts of gold. To look at them, they might all have been brothers, or at least members of one and the same family—fair, tall, muscular and lithe, always keeping together, sharing what they had, and defending each other against anyone who dared mistreat them.

The very first day we met, Carl invited me to come with him to his barracks after work. When we got there, he carefully examined my swollen legs and feet, and gave me a bottle of vitamin pills. He said that these pills would rid my system of the excess water that had accumulated in my legs. I was stunned. One such pill was considered a treasure in the camp and here was Carl, giving me a whole bottle of them—as a gift. He also gave me some dry Norwegian bread, dried fruits, and sprats. As I ate, I could not believe that the taste of these delicacies in my mouth was real and not a figment of my imagination. Afterwards we sat on his bunk and talked—about Poland, Norway, and our lives since the beginning of the war. We talked and talked until the "lights out" bell signalled that it was time to go to bed.

Carl Jantzen was a pharmacist by profession. He had just completed his studies when the Germans invaded his country. He was inducted into the army but was captured by the Germans almost immediately. Ever since then, he had been a prisoner of war. He came of a devout Protestant family and, before the war, had been active in the YMCA of Trondheim. He had never been able to understand why the Germans should hate the Jews and Poles so much. It only made him hate the Nazis all the more. He had fought the Germans because they had enslaved his country and his people. "There's no other way," he would tell me. "They have to lose the war; then we will be free." Once we would be back home in our countries, he told me, we would keep in touch; he was very prompt in answering letters, he said. In the meantime, we must stand firm and not give in; above all, we had to keep our bodies clean by washing ourselves at least once each day. As he talked, he took a bar of fragrant soap and a towel and handed them to me. It was downright embarrassing, and I felt like a beggar, but it was beyond my strength to refuse these precious gifts.

The Germans treated the West European prisoners of war as privileged characters compared with the concentration camp inmates from the East European countries—not to speak of the Jews. Families in Norway, Holland, Denmark, France and Belgium were permitted to send gift packages to relatives in concentration camps in Germany. As a result, my friend Carl received a package from home each week—food, fresh underwear and various toilet articles. In exchange for bread and sprats, Carl managed to get clean prison uniforms. We all had to wear the same striped cotton shirts and pants, but the ones Carl wore had a certain elegance: they seemed tailored to his figure, and they were always clean and well-pressed.

I awoke each morning looking forward eagerly to spending the day at work with my new-found friend. Every day, without fail, he brought with him three little parcels of food, one for each of us three Poles. We could hardly wait until the moment when no one was looking and he could slip the precious bundles into our hands. But it was not merely the food from Norway that gave us new strength. It was Carl Jantzen himself, simply by being what he was. His human kindness, his words of encouragement, and his concern for our well-being sustained us and fired us with the will to hold out until freedom came.

If Carl Jantzen had not received food packages from home, and would have had to undergo the tortures of slow starvation like ourselves, would he have behaved differently?

No. He would have been the same Carl Jantzen—kind, honest, clean of body and mind, no matter what befell. Of that we were sure beyond the shadow of a doubt.

217

17

From the Diary of
a Former Aryan

IF YOU WERE a Jew in Hitler's Poland and wanted to "pas"as an Aryan, you had to meet some harsh requirements. To begin with, of course, you had to possess good—meaning credible—"Aryan" papers, which in many instances cost tens of thousands of zlotys to obtain. You also had to have complete mastery of the Polish language, without a trace of a Yiddish accent. In addition, you had to be thoroughly familiar with the psychology of the average Polish Gentile—his attitudes, his religious customs, and his social behavior. Above all, you had to school yourself to listen without emotion when people spoke of the liquidation of entire Jewish families and communities. It was very easy to give yourself away. If and when you were found out, bribery was a hindrance rather than a help; "Aryan" Jews who attempted to bribe informers with dollars or diamonds were summarily turned over to the Gestapo—after having been milked dry of all they possessed. This is the reason why so few of the Polish Jews who tried to "pass" as Aryans—and there were relatively many who made the attempt—survived to tell the tale.

Sadder still was the fate of the "Aryan" Jews who were unfortunate enough to land in a concentration camp for such crimes as underground activities. Once in a death camp, the would-be Aryan had to transform himself into a first-rate actor; if he forgot his part so much as just once, he ended up in the crematorium.

219

Above all else, he had to employ every imaginable ruse to avoid being examined by the camp medicos and using the communal showers together with other inmates, for then the evidence of his circumcision would have been exposed for all to see. Nor could he undress in his barrack while others were watching because many inmates were ready to inform on each other for a piece of bread or a bowl of soup.

In that poisoned atmosphere, the "Aryan" Jew had his work cut out for him—forever thinking up ways of avoiding discovery, yet never betraying by a look or an act the stress under which he lived in order to survive. He knew that any loss of nerve meant death.

I, Pinkhas Lazarovich Trepman, lived for four years as an Aryan—two years in freedom, if one may call it that, and the next two in a sequence of seven concentration camps. While I was in Sachsenhausen, I began to keep a diary, which eventually filled over one hundred pages. But when our transport arrived in Camp Ellrich, I destroyed my diary for fear that I might suffer the same fate as my friend Janek, a pure-blooded Pole, who was hanged because he was discovered to be keeping a diary which did not have much good to say of our Nazi captors.

But in Bergen-Belsen, only a few days before our liberation, I began to keep a diary again. It is a record of how the terror ended and a new life began for me.

Friday, April 13, 1945

We are now in the artillery barracks of Bergen-Belsen, two kilometers away from the death camp of Belsen proper. More than 40,000 concentration camp prisoners are here. In our own "room" there are 34 men. The air is stifling and fetid with the stench from our feet, our clothes and our bodies. The lice are eating us up alive. We have no food, only water—just enough to quiet our thirst and to moisten our bodies. We do not know what tomorrow will bring. We feel that the war is coming to an end. Perhaps our own end is not far off, either: we are prepared for it to happen any moment. It's all the same to us. We've ceased caring long ago about what may happen to us; nowadays, we care even less.

The German army left as soon as we arrived here. The only soldiers still remaining are a few dozen Hungarians, and some S.S. men. They are wearing white bands on their right sleeves. So it must be true, then, that the war is over, at least hereabouts. We can't believe it. Have we actually survived this hell in one piece? It can't be. I feel sure there is one more bitter drop—the bitterest of all—that we have yet to swallow.

The hunger is terrible. I have never been so hungry in my life as I am today. It's even worse than in Camp Ellrich. I really don't know whether I'll be able to stand it any longer.

There were rumors that the International Red Cross has already taken over the supervision of the camp. We don't want to die. Just now our will to live is stronger than ever before. But the journey from Ellrich to Bergen-Belsen, and the death march, have drained us completely. I can't stand on my legs for more than a few minutes, I have become a real "Muselmann"—a creature whom hunger has deprived of the last vestige of humanity. Never did I pray so fervently for death as I did in the cattle car on the way to Belsen. And now we are waiting. How much longer will we still have to wait? What will happen to us here? How will it all end? We lie on our bunks for days on end. It's a shame to waste any energy. So we lie here, just like cattle. . .

Sunday, April 15, 1945

Wild shouts startle us out of our stupor. What joy! I look out the window of the barrack. People are running like crazy. What's going on? It seems that a minute or two ago some British armored cars pulled up at the gates of the camp, and everybody's running to welcome them. People are going crazy with joy, really crazy. They cry, laugh, hug, kiss, and roll on the ground—they don't know what to do with themselves. So it's all over; our slavery has come to an end.

"Down with German Fascism and with all the other Fascists!"
I shout to the others. "Long live freedom! Long live democracy!
Long live all of us!"

They stare at me as if I'd lost my senses. Can it be only a dream,
just another one of the many dreams of freedom we have had in
concentration camp? The hunger is gone. I no longer think about
food. We're all thinking about the same things now—a clean bed of
one's own to sleep in, a sunny street to walk in, and a table
groaning with good things to eat. But with it all, there is an
undercurrent of fear; we are afraid of freedom. Where shall we
go tomorrow? Will we find our loved ones? How will we behave
when we are free again? Will we be able to enjoy our freedom?
That is what we Poles have been thinking about.

But for me, on my iron cot, there are other things to ponder
as well. Where is my home? To whom shall I go? How shall I
start life all over again without the people and the things I've
lost? Sure, I'm alive, I've survived the war—but was it worth it?
What kind of a life will I have with my heart bleeding and my
spirit broken? Now that I'm free, all I feel is a terrible ache of
loneliness. It seems that you can become accustomed to trouble
and even get so attached to it that you're afraid to have it end
because you don't know what will follow.

Monday, April 16, 1945

Monday morning. Whoever is able to do so goes outside. Groups
of prisoners stand around the barracks talking, or thinking out
loud, about our liberation. Suddenly, there is a commotion. The
first British soldiers and officers have driven into the camp. They
are sitting in a small open military car which has come to a stop
outside Canteen No. 3. Prisoners are crowding around the car;
everybody wants to have a look at them, to see with his own
eyes the liberators of whom we've dreamed for so long. One of the
prisoners, who knows some English, is talking with them. They
smile and wave to us, and they promise us freedom and food. I
really don't understand how I can take all this so calmly, without

ecstasy, without any excitement. Maybe it is because I am so terribly hungry and because my legs are swollen like a pair of barrels, and they are shaking with weakness and pain. But I hope that my strength will return and then my spirits will also improve. . . .

Wednesday, April 19, 1945

Today they are going to divide us up and assign us to various camps according to nationality. We Poles already have a committee working on our behalf with the British authorities. Our food situation hasn't improved, although we were promised everything under the sun. The camp is bathed in a sea of colors. Every prisoner is wearing in his lapel his national colors—red and white, blue and white, red, white and black, and so forth. There is singing everywhere; we're all singing the songs and the national anthems of our countries. The few dozen S.S. men—all high-ranking officers—who're still here in Bergen-Belsen have to work like mules. They're "cleaning up" the camp, gathering up the unburied corpses of inmates and piling them up in one place. A mountain of corpses—a sacred mountain. Then a second and a third. Dozens of mountains of dead bodies. One of the prisoners recognizes his brother among the bodies; another has found his father, yet another his sister. Heart-rending cries everywhere. The ex-prisoners fall on the S.S. officers and strike them with their bare fists. The Germans don't even try to fight back; they say nothing. Young Jewish ex-prisoners are watching the S.S. officers to make sure they are working good and proper. The sight is so unreal, it is hard to digest all at once.

Saturday, April 21, 1945

For the past two days there has been panic in the camp. Everybody's talking in whispers; no one wants the rumor to spread. We're afraid of what tomorrow will bring. What's going on? There was a rumor that a group of German soldiers has broken through the forests around Bergen-Belsen. They're on their way to our camp to settle their accounts with us, the prisoners. The story is that they're former S.S. men who want to stop us from telling the world about their crimes. We are mortally afraid. If they really get through to us, they will kill every last one of us. Didn't the Nazis poison thousands of prisoners in Dora and in Buchenwald when they knew the Russians were coming? There were rumors that even here in Belsen, thousands of loaves of poisoned bread were prepared by the Germans to be given out to the prisoners on April 17.

Jozef Kramer, the bloodthirsty commander of Belsen, Irma Grese, "the beast of Belsen," the sadistic S.S. woman, and dozens of other former camp "officers" are now working under the supervision of Jewish exinmates. But our fear of the Germans who we hear are advancing toward Bergen-Belsen allows us no peace. Many of the prisoners are escaping from the camp. Where are they going? No one knows.

Fear of the Germans has also kept me from going to the committee of Jewish ex-inmates and telling them that I am a Jew. The days drag on as we wait for a better tomorrow. We are hungry and anxious. What we find most infuriating is that fact that, although we are supposedly free and under the care of the British, we are still being guarded by Hungarian S.S. men, who are standing on guard duty at the camp gates, their guns at the ready. These Hungarians, who were Hitler's allies, have already shot dozens of starving prisoners who, just before liberation, had made a rush for the food left by the fleeing S.S. men. The Hungarians shot at them as if they had been out hunting animals, and now they smoke English cigarettes and continue standing guard over us.

Sunday, April 22, 1945

This is the first Sunday after our liberation. Once there was a popular tango tune in Poland, "The Last Sunday;" now we're singing "The First Sunday." The tune is the same but the words are new; they were written by one of the Polish prisoners. Today there'll be a prayer service for the Polish inmates in the main square of the "Polish" camp. An altar and a huge cross have already been set up. This afternoon the Auschwitz orchestra, which is also here in Belsen, will present a concert of vocal music. There is a festive atmosphere in the place, but right now a big piece of bread would make us far happier than the promised concert. All of us are terribly hungry and apathetic. After all these years of starvation we had hoped for something better. They keep telling us that things will be better soon. But how can we accept the idea that in this respect the British should be treating us even worse than the Nazis? This morning a British officer gave us a pep talk in German in an attempt to calm us down. For the present, he told us, it is impossible to bring larger shipments of food into the camp because the battle lines are still close by and as a result transportation isn't normal yet. He also warned us that once we get the food— in a week or so—we should go easy in the beginning because our stomachs had shrunk from lack of food and eating too much at once might kill us. So we'll just suffer a little while longer.

I'm really sorry now that I destroyed my Sachsenhausen diary when I got to Camp Ellrich. I had torn it into small pieces for fear that the work-assignment chief might discover it during an inspection. That diary contained descriptions of the days and nights I spent in that death camp in the Hartz mountains. As for the evacuation from Ellrich to Bergen-Belsen—that was the peak of all my sufferings. The German prisoners trampled us with their boots, the S.S. officers kept shooting at us, and all the while we weren't even able to move. We were 120 men in one cattle car, filthy with our own excrement and literally reduced to drinking our own urine. When we were herded out of the train at the Bergen station, we found to our horror that our legs folded beneath us. I was unable to walk. My legs seemed to be paralyzed; they were stiff like logs. I remember that I started to cry like a helpless baby. The S.S. men were shooting down those who couldn't walk. Who took pity on me? Genek, a pickpocket from Lodz, and Witek, another Polish prisoner from Posen. They grabbed me under my arms and literally dragged me along until the circulation in my legs began to work and I was able to move under my own power. That's how I got here alive.

Sunday, April 29, 1945

We will have to leave Bergen-Belsen within the next eight days. The barracks in which we are now living have to be cleaned and prepared to receive the sick and exhausted ex-inmates of Camp No. 1, the actual death camp of Belsen. We are supposed to be the healthy ones, so I can just imagine what the sick ones look like. We have been forbidden to enter Camp 1 because a typhus epidemic is raging there. We hear that hundreds are dying there each day. Many of the sick are lying on the bare floor because there aren't enough beds. Water is brought to them in barrels from our camp. British Red Cross volunteers have already placed barbed wire fences around some 20 of the barracks in our own camp and put up a sign: "Do not enter. Danger of typhus." So that's where they'll move the typhus patients because the sanitary facilities in our barracks, which were originally built for German soldiers, are much better than those elsewhere in the camp.

We will be moved to Celle, a little town some 24 kilometers from Belsen. We hear that all the Germans have been evacuated from Celle and the place will be turned into an ex-prisoners' town. We're impatient to start out on the way.

Life in Belsen is much better already. At long last we get a third of a loaf of bread and a quart of very good soup every day.

Today I visited one of the "Jewish" barracks. I sought out the block elder and asked to speak with him in private. He asked everyone else in the room to leave and we remained alone. He is a very nice man; his name is Kurt Fuchs and he's from Czechoslovakia. In a shaking voice I told him my secret which I had kept locked in my heart for four long years. I told him something of what I had gone through. Now that we were free, I said, I was anxious to be a Jew again. Kurt sat speechless, unable to believe his eyes and ears. Tears were rolling down his cheeks. He put his arms around me, patted my shoulders, and didn't know what to do with me. He then told me his own story; he has suffered a lot, too. He advised me to wait a little longer before officially announcing that I was a Jew. Better wait until the situation stabilizes, he said. He was, of course, referring to the rumors about the German soldiers near the camp. If I had waited for so many years I could surely manage to hold out another few days. Then he took half a loaf of bread from his cupboard, handed it to me, and asked me to come and see him in his room every day.

How good it is to be with Jewish people again! I've had enough of the play-acting! Just a little longer, and I'll be able to be myself again at long last.

Saturday, May 5, 1945

The British have increased our food rations but it still is nowhere nearly enough to satisfy our hunger. The Russian prisoners were the first to rush out of the camp to get some food from the German peasants in nearby villages. The Hungarian guards threaten to shoot us if we walk out of the camp, but we go out just the same. Some of the inmates have already collected bacon, eggs, honey, preserves, and bread. They go from village to village and force the German peasants to give them food. The Germans aren't anxious to comply, but they do as they are told because they're afraid of getting beaten up or having their homes set on fire. That's what has been happening to farmers who refused to give food to the Russian ex-prisoners.

The prisoners are doing their cooking in large kettles outdoors —thick soups with chunks of meat and fat floating about in them. It's too much for me; the aroma of all this precious food makes me dizzy. But for the time being I am unable to go out of the camp by myself to "organize" some food. My legs are still badly swollen and I can't walk much yet.

Still, one day, I couldn't contain myself any longer. I got together with Zygmunt Gandecki, a boy of sixteen, and we prepared for our "outing." At sunrise the next day we set out while the Hungarian guards weren't watching. We walked all day long, stopping to rest now and then. I was soaked with sweat and I could hardly stand the pain in my legs. In fact, I was ready to turn back, but Zygmunt urged me to keep going. At 11 o'clock that night we reached Falingbostel, a camp of French, Russian, Yugoslav and Italian prisoners of war. These POW's had lots of food because they have been getting food packages regularly from the International Red Cross. They loaded us down with food, cramming into our rucksacks cans of meat and fish, prunes, raisins, crackers and other delicacies we hadn't seen in six years. We got hold of a hand cart, put all our "loot" on it and went over to the Russian part of the camp to get a pass from the commanding officer. This pass, we felt, would serve to protect us from Russian ex-prisoners who roamed the highways and robbed other prisoners they met on the road. The Russian commander was very kind. The interpreter, who spoke both English and German fluently, gave us the pass and bade us a cordial farewell.

The trip back to Belsen was difficult. The sun was burning, we could find no water on the way, and we were close to exhaustion. The road back led through a forest and we were terrified that we might run afoul of S.S. men who might be hiding out in the woods. Such things have happened to other concentration camp inmates. In the end, however, we arrived safely in Belsen. The others received us with great rejoicing and we had a real banquet.

Today we're supposed to be leaving for Celle. There, we will be assigned private quarters and we'll be able to live like normal, free people. At least that's what they've been promising us.

Tuesday, May 8, 1945

We've been in Celle two days now. The British have put us up in quarters that used to be occupied by German soldiers. Its called Heidekaserne—military barracks. We have no guards. Only at the entrance to the barracks there is a British soldier with a gun, on guard duty. He is very friendly; he smiles at us and tells us in sign language that it is all right for us to go out into the town.

Yesterday I took a walk about Celle. It is hard to describe my feelings as I walked about the streets of Celle, a free man. My dreams of freedom have come true. At last I'm free and don't have to be afraid of the Gestapo and all the other devils of Hitler's Third Reich. There's plenty of life in this town. The streets are crowded with ex-concentration camp inmates. It is a veritable

Tower of Babel. Hitler had brought together people from all over Europe into his concentration camps. Now the camps have been thrown open and the German towns are flooded with foreigners. The prisoners are walking about with their heads held high, partic-front, but the loss of morale on their home front is even worse. The prisoners are walking about with their heads held high, partiularly the Jews. We walk as if we were strolling through the streets of Tel Aviv. After all, we're the Jews who have come back to life from among the dead. You hardly see any Germans in the streets. Those few who do appear scurry by, in terror that one of the ex-prisoners may attack them. The doors of their homes are boarded up. The few Germàns we see in the streets are nauseatingly polite. Some of them stop us and assure us that Hitlerism was a foreign growth on the body of Germany, and that they always listened to the B.B.C. broadcasts during the war. We see German women wearing black because they've lost their husbads in the war; but now they're finding solace in the arms of British "Tommies." How low these proud German women have sunk!

I am lying on my bed. There is some commotion in the corridor, and I hear happy shouts. The block supervisor comes in to tell us that the radio has just announced the news that Germany has officially surrendered to the Allies. I can't describe our rejoicing. This afternoon, at 5:30, there will be a victory celebration in the open square. We are jubilant. Hurrah! Hurrah! Long live—long live—EVERYBODY!

ABOUT THE AUTHOR

Paul Trepman presently resides in Montreal, Canada with his wife and two children where he occupies the position of Director of the Jewish Public Library.

Following his liberation, Paul Trepman served as Editor of *Unzer Shtimme* (Our Voice), a Yiddish newsletter which was the first Jewish periodical to be published in Germany after the war. Later, he edited the *Vochenblatt* (Weekly Journal). Both these publications were organs of the Central Committee of Liberated Jews in Bergen-Belsen, which represented all Jews in the displaced persons camps and the Jewish-German community of the British occupation zone. He was also a member of the Central Committee of the Liberated Jews of the British Zone of Germany, and was President of the Association of Jewish Sport Clubs in the British zone.

Paul Trepman was born in Warsaw where he graduated from the Rabbinical Seminary 'Tachkemoni' and attended the University of Stefan Batory in Vilno; his studies at the university were interrupted by the outbreak of the second world war.

Paul Trepman left Europe in 1948 together with his wife, the former Babey Widuchinsky whom he met and married in Bergen-Belsen—and settled in Montreal. He was a teacher in the Jewish People's Schools for twenty-four years, and Director of Unzer Camp (later Camp Dan), the summer home of the Labor Zionist Movement—for eighteen seasons.

He has written three books and had numerous articles published in various Yiddish periodicals all over the world.